A Brit's (..... ..
Las Vegas
and the West
2000

A Brit's Guide to Las Vegas and the West 2000

Karen Marchbank

foulsham
LONDON • NEW YORK • TORONTO • SYDNEY

foulsham

The Publishing House, Bennetts Close, Cippenham,
Berkshire, SL1 5AP, England

ISBN 0-572-02554-0

Printed in Great Britain by St. Edmundsbury Press, Bury St. Edmunds, Suffolk.

CONTENTS

For Jennifer, who, admittedly, is not quite old enough to enjoy all the delights of Las Vegas, but who is still game for anything.

1

WHAT'S IT ALL ABOUT?

Why go to Vegas? – the resorts, the weather, the best times to go

Las Vegas is America's best-kept secret. Sure we know it's got some big hotels, that this is where Bugsy Siegel and a bunch of mobsters set up shop in the 1940s and 1950s, that the casinos are amazing and you get lots of free drinks to while away the time while you spend your £20 gambling. But it's not until you have driven down the Strip or flown into the McCarran International Airport and seen the staggering line-up of theme hotels that you have any idea of the enormity of the place. This truly is the all-singing, all-dancing, top-of-the-pile city for tourism in America.

As you drive up Las Vegas Boulevard South – the Strip, as it is known – from the airport, you'll encounter the amazing pyramid of the Luxor on your left and the gigantic golden lion of the MGM Grand to your right. Other spectacular sights follow, including the beautiful drawbridge-castle of the Excalibur, the tropical paradise of the Tropicana (one of the oldest surviving hotels), a complete replica of New York's skyline at the New York-New York resort and the beautiful Treasure Island, with its amazing pirate battle at Buccaneer Bay. And that is before you even get to what used to be the most famous part of the Strip – the old Four Corners that include the Greco-Roman empire of Caesars Palace and the Flamingo Hilton. Towering over it all, of course, is the Stratosphere, the world's tallest free-standing observation tower at the top end of the Strip near to downtown Las Vegas. Here you'll find the last vestiges of Las Vegas' former neon culture known as Glitter Gulch in the recently-opened Fremont Street Experience that totally encloses Fremont Street.

There are nearly 120,000 hotel beds in the city and the number keeps on rising as older hotels are taken over, imploded and replaced by more and more giant resorts. Even so, occupancy was a staggering 91% in 1998 and more than 30 million visitors spent $24.6 BILLION in the city in the same year.

Las Vegas is also a great place to work. Up to 8,000 people move into the Las Vegas area every month from southern California, Utah and beyond. The predictions are that the current population of 1.2 million in Clark County, which encompasses Las Vegas, will more than double to 2.7 million by the year 2018. It's not surprising, given that the unemployment rate of 4.2% is the lowest in the country, that the number of jobs will grow by 5.2% every year over the next decade and that the lifestyle is just so good.

But not all the jobs are in the gambling industry. Many other businesses, especially those in the hi-tech industry, are attracted by the low property tax and the lack of income or corporate income taxes. For the sixth year in a row *POV* – the New York business magazine for young entrepreneurs with a smart Point of View – ranks Las Vegas in its top five cities for new businesses. This is based on 19 factors, including quality of life, 'coolness', infrastructure, educated workforce, success rate and taxes.

As a result, a large part of the workforce consists of smart, young professional types, who are lured by the huge wages – salaries in the hi-tech sector average out at around $56,000 per annum in comparison with the country-wide norm of $29,000. And that has given rise to a huge number of trendy bars, delis, cafés and restaurants including Spielberg's submarine-themed restaurant, Dive!, Andre Agassi's All Star Sports Café and most recently Dan Aykroyd's House of Blues.

An increase in younger, trendier visitors has also played a part in the growth of thrill rides, such as the heartline-twister Manhattan Express around New York-New York, the heartstopping Big Shot at the Stratosphere and Sky Screamer at the MGM Grand. There are now so many family attractions that it really is possible to have a family holiday here – and see the fabulous nearby natural sights of the Red Rock Canyon, Valley of Fire, Grand Canyon (by helicopter or plane in a day) and Mount Charleston. You can find a venue for nearly every activity you want to participate in and there are plenty of opportunities to experience the real West. You can go horse riding at any of the national parks mentioned, go on a cowboy trail, meet the Native American tribes north and south of the city, go swimming, waterskiing and fishing at Lake Mead and even go skiing in Lee Canyon during the winter months. If that's not enough action for you, then try the skydiving that's on offer from Boulder City Airport near the Hoover Dam.

The power of plastic comes into its own in the myriad of shopping centres that have sprung up since Caesars Palace's Forum Shops gave a whole new meaning to the word 'mall'. Now locals and tourists spend even more money in these 'super' shopping centres than they do on gambling, making Las Vegas the most successful place for the retail industry in all of America.

It's all a long way from the days of Bugsy and, before him, the railroad settlers and Mormons. In fact, southern Nevada has a history that reaches back into prehistoric times when it was a virtual marsh of abundant water and lush vegetation that formed a home to dinosaurs. Eventually, as millions of years went by, the marsh receded, rivers disappeared beneath the surface and the wetlands evolved into a parched, arid landscape that can now only support the hardiest of plants and animals. Water trapped underground in the geological formations of the Las Vegas Valley sporadically surfaced to nourish plants and create an oasis in the desert, while life-giving water flowed to the Colorado River.

Hidden for centuries from all but Native Americans, the Las Vegas Valley oasis was protected from discovery by the surrounding harsh and unforgiving Mojave Desert until around 1829 when Mexican trader Antonio Armigo, leading a 60-man party along the Spanish Trail to Los Angeles, veered from the accepted route and discovered Las Vegas Springs.

Finding this oasis shortened the Spanish Trail to Los Angeles and hastened the rush west for the California gold. Between 1830 and 1848, the name Vegas was changed to Las Vegas, which means 'the meadows' in Spanish. In 1844 John C Fremont camped at the Springs while leading an overland expedition west and his name is remembered in the city at the downtown Fremont Hotel and Fremont Street.

In 1855, Mormon settlers from Salt Lake City started to build a fort of sun-dried adobe bricks in Las Vegas to protect pioneers travelling between Utah and Los Angeles. They planted fruit trees and vegetables and made bullets from lead mined at Potosi Mountain, 30 miles from the fort. They abandoned the settlement in 1858, largely because of Indian raids, but it remains as the oldest non-Indian structure in Las Vegas and has been designated a historic monument.

By 1890, railroad developers had chosen the water-rich valley as a prime location for a stop facility and town. When work on the first railroad into Las Vegas began in 1904, a tent-town sprouted, with saloons, stores and boarding houses, and the San

Pedro, Los Angeles and Salt Lake Railroad (later absorbed by Union Pacific) made its first run east from California. The advent of the railroad led to the founding of Las Vegas on 15 May 1905. The Union Pacific auctioned off 1,200 lots in a single day in an area that is now known as the Fremont Street Experience.

Gambling got off to a shaky start in the state, which introduced anti-gambling laws in 1910. They were so strict that even the western custom of flipping a coin for a drink was banned. But the locals set up under-ground gambling dens for their roulette wheels, dice and card games. They stayed illegal but were largely accepted, and flourished until 1931 when the Nevada Legislature approved a legalised gambling bill that was designed to generate tax revenue to support local schools. Now more than 43% of Nevada's income comes from gambling tax revenue and more than 34% of its fund is used to provide state education.

In the same year, construction work began on the Hoover Dam project, which at its peak employed more than 5,000 people, so the young town of Las Vegas was protected from the harsh realities of America's Great Depression. World War Two delayed major resort growth but the seeds for development were sown when Tommy Hull opened the El Rancho Vegas Casino in 1941 on land opposite what is now the Sahara Hotel. During World War Two, the nearby Nellis Air Force Base was a key military installation and later became a training ground for American fighter pilots.

The success of El Rancho Vegas triggered a small building boom in the late 1940s including several hotel-casinos on the two-lane highway leading into Las Vegas from Los Angeles that has evolved into today's Strip. Early hotels included the Last Frontier, Thunderbird and Club Bingo. By far the most famous was the Flamingo Hotel, built by mobster

Benjamin 'Bugsy' Siegel, a member of the Meyer Lanksy crime family. With its giant pink neon sign and replicas of pink flamingos on the lawn, it opened on New Year's Eve in 1946, complete with a bullet-proof, high-security apartment for Bugsy. He was gunned down six months later as he sat in the living room of his girlfriend's home in Beverly Hills. After numerous changes in ownership, the Flamingo is now owned and run by the Hilton Hotel Group. Now only the name remains as the last of the original motel-like buildings were removed and replaced by a $104-million tower in 1995.

The early building boom continued and Wilbur Clark, a former hotel bellman, opened the Desert Inn in 1950. Two years later, Milton Prell opened the Sahara Hotel on the site of the old Club Bingo. Despite numerous ownership changes, both hotels have survived and in 1997 the Desert Inn completed a $200-million remodelling and construction programme to turn it into a five-star luxury resort. The Sands Hotel, a showroom and once the playground for the 'Rat Pack' of Frank Sinatra and his buddies, high rollers and Hollywood stars, opened in 1952. It has not been as fortunate as the Sahara and Desert Inn and in 1996 was demolished to make way for the fabulous new Venetian.

In 1976, Atlantic City legalised gambling and so began a new era in Las Vegas' history as hotel-casinos realised they would need to create a true resort destination to compete. Caesars Palace had been the first hotel on the Strip to create a specific theme for its resort hotel when it opened in 1966 and two years later Circus Circus opened its tent-shaped casino with carnival games and rides. But it was not until the late 1980s and early 1990s that the boom in resort hotels began in earnest.

In 1989, the $630-million upmarket Mirage Hotel opened with a white tiger habitat, dolphin pool, elaborate swimming pool and waterfall and a man-made volcano that belched fire and water. Mirage owner Steve Wynn then built the $430-million Treasure Island resort next door, complete with the Buccaneer Bay and its exciting battles between a pirate ship and British frigate (the Brits always lose!). Wynn also went into a joint venture with Circus Circus Enterprises to develop another luxury resort hotel – the Monte Carlo, which opened in 1996 – and his latest venture is the Bellagio, which opened in 1998 on the site of the former Dunes Hotel.

The Excalibur medieval castle opened in 1990 with court jesters and King Arthur's jousting knights entertaining visitors to the massive $290-million complex. Circus Circus Enterprises then developed the amazing $375-million Luxor next door to the Excalibur and it opened in 1993. In the same year, Grand Slam Canyon Adventuredome opened at Circus Circus Hotel, and Treasure Island, the MGM Grand Hotel and Theme Park all opened their doors. Now one of the world's largest resorts, the MGM Grand has three of the largest concert and sports venues in Las Vegas, some of the top restaurants and a myriad of swimming pools and tennis courts.

In 1997, the £460-million resort hotel New York-New York, which recreates the Big Apple's skyline, added 2,000 rooms. Then came a whole raft of luxury resorts aimed specifically at the sophisticated traveller – the Bellagio in 1998, followed by Mandalay Bay, Paris and the Venetian in 1999. These hotels are not just the last word in luxury, nor magnificent creations of a theme – an Italian lakeside village, South Seas Island, the French capital and Venice respectively – they have also swelled the cultural and dining coffers of the city.

Bellagio has *O*, a fabulous theatrical feast of human feats by the world-acclaimed Cirque du Soleil in,

on and above water – *eau* in French. Mandalay Bay not only has the House of Blues restaurant and live gig joint, but also the award-winning musical *Chicago*, direct from Broadway. And between the four of them they have enticed more than a dozen top-notch and celebrity chefs from New York, Los Angeles, San Francisco and New Orleans to open fine restaurants, including Wolfgang Puck, Joachim Splichal, Charlie Palmer, Jean-Louis Palladin and Julian Serrano.

It seems after going through all its different marketing ploys – the city that never sleeps, a family town, adults only – Las Vegas has finally become the sophisticated Mecca of fun Bugsy Siegel envisaged so many decades ago.

Events

Las Vegas may have a staggering 120,000 rooms, but at certain times of the year it still gets absolutely packed. The busiest times are Christmas, July, August, Easter and the American bank holidays which are: President's Day (George Washington's birthday) – the third Monday in February; Memorial Day – the last Monday in May and the official start of the summer season; Independence Day – 4 July (slap bang in the middle of the high season anyway); Labor Day – the first Monday in September and last holiday of summer; and Thanksgiving – always the fourth Thursday in November.

The best times to visit Las Vegas – providing there are no major conferences or boxing matches going on – are from January to the end of April excluding the bank holidays and Easter, October and November. May, June and September are busier, but are still good times to go.

Getting around

Las Vegas has been growing at such a phenomenal rate in the last six years that it has not been able to keep up in terms of providing the necessary road systems. At peak times, and during the early evening in particular, the Strip gets so crowded that you'll be lucky to move at a snail's pace. The busiest intersection is Tropicana Avenue and the Strip, which is used by an average of 148,000 vehicles a day. This affects the MGM Grand, Tropicana, Excalibur, Luxor, New York-New York and Monte Carlo resort hotels. And getting in and out of the car parks of these major resorts is also a total nightmare during the early evening as people arrive for shows and dinner.

The $92-million Desert Inn Super Arterial, designed to remove traffic from the Strip, opened in April last year and has certainly relieved some congestion. But it is unlikely to help tourists staying on the Strip. For all these reasons, even if you rolled into Las Vegas by car, I recommend you leave it in your hotel car park for the duration of the trip. (Unlike many other cities in America, most of the hotels in Las Vegas provide free parking for residents.)

If you arrive by plane, a taxi ride to a Strip hotel (where most of the major theme resorts are located) will cost $7 to $10, and $10 to $18 to a downtown hotel, depending on the route. Airport shuttle fares are $3.50 to Strip hotels and $4.75 to downtown hotels.

The forecasts are that there will be some relief from the congestion in the future. A tunnel is planned to go under the Strip at Harmon Avenue

and a 16-mile transportation system has been proposed from the airport to Downtown via the Strip.

Buses, taxis, trolley and monorail

Despite the size of the hotels, the Strip is still a relatively compact area so you can often walk to your destination – something I'd never recommend anywhere else in America! But there are other alternatives.

The **Las Vegas Trolley** now has two routes, which will allow you to travel all the way from the Luxor to the Sahara Hotel on the Strip and from the Stratosphere to Downtown. Trolleys run every 15 to 20 minutes and stop at every hotel/casino en route. It will cost you $1.30 to ride the Strip and another $1.30 to go all the way Downtown. The service runs from 9.30am to 2am, daily.

The city bus service – **Citizens Area Transit** (CAT) – has a 24-hour service on the Strip and Downtown, plus 40 other routes that run from 5.30am to 1.30am, seven days a week. For information about routes and schedules, phone 702-228 7433.

There is also an armada of **taxis** – over 1,100 service the city – and here are some of their numbers: ABC Union: 702-736 8444; Ace Cab Co: 702-736 8383; A North Las Vegas Cab Co: 702-643 1041; A Vegas Western Cab Co: 702-736 6121; Checker Yellow Star: 702-873 2227; Desert Cab: 702-386 9102; Western Cab Co: 702-736 8000; Whittlesea Blue Cab 702-384 6111.

The smart new **Monorail**, which opened in 1995 at a cost of $25 million, currently links the MGM Grand Hotel on Tropicana and the Strip to Bally's Hotel Casino on Flamingo Road and the Strip, and there are plans for an extension to the Las Vegas Hilton. These have been held up while planners decide if they will allow the hotel-operated transport system to expand when there are proposals afoot for a massive public rail system that would run from the airport to Downtown.

A new five-car shuttle now transports people free of charge between Mandalay Bay, Luxor and the Excalibur. In the meantime pedestrian footbridges have been built over the Strip, and it is wise to use them as nearly 50 pedestrians were killed in road traffic accidents on the Strip in 1998.

Car rental

If you intend to arrive in Las Vegas and experience the city in full before starting a tour of the region, I recommend that you do not arrange to collect your car until you are ready to leave the city. This way you will save vital pounds on insurance, tax, surcharges and hire costs (see Chapter 10 for full details).

★ ★ ★ **INSIDE TRACK** ★ ★ ★

If you plan to arrange car rental on arrival in Las Vegas, look out for special deals advertised in local papers and magazines – you may find excellent prices and extras such as free long-distance phone cards.

★ ★ ★ ★ ★ ★ ★ ★ ★ ★ ★ ★ ★ ★ ★ ★ ★

You may also decide not to book a car in advance, but hire one once you arrive (still read Chapter 10 please!), so here are the local car rental companies and their numbers: Airport Rent-A-Car: 702-795 0800; Alamo: 702-263 8411; All State: 702-736 6147; Avis: 702-261 5995; Budget: 702-736 1212; Dollar: 702-739 8408; Enterprise: 702-795 8842; Hertz: 702-736 4900; National: 702-261 5391; Practical: 702-798 5253; Rent A Vette Sports Cars/Exotics/Motorcycle Rentals: 702-736 2592; Thrifty: 702-896 7600.

Some companies have rental sites at many of the major resort hotels. If

booking on site in Las Vegas at a quiet time, you may be offered very cheap upgrades, but beware of hard-sell tactics and if you're certain you don't want or need a bigger car, stick to your guns.

★ ★ ★ **INSIDE TRACK** ★ ★ ★

Some of the smaller rental companies may be cheaper, but always ensure that your rental agreement will allow you to drive outside the state of Nevada.

★ ★ ★ ★ ★ ★ ★ ★ ★ ★ ★ ★ ★ ★ ★ ★ ★ ★

Limos

It won't cost you an arm and a leg to travel in style in Las Vegas – you can rent a limo for the ride into town from the airport for as little as $5 a person if there are several of you. Check out the deals available on arrival. And if you're having a big night out on the town and want to have a drink, it often works out about the same price to hire a limo for the night. Here are some limo companies: Ambassador Limousines: 702-362 6200; Bell Trans/ Limousines and Buses: 702-739 7990 or toll-free 1-800 274 7433; Las Vegas Limousines: 702-736 7990 or toll-free 1-800 274 7433; On Demand Sedan-Black Car Service: 702-876 2222; Presidential Limousines: 702-731 5577 or toll-free 1-800 423 1429.

Tips on tipping

Tipping is not just a way of life in America, but a genuine source of income for most employees in the hotel and casino services and they are even taxed on an expectation of tips received. Sadly, tipping is something that we Brits tend to overlook. There are some fairly loose customs in Las Vegas, but here is a guide to how much we should tip.

Bartenders and cocktail waitresses generally get around $1 a round for parties of two to four people, more for larger groups. It is usual to tip keno runners (see Chapter 4, Gambling), slot machine change girls or casino dealers. Some gamblers who play for long periods of time tip casino staff even if they've lost! Hotel maids expect $2 a day at the end of a visit, pool attendants get 50 cents to $1 for towels, pads, loungers, etc. For food servers and room service, the standard 15–20% rule applies.

★ ★ ★ **INSIDE TRACK** ★ ★ ★

When buying US$ before your trip always ask for plenty of $1 bills so you can tip porters and taxi drivers on arrival. It is also useful to bear in mind that at many American airports it will cost you a $1 bill to use a baggage trolley, so it's better to be safe than sorry!

Many showrooms sell assigned seating tickets, which may include the tip. In resort showrooms that have restaurant-style reservations and seating, you can tip the maître d' (Americans don't have head waiters, they have maître d's like the French!) $5 to $20 to improve your seats. Showroom servers get $5 to $10 for a party of two to four people at a cocktails-only show, or $10 to $20 for a dinner show depending on the service and quality of food. Taxi drivers expect $1 to $2 per person at the end of the trip. It is normal to tip valet parkers $1 to $2, depending on how quick the service has been.

Medical Emergencies

The number you need to know is 911, though I sincerely hope you won't need to use it. If you take any kind of regular medication, eg for a heart condition or epilepsy, you need to know that the same drugs are produced under different generic names In America to here in Britain. This means that if you are involved in an accident in America, doctors will not be able to define your condition via your medication. It is a good idea to ask your doctor or pharmacy to find out the name of your particular prescription drug in America. Keep this written down with your prescription or put both English and American drug names inside a clear plastic case that is easily accessible to medical crews.

Weather

One thing you can be sure of – you're not going to freeze! Having said that, in November 1995, temperatures only got as high as 7°C/45°F – 6°C/21°F below the daytime norm – and there was the briefest flurry of snow. You'll be pleased to know that those poor Las Vegans got over their small taste of what we live with in a normal springtime! On average, Las Vegas has about 300 days of sunshine a year, with an average rainfall of 10.2 cm/4.2 in throughout the year, making it an arid climate. June to September tend to be the hottest months with daytime temperatures above 38°C/100°F in July and August, so if you're going out and about for the day, always make sure you put a decent sunblock on before you leave your hotel.

Dress code

Fortunately, given the climate, the dress code is pretty relaxed in Las Vegas with casual clothes permitted around the clock. But wearing swimming costumes inside a casino or restaurant is not acceptable and it is normal to go a bit dressy for a big evening out. If you're intending to visit in early spring or late autumn, take a cardigan or lightweight jacket for the evening and something a bit heavier for winter.

MONTH	TEMPERATURE °C/°F MIN MAX	HUMIDITY % AM/PM	PRECIP. INCHES	SUNSHINE %
January	1/33 13/56	41/30	.50	77
February	3/37 19/67	36/26	.46	80
March	5/42 20/68	30/22	.41	83
April	9/49 25/77	22/15	.22	87
May	15/59 30/87	19/13	.22	88
June	20/68 36/98	15/10	.09	92
July	24/75 40/104	19/15	.45	87
August	22/73 38/101	14/18	.54	88
September	18/65 34/94	23/17	.32	91
October	11/53 27/81	25/19	.25	87
November	5/41 19/66	33/27	.43	80
December	1/33 14/57	41/33	.32	77

Useful numbers

Airport information	702-261 5743
Airport parking	702-261 5121
Citizens Area Transit	702-228 7433
Convention information	702-892 0711
Directory assistance	702-555 1212
Emergency Service Dispatch	911
Highway Patrol	702-385 0311
Las Vegas Fire Department	702-383 2888
Las Vegas Transit System	702-228 7433
Marriage License Bureau	702-455 4415
Metro Police	702-795 3111
Poison Information Center	702-732 4989
Road conditions	702-486 3116
Show Hot Line	702-225 5554
Tourist information	702-892 7575
Weather	702-736 3854

Vocabulary

It has often been said that Brits and Americans are divided by a common language and when you make an unexpected *faux pas* you'll certainly learn how true this is. For instance, never, ever ask for a packet of fags as this is the American slang word for gays and a sense of humour is not their strong point! There are plenty of other differences, too, which may not necessarily cause offence, but which will cause confusion, so to help you on your way, here is a guide to American-speak. There are some words, like fuel, which are just spelt differently. These have not been listed as they are mostly self-explanatory, but it helps to remember that spellings do sometimes vary.

Travelling around:

Aerial	Antenna	Motorway	Superhighway,
Articulated Truck	Semi		freeway, expressway
Bonnet	Hood	No parking or stopping	No standing
Boot	Trunk	Pavement	Sidewalk
Caravan	House trailer	Petrol station	Gas station
Car park	Parking lot	Request stop	Flag stop
Car silencer	Muffler	Ring road	Beltway
Crossroads/junction	Intersection	Run in (engine)	Break in
Demister	Defogger	Slip road	Ramp
Dipswitch	Dimmer	Subway	Pedestrian underpass
Dual carriageway	Four-lane	Transport	Transportation
	or divided highway	Turning	Turnoff
Flyover	Overpass	Tyre	Tire
Give way	Yield	Underground	Subway
Jump leads	Jumper cables	Walk	Hike
Lay-by	Turn-out	Wheel clamp	Denver boot
Lorry	Truck	Windscreen	Windshield
Manual transmission	Stick shift	Wing	Fender

Eating and stuff:

One of the biggest disappointments I had on my first American trip was to use what I thought was the correct lingo when ordering my breakfast eggs 'sunny side up' one morning, only to end up with what seemed like a half-cooked egg! The Americans don't flick fat over the top of the egg when frying it, but turn it over to cook on both sides. So for eggs the way I like them, cooked on both sides but soft, I have to order eggs 'over easy' and if you like yours well done, then ask for eggs 'over hard'.

There are plenty of other anomalies. Many standard American dishes come with a biscuit – which is a corn scone to us and all the more strange for breakfast! They also have something called grits, which is a porridge-like breakfast dish made out of ground, boiled corn, plus hash browns – grated, fried potatoes. Here are some other differences in food-speak.

Aubergine	Eggplant	Essence (eg vanilla)	Extract
Bill	Check or tab	Golden syrup	Corn syrup
Biscuit (sweet)	Cookie	Grated, fried potatoes	Hash browns
Biscuit (savoury)	Cracker	Grilled	Broiled
Chickpea	Garbanzo bean	Icing sugar	Confectioner's sugar
Chips	French fries	Jam	Jelly
Choux bun	Cream puff	Ketchup	Catsup
Cling film	Plastic wrap	King prawn	Shrimp
Coriander	Cilantro	Main course	Entree
Corn	Wheat	Measure	Shot
Cornflour	Cornstarch	Minced meat	Ground meat
Courgette	Zucchini	Off-licence	Liquor store
Crayfish	Crawfish	Pastry case	Pie shell
Crisps	Chips	Pips	Seeds (in fruit)
Crystallised	Candied	Plain/dark chocolate	Semi-sweet
Cutlery	Silverware or place-setting		or unsweetened chocolate
Demerera sugar	Light-brown sugar	Pumpkin	Squash
Desiccated coconut	Shredded coconut	Scone	Biscuit
Digestive biscuit	Graham cracker	Shortcrust pastry	Pie dough
Double cream	Heavy cream	Single cream	Light cream

Soda water	Seltzer
Soya	Soy
Sorbet	Sherbet
Spirits	Liquor
Sponge finger biscuits	Ladyfingers
Spring onion	Scallion
Starter	Appetiser
Stoned (cherries, etc.)	Pitted
Sultana	Golden raisin
Sweet shop	Candy store
Take-away	To go
Tomato purée	Tomato paste
Water biscuit	Cracker

Shopping

Bumbag	Fanny pack
Chemist	Drug store
Ground floor	First floor
Handbag	Purse
High Street	Main Street
In (Fifth Avenue, etc.)	On
Jumper	Sweater
Muslin	Cheesecloth
Pants	Underpants
Suspenders	Garters
Tights	Pantyhose
Till	Check-out
Trainers	Sneakers
Trousers	Pants
Underpants	Shorts
Vest	Undershirt
Waistcoat	Vest
Zip	Zipper

Money

Bill	Check
Banknote	Bill
Cheque	Check
10 cents	Dime
5 cents	Nickel
1 cent	Penny
25 cents	Quarter

General

Air hostess	Flight attendant
Anti-clockwise	Counterclockwise
At weekends	On weekends
Autumn	Fall
Behind	In back of
Camp bed	Cot
Cinema	Movie theater
Coach	Bus
Cot	Crib
Diary (appointments)	Calendar
Diary (records)	Journal
Doctor	Physician
City/town centre	Downtown (not the run-down bit!)
Fold-up bed	Cot
From … to …	Through
Lift	Elevator
Long-distance call	Trunk call
Nappy	Diaper
Ordinary	Regular, normal
Paddling pool	Wading pool
Post, postbox	Mail, mailbox
Pram, pushchair	Stroller
Queue	Line, line up
Tap	Faucet
Toilet	Restroom (public) Bathroom (private)

A Note on *The Brit's Guide*

This *Brit's Guide* is one of an innovative series of travel guides which aim to offer practical, user-friendly guidance for the British traveller abroad. Focusing on clear, honest information, it is one British traveller's advice to another – without the jargon or sales pitch of the brochures. *A Brit's Guide to Las Vegas and the West 2000* gives you the complete rundown on the hotels, restaurants and shows in Las Vegas, plus help in planning a grand tour of the West Coast. The colour plates are organised thematically, so do consult them as you read.

RESORT HOTELS

Choosing the right resort hotel for your holiday

Try, if you can, to fly into Las Vegas. That way you'll get a bird's-eye view of one of the most amazing man-made sights in the world as a mirage-like image of the most spectacular collection of buildings ever crowded into one six-mile stretch of land shimmers up at you from the desert landscape. Once you've landed, you can go round the world – and its history – in a few hours, thanks to the splendours of the new breed of theme resort hotels Las Vegas has to offer.

As you drive north on the Strip from the airport, you'll pass the South Seas paradise of Mandalay Bay on your left, before spotting the unmissable pyramid of the Luxor and the castle-like vistas of Camelot at Excalibur. By now you'll be at the new Four Corners of Las Vegas on the Strip and Tropicana. Before you've had time to let out a sigh of amazement you'll be passing the lion of MGM Grand on the right, opposite the towers of New York-New York and its famous Big Apple landmarks. The Monte Carlo is next, a fine recreation of the ritzy Place du Monaco, then there is the Eiffel Tower at Paris on the right, before the Italian village of Bellagio looms up on your left.

Now you've reached the old Four Corners, the original section of the Strip that was home to Bugsy Siegel's Flamingo and the first you'll know of it is seeing the majestic Caesars Palace with its Greco-Roman empire theme on the left. Opposite the Forum Shops at Caesars is the modern Flamingo Hilton. Then, further north on the right, is the Japanese-inspired Imperial Palace opposite the posh Polynesian resort of the Mirage and its exploding volcano. If arriving any time after 4pm, Treasure Island's

pirates of the Caribbean could well be in action at Buccaneer Bay, but don't forget to look right to see the spectacular Venetian with its recreation of St Mark's Square and the Doge's Palace.

Further north on the right is the beautiful Desert Inn, home to one of the few golf courses on the Strip. Then on the left you'll see the circus dome shape of the Grand Slam Canyon and Circus Circus, a classic family resort on the theme of a turn-of-the-century travelling circus, before you finally reach the spire of the Stratosphere Hotel, the tallest free-standing tower in America.

★ ★ ★  ★ ★ ★
★   ★
★   ★
★ The term 'the Strip' was coined by ★
★ a former Los Angeles police ★
★ captain in 1938. Guy McAfee said ★
★ the stretch of road with its ★
★ brightly lit hotels and casinos ★
★ reminded him of Hollywood's ★
★ Sunset Strip, another Mecca for ★
★ night owls! ★
★ ★ ★ ★ ★ ★ ★ ★ ★ ★ ★ ★ ★ ★ ★ ★

It's an amazing line-up – and it's all thanks to money and the making of it. It was in the 1980s that the city and its hotel owners realised that they would have to do more than just provide plush casinos to lure gamblers way from their rival gambling destination of Atlanta. Since then, more and more states have legalised gambling, so the competition has stiffened further. To fight back, the hotels have tried every marketing trick in the book – first labelling the city as a 24-hour destination. This epithet may be true, yet sadly most top-notch restaurants and attractions are closed by 11pm.

Then it was as a 'family destination' that Las Vegas tried to lure in more punters, but they found that families don't tend to part with big wads of cash in the same way as adults do.

Now, as the city enters the new Millennium, it is repositioning itself once again as an 'adults only' city, while plush new resorts – the Bellagio, Mandalay Bay and the Venetian – are aimed at the more sophisticated affluent traveller. It means that for us punters there is more choice than ever.

So where do you stay? The choice is endless, but the point of being in Las Vegas is to 'experience' the attractions too, so I've stuck to the most important hotels. Here's a complete rundown of each of the major theme resorts, their facilities and roughly how much it costs to stay there. I have not given each of the major resorts a rating, for the simple reason that they are aimed at different types of people, so a comparison would not really be appropriate. Also do remember that in Las Vegas, as in no other city on earth, supply and demand vary greatly and the differences are reflected in hugely fluctuating room prices. My notes on booking your hotel room in Chapter 9 give a more detailed picture of how to get a room not only at the inn of your choice, but also at the right price.

The Best Theme Hotels

The Bellagio

A once-in-a-lifetime treat for romantics everywhere!
Location: The Strip at the corner of West Flamingo
Theme: Upmarket, romantic Italian lakeside village
Cost: $1.7 billion
Rooms: 2,688
Shows: New Cirque du Soleil theatrical circus spectacular, O
Entertainments: Nightly water ballet by thousands of fountains and lights

in the lake with classical music
Restaurants: 12 dining outlets
Chilling out: Five outdoor pool areas plus full-service beauty salon and spa
Shopping: Esplanade filled with designer shops
Wedding chapels: Two
Room rates: From $150 Monday to Thursday; from $500 Friday to Sunday
Reservations: 702-693 7111

For the ultimate romantic experience in a luxurious setting, this brand new hotel, which only opened in October 1998 and is based on an entire village in north Italy, is the place to go. The real crowd-puller is O, the new show by the world-famous Cirque du Soleil. A special $70-million theatre, modelled on the Paris Opera House, has been built as a permanent home for the theatrical acrobatics and breathtaking stunts that make Cirque shows so spectacular. Their new show – Mystère will continue at Treasure Island – involves breathtaking maneouvres in, on and above water.

The free 'signature' show of the resort is the $30-million night-time spectacle created by colourful, soaring fountains in a water ballet accompanied by lights and classical music by Copland and Strauss.

Here, at the Bellagio, the emphasis is on the finest things that money can buy. Everything is so seriously upscale it almost makes Beverly Hills' Rodeo Drive look downmarket! Mirage Resorts chairman Steve Wynn is said to have spent more than $72 million of his own money buying up original works by Van Gogh, Monet, Manet, Renoir, Cézanne and Gauguin for the gallery that houses impressionist and abstract expressionist paintings from 1870 to 1970. Stretching across the lobby ceiling is a fabulous, hand-blown multi-coloured glass sculpture and the nearby botanical conservatory is replanted several times a year to keep its blooms perfect all year round.

From each of the many rooms are panoramic views of the 8.5-acre lake, classical gardens, elegant pools and landscaped grounds filled with fountains, waterfalls and pools. The restaurants range from casual bistros to gourmet restaurants Le Cirque and Picasso, which is filled with paintings and ceramics by the artist. When you have a spare moment (and a spare million), try browsing round the esplanade filled with gorgeous Chanel, Armani, Gucci, Prada and Tiffany boutiques, before taking afternoon tea – one of the more affordable pleasures of the Bellagio!

INSIDE TRACK

You've got more chance of getting a room – and cheaply – at the resort hotels if you go between Monday and Thursday.

Caesars Palace

Originally designed for high rollers, it's now accessible to all and should at least be on your must-see list.
Location: On the Strip at the famous Four Corners with Flamingo
Theme: Greco-Roman Empire
Rooms: 2,471
Showrooms: Circus Maximus Showroom, Caesars Magical Empire, Omnimax® Theater
Entertainments: Cleopatra's Barge Nightclub, Adventure Arcade, CyberStation
Restaurants: 18
Chilling out: Garden of the Gods pools and spa
Shopping: Appian Way and The Forum Shops
Wedding Chapels: One
Other facilities: Four late-night lounges featuring live music, lighted outdoor amphitheatre
Room rates: From $109 Monday to Thursday; from $179 Friday to Sunday

Reservations: 702-731 7110
The first-ever theme hotel of Las Vegas, Caesars Palace opened in 1966 specifically aimed at big-money gamblers. Although it allows more ordinary mortals to enter its palatial doors these days, the emphasis is still very much on luxury and opulence. The Palace has recently undergone a $600-million expansion, which included building the 17-storey Palace Tower, a new Garden of the Gods outdoor area, with pools and landscaped gardens, and a wedding chapel, Neptune's Villa. You enter this monument to the ancient gods of Europe through the central People Mover, which takes you to the World of Caesar. The round centrepiece houses a miniature city of Rome as it may have looked 2,000 years ago, while fibre optics, three-dimensional video projection and other special effects recreate the feeling of guests approaching a celebration at a mighty emperor's palace. Throughout the 80-acre resort are spectacular fountains, majestic cypress trees, gleaming marble statues and beautiful landscaping. The Garden of the Gods area has three outdoor swimming pools inlaid with marble and granite, adjoined by two whirlpool spas and rimmed by lush gardens. There are also three lighted tennis courts and an intimate outdoor amphitheatre. In addition to big-star concerts – Caesars Palace has played host to Natalie Cole, Celine Dion and David Copperfield – the new multi-chambered Caesars Magical Empire provides dining and live magical entertainment in a fabulous setting. All of the rooms have jacuzzi tubs and the latest fax/phone gadgetry, while the fabulous Forum Shops are also known as the Shopping Wonder of the World (see Chapter 7). If you want to see how the other half live, take a wiggle on down to the posh baccarat and VIP high-roller areas. You never know, you may just get a proposal of sorts!

Circus Circus

A good-value, family-fun destination.
Location: The Strip between West Sahara and Convention Center
Theme: Circus carnival featuring the world's largest permanent circus
Rooms: 3,744
Entertainments: Free circus acts; IMAX® theatre and Grand Slam Canyon theme park
Casinos: Three, covering 107,500 square feet
Restaurants: Six restaurants, four snack bars and six bars and lounges
Chilling out: Three swimming pools
Shopping: 20 retail outlets in a 40,000-square-foot promenade
Wedding chapels: One
Other facilities: Beauty salon
Room rates: From $39 Sunday to Thursday; from $59 Friday and Saturday
Reservations: 702-734 0410

The owners of Circus Circus were the second operators to build a theme casino on the Strip and it originally opened in 1968 with the world's largest permanent circus tent plus casino but no hotel rooms. Now it has two 15-storey towers housing nearly 4,000 rooms, three major gambling areas, a whole raft of shops and some major family attractions, and there are plans for further expansions! Circus Circus was inspired by the turn-of-the-century circuses that used to visit towns throughout America, and aims its services directly at the cost-conscious family market.

The Circus Arena appears in the *Guinness Book of World Records* as the world's largest permanent circus and covers 120,000 square feet with a 90-foot-high tent-shaped roof. The Carnival Midway is a circus-themed amusement arcade and the centre stage of Carnival Midway is where free half-hourly shows are presented from 11am to midnight by top circus acts, from high-wire daredevils to flying trapeze artists, acrobats, magicians and jugglers.

The Circus Circus Theme Park – the Grand Slam Canyon – is a fully enclosed five-acre elevated theme park which is climate-controlled to provide temperatures of 21°C/70°F all the year round. This first-ever Las Vegas amusement park has been improved over the years and now has thrilling rides in a canyon-like setting (see Chapter 6 for details).

What the resort is about is providing entertainment in a friendly, low-cost way. If you're a novice and fancy a flutter on the Strip, this is the place to try out your luck on the roulette wheels before moving on to a high-stakes poker game elsewhere (we can dream, can't we?).

The hotel has implemented a fast-track check-in and check-out facility. If your reservation is pre-paid or a credit card number has been given, you can avoid long queues at reception by phoning 1-800 5NO WAIT between 8am and midnight on the day you intend to check in. Allow at least one hour and you will be able to pick up your keys at the special NO WAIT window in the hotel lobby between 2pm and midnight.

★ ★ ★ ★ **INSIDE TRACK** ★ ★ ★
★   ★
★   ★
★   Be warned, Circus Circus is so   ★
★   popular with families that it can ★
★   seem like you're surrounded by   ★
★   wall-to-wall kids!   ★
★ ★ ★ ★ ★ ★ ★ ★ ★ ★ ★ ★ ★ ★ ★ ★ ★

The Desert Inn

Not cheap but worth every penny, so really good value.
Location: The Strip, just north of Sands
Theme: If anything, a golf resort in the grand Palm Beach style
Rooms: 715
Shows: Headliners at the Crystal Showroom and nightly live music in the Starlight Lounge
Restaurants: Four gourmet restaurants
Chilling out: Luxurious spa, pool and jogging track
Shopping: Award-winning golf shop

Other facilities: Championship golf course and tennis courts
Room rates: From$155 Monday to Thursday; from $205 Friday to Sunday
Reservations: 702-733 4444

An older-generation hotel frequented by the 'Rat Pack' of Sinatra and his buddies, this is one of the few that has stood the test of time – and which has adapted to meet the changing face of visitors to Las Vegas. Wilbur Clark began building the Desert Inn Hotel in 1946 and it opened in 1950 at a cost of $4.5 million. Frank Sinatra made his Las Vegas début at the hotel in 1951 and from then on it became a famous landmark on the Strip.

A recent $200-million renovation has created an opulent and elegant resort with a fabulous Grand Lobby atrium, complete with stunning 30-foot murals, marble floors and large windows that provide breathtaking views of the lagoon and golf course, lagoon-style pool and gardens, a new Starlight Lounge, a nine-storey Palm Tower and new villas. The name of the game is now luxury and the new accommodations reflect that with 715 rooms and suites housed in five beautiful buildings designed and built in Spanish/Moorish architectural style.

Once you've learnt how to handle yourself at the baccarat and blackjack tables, then you can gamble to your heart's content in the most sophisticated settings of the Desert Inn Casino, where the dome-shaped ceilings are hand-painted in royal blue and gold leaf to create a night sky, magnificent chandeliers add a stately touch, and rich, gold velvet curtains over organic iron railings for the two private baccarat parlours add a certain splendour to the proceedings of parting with your cash.

Golfers will be in heaven on the golf course – the only one on the Strip – which annually hosts top PGA tournaments, while beyond the lakes, trees and fairways are four tournament-class tennis courts

specially lit for night play. And another thing, parking is actually quite close to the hotel, while the valet service is free (don't forget to tip).

Excalibur

Great for family fun at reasonable prices, it should also be on your must-visit list.
Location: The Strip at West Tropicana
Theme: King Arthur and the Knights of the Round Table
Cost: $290 million
Rooms: 4,032
Shows: *King Arthur's Tournament* and two magic-motion cinemas
Entertainments: Free fire-breathing dragon show and strolling entertainers
Restaurants: Six
Chilling out: Two swimming pools
Shopping: The Medieval Village
Wedding chapels: Two
Room rates: From $45 Monday to Thursday; from $75 Friday to Sunday
Reservations: 702-597 7777

The beautiful spires of the Camelot-style entrance building are set between two huge castle-like towers that house the 4,000-odd rooms available at this family-orientated resort. Make no mistake, though, the free Dragon Battle that takes place every hour on the hour from 10am until 10pm and draws crowds from far and wide has the sole purpose of inviting you in to part with your cash in the 100,000-square-foot casino. But there are plenty of other free entertainments to keep you amused as you wander round the Medieval Village of shops and restaurants, from the strolling entertainers to the free variety acts on the Court Jester's Stage from 10am every day or the pretty Glockenspiel Fairy Tale that is played out over the giant clock at the back entrance on the hour and half hour from 10am to 10pm. You can eat dinner and see King Arthur's Tournament at either 6pm or 8.30pm any day of the week, or bop along to live music at the Minstrel's Lounge or Wild Bill's Saloon and Steakhouse. The house of fun also has six restaurants and parking is free and relatively accessible by Las Vegas standards!

Don't miss the medieval-costumed staff at the Excalibur, where entertainers wander around playing medieval trumpets!

Imperial Palace

Friendly, reasonably priced hotel in prime location.
Location: The Strip at West Flamingo
Theme: Japanese
Rooms: 2,700
Shows: *Legends in Concert*
Entertainments: Auto Collection
Restaurants: Nine
Chilling out: Olympic-size swimming pool with waterfall and heated spa
Wedding chapels: One
Other facilities: The only 24-hour medical facility on the Strip, phone direct on 702-735 3600.
Room rates: From $45 Monday to Thursday; from $100 Friday to Sunday
Reservations: 702-731 3311

When the reviews of Las Vegas accommodation are done, the Imperial Palace hardly takes centre stage, yet after Circus Circus and Caesars Palace, it was actually one of the first hotels to adopt a theme and is the largest privately-owned hotel in the world. Owner Ralph Engelstad favoured the clean lines of oriental design and plumped for a theme based on Japanese temple architecture. Now the resort is home to one of the longest-running shows on the Strip, houses a collection of vintage and special-interest cars and has a good-value full-service spa.

Las Vegas Hilton

Filled with conventioners; best just to visit for the *Star Trek* experience.
Location: Paradise Road and Karen Avenue (behind the Strip)
Rooms: 3,174
Shows: *Star Trek: The Experience*
Entertainments: The Nightclub
Restaurants: 12
Chilling out: Pool, spa, tennis courts
Shopping: Two promenades
Room rates: From $89 Monday to Thursday; from $269 Friday to Sunday
Reservations: 702-732 5111

An understated elegance pervades what is ostensibly an upmarket hotel resort for business people visiting one of the millions of conventions held in Las Vegas. For them its location near the Convention Center is perfect, but it's about a 10–12-minute walk to the Strip, so it's a little off the beaten track for real tourists. The rooftop recreation deck includes a health club, massive swimming pool, six lighted tennis courts and a putting green, while the Nightclub has all the latest hi-tech nightlife gadgetry and is one of the in-places to be seen. Now, following a collaboration with Paramount Parks, the hotel is home to one of the most exciting theme entertainments in Las Vegas – *Star Trek: The Experience*.

When Elvis first appeared in Las Vegas at the Last Frontier Hotel on the Strip in 1956 he was a flop. He didn't return until 1969 when he mostly appeared – to great acclaim, of course – at the Las Vegas Hilton.

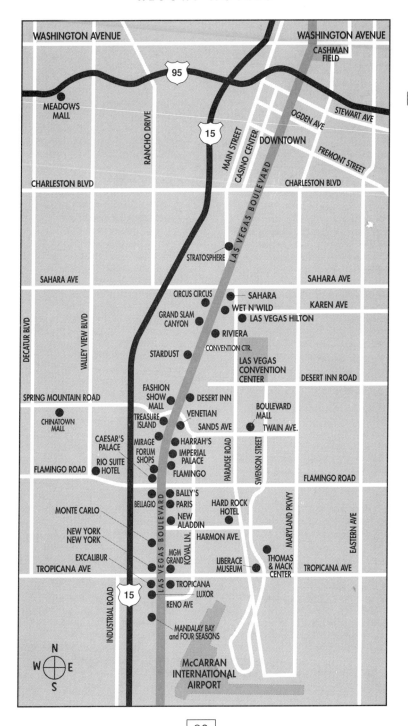

2

WASHINGTON AVENUE   WASHINGTON AVENUE

CASHMAN FIELD

95

STEWART AVE

MEADOWS MALL

RANCHO DRIVE

15

OGDEN AVE

MAIN STREET

CASINO CENTER

DOWNTOWN

FREMONT STREET

CHARLESTON BLVD   CHARLESTON BLVD

LAS VEGAS BOULEVARD

SAHARA AVE   SAHARA AVE

STRATOSPHERE

DECATUR BLVD

VALLEY VIEW BLVD

CIRCUS CIRCUS   SAHARA
                       WET N'WILD   KAREN AVE
GRAND SLAM CANYON   LAS VEGAS HILTON

RIVIERA
CONVENTION CTR.
STARDUST
                       LAS VEGAS CONVENTION CENTER   DESERT INN ROAD

SPRING MOUNTAIN ROAD
FASHION SHOW MALL   DESERT INN
                       VENETIAN   BOULEVARD MALL
TREASURE ISLAND
CHINATOWN MALL   SANDS AVE   TWAIN AVE.
CAESAR'S PALACE
MIRAGE FORUM SHOPS   HARRAH'S
RIO SUITE HOTEL   IMPERIAL PALACE

PARADISE ROAD

SWENSON STREET

FLAMINGO ROAD   FLAMINGO   FLAMINGO ROAD

BALLY'S
BELLAGIO   PARIS   HARD ROCK HOTEL
MONTE CARLO   NEW ALADDIN

MARYLAND PKWY

EASTERN AVE

NEW YORK NEW YORK   HARMON AVE.

KOVAL LN.

EXCALIBUR   MGM GRAND
TROPICANA AVE   LIBERACE MUSEUM   THOMAS & MACK CENTER   TROPICANA AVE

TROPICANA
INDUSTRIAL ROAD

15   LUXOR
                      RENO AVE

MANDALAY BAY and FOUR SEASONS

N
W   E
S

McCARRAN INTERNATIONAL AIRPORT

Luxor

Tastefully done theme resort at good value-for-money prices.
Location: The Strip between Tropicana and Reno
Theme: Ancient Egypt
Cost: $375 million, plus a $240-million expansion
Rooms: 4,427
Shows: *Imagine: A Theatrical Odyssey*
Entertainments: Ra nightclub, Nefertiti's Lounge for live music and dancing, Sega® VirtuaLand arcade, IMAX® cinema
Restaurants: Six
Chilling out: Swimming pool and spa
Shopping: Giza Galleria promenade plus Luxor shops in the pyramid
Other facilities: Enclosed moving walkway to the Excalibur next door
Room rates: From $59 Monday to Thursday; from $170 Friday to Sunday
Reservations: 702-262 4444

For us Brits this is the hotel that is synonymous with Las Vegas extravagance, and staying in the fabulous replica of a pyramid is up there on your must-do list for Las Vegas, along with visiting the Liberace museum and flying out to see the Grand Canyon. With its trademark beacon of light that shoots ten miles into space, the hotel is one of the most tastefully executed theme resorts in the middle-market sector. But nothing ever stays the same for long in this city and the Luxor has been no exception to the rounds of upgrade and expansion projects carried out in the late 1990s. At the beginning of 1998, a new computer-controlled lighting system on the exterior of the pyramid was installed, which means the resort can be seen up to 50 miles away, and a new nightclub – called Ra after the Egyptian God, of course – was opened with a stage, dance floor, bars, cigar lounge and a 110-seater sushi and oyster bar.

You can now enter the beautiful structure through a new life-size replica of the great Temple of Rameses II, which takes you directly into the casino (funny that!) where 120,000 square feet of gambling space are home to slot and video machines, gaming tables, a sports book, poker and keno. Attractions include a motion-based simulator ride called In Search of the Obelisk, the first IMAX 3-D cinema in the city with an eight-channel, multi-dimensional digital sound system, and the museum replica of King Tut's tomb. Sega VirtuaLand is a prototype high-tech entertainment centre that showcases the very latest in Sega technology. You can try the dog-fight simulator with gyro-moving spherical cockpit and other three-dimensional interactive arcade games. The resort's headliner show *Imagine: A Theatrical Odyssey* can be seen in the new Luxor Theater that has comfy seats, cup-holder armrests and state-of-the-art lighting and sound systems.

To get to your room, you'll travel at a bizarre 39-degree angle, while a huge pool with private cabanas offers a good place to just chill out and relax. All this and shops selling Egyptian antiquities, gemstones and charms and limited edition art, while one of the restaurants, Isis, is consistently voted among the top ten restaurants in America.

★ ★ ★ **INSIDE TRACK** ★ ★ ★
★ ★
★ ★
★ The light beam from the Luxor ★
★ pyramid is so bright it is ★
★ equivalent to the power of ★
★ 40 billion candles and provides ★
★ enough light to read a ★
★ newspaper 10 miles up in space! ★
★ ★ ★ ★ ★ ★ ★ ★ ★ ★ ★ ★ ★ ★ ★ ★ ★

Mandalay Bay

A luxury resort filled with must-see shows and must-eat-at restaurants.
Location: The Strip, just south of West Tropicana Avenue (entrance off Hacienda Drive)
Theme: South Sea Islands
Cost: $950 million

Rooms: 3,700
Shows: Broadway smash hit musical *Chicago*
Entertainments: House of Blues entertainment venue and restaurant, Rum Jungle nightclub and lounges
Restaurants: 14 eating outlets including two celebrity-chef restaurants and a vodka and caviar bar
Chilling out: Sand-and-surf beach, lazy river ride and luxury spa
Shopping: A selection of shops on the South Seas theme selling everything from cigars to Bali treasures
Room rates: From $99 Sunday to Thursday; from $139 Friday and Saturday
Reservations: 702-632 7777

You just won't know where to start at this hotel, one of the latest in a raft of top-notch establishments aimed at the more sophisticated traveller.

The Broadway musical smash hit, *Chicago*, is bound to be a big draw and deservedly so. Since opening in New York in 1996, it has won the Grammy Award for Best Musical Show Album, six Drama Desk Awards, three Astaire Awards and six Tony Awards, among others. The entire cast that made the production a legend has moved lock, stock and barrel to Las Vegas to play at Mandalay Bay's 1,700-seat theatre for a lengthy engagement.

When the owners of the House of Blues (the famous dinner and entertainment venue on Los Angeles' Sunset Strip) first announced it would be opening an outfit in Las Vegas, such was the excitement that James Brown, Natalie Cole and Jim Belushi all turned out to the launch party. Despite the competition, the live music venue is drawing such crowds that a reservation is needed at least four weeks in advance. And if you just can't get enough of the blues, then ask for a room on the 34th floor of the hotel – it's filled with themed House of Blues guestrooms.

Then there are the two celebrity-chef restaurants, Charlie Palmer's

Aureole, consistently vo[...] one in New York for Ar[...] by the Zagat restauran[...] Trattoria del Lupo, owned by, Wolfgang Puck, one of the most influential chefs in the States. Or try Red Square, the Russian-inspired homage to vodka and caviar. Celebrities have their own private vodka lockers, but the less well-to-do can still partake at the frozen ice bar where there is a selection of more than 100 frozen vodkas and infusions, martinis and Russian-inspired cocktails. You can also dine – for a price – on an extensive selection of caviars or Russian classics.

Still not enough fun? Then try Rum Jungle for a bit of dinner and dancing. Here the food and drinks are turned into works or art from a flaming wall to cascading waterfalls, while volcanic mountains of rum and spirits rise before you at the illuminated bar. Many of the sizzling meals are cooked over a giant open fire pit for that authentic South Seas flavour, while there is dancing to Latin, Caribbean and African beats until the wee small hours of the morning. It's not all fast-paced at the Mandalay though, as there are plenty of ways to unwind in the 11-acre tropical water environment. Try out the city's first sand-and-surf beach, take a dip in one of the many swimming pools or just go for a lazy river ride.

Incorporated into the Mandalay Bar, but with its own entrance and reception area is the:

Four Seasons at Mandalay Bay

Provides an oasis of elegance as the first non-gambling hotel on the Strip. Guests have access to all the facilities of the Mandalay Bay, but have their own exclusive facilities too!
Location: Mandalay Bay (Floors 35 to 39)
Theme: Understated luxury
Cost: (part of Mandalay Bay)
Rooms: 424

Restaurants: Four restaurants and lounges including the Lobby Lounge for afternoon tea and Club Bar, the new Las Vegas power spot.
Chilling out: Pool and health and fitness club
Room rates: From $200 Sunday to Thursday; from $300 Friday and Saturday
Reservations: 702-632 5000

MGM Grand

Seriously major resort hotel that is good fun for the whole family.
Location: The Strip at the new Four Corners with East Tropicana
Cost: Originally $1 billion plus $950-million expansion and theme transformation
Theme: The City of Entertainment
Rooms: 5,005
Shows: EFX in the Grand Theater, sporting events and major concerts in the Grand Garden Arena (which seats 16,325), plus smaller gigs in the 650-seat Hollywood Theater and a Comedy Club
Entertainments: Studio 54 nightclub with live dancers
Restaurants: 10 restaurants, with three managed by celebrity chefs
Chilling out: Grand pool and spa
Wedding chapels: Two
Other facilities: The MGM Grand Adventures entertainment complex, arcade and youth activity centre
Room rates: From $69 Monday to Thursday; from $129 Friday to Sunday
Reservations: 702-891 1111

When the MGM Grand first opened in 1993 as one of the new mega-resorts of Las Vegas, it came with a 33-acre themed amusement park specifically aimed at the family market. But it was not to be. Okay, so families do visit Las Vegas, and in ever-increasing numbers, but they are not the big casino-using money generators that your good old regular gamblers are, so the resort had a change of heart. All the same, the MGM Grand still has an entertainment complex, but by and large the entertainments are aimed more at adults than children and a recent $950-million project has completed its transformation into a City of Entertainment theme.

Taking the lion's share of funds was the new 45-foot-tall, 50-foot-long golden lion perched on a 25-foot-high pedestal at the entrance to the resort – the largest lion statue in the world – that replaced the old fibreglass lion. Already in place as part of the new programme is the 6.6-acre Grand Pool and Spa complex, which features five pools, lush landscaping, a lazy river, bridges, fountains and waterfalls, while you can check out your cardiovascular rating in the state-of-the-art fitness centre at the Grand Spa. The MGM Grand Arena is where you get to watch boxers punch the living daylights out of each other in search of a world title, while the Grand Theater is home to one of the most spectacular and not-to-be-missed shows in town – EFX.

Then there is the Hollywood Theater that is home to legendary headline entertainers and the Center Stage Cabaret where rising comics get to try out their routines.

★★★ **INSIDE TRACK** ★★★
★ ★
★ ★
★ Some people find the awesome ★
★ MGM Grand both way too big ★
★ and way too crowded. ★
★★★★★★★★★★★★★★★★★★

Top restaurants include the Wolfgang Puck Café, the Brown Derby and Gatsby's. Family fun includes the MGM Grand Adventures, an outdoor entertainment complex that is home to the world's largest skycoaster – Sky Screamer – plus other rides, entertainment, restaurants and shops. The arcade provides all the latest in arcade technology and the MGM Grand Youth Activitiy Center offers plenty of fun activities to keep 3- to 12-year-olds happy.

As if the current 5,000 beds were not enough, a new Marriott-run Marriott Marquis is due to open in the year 2000 with 1,500 beds, and there are plans for a 500-room Ritz-Carlton Hotel after that!

Mirage

An elegant taste of paradise, well within reach of most budgets.
Location: The Strip, between Flamingo and Spring Mountain
Theme: Polynesian, South Seas oasis
Cost: $730 million
Rooms: 3,044
Shows: *Siegfried and Roy*, internationally renowned illusionists
Entertainments: The White Tiger Habitat, the Dolphin Habitat
Restaurants: 12
Chilling out: Pool and cabanas
Shopping: The Street of Shops promenade
Other facilities: Spa and salon
Room rates: From $79 Monday to Thursday; from $350 Friday to Sunday
Reservations: 702-791 7111

The entrance garden surrounds you with a mass of foliage and waterfalls that cascade over 50-foot rocks to the lagoon below before you reach the Mirage 'signature', the volcano. This erupts every few minutes, spewing smoke and fire 100 feet above the water. The reception is a tropical rainforest, filled with 60-foot-high palm trees, more waterfalls, banana trees and tropical orchids. The forest is kept in perfect condition by plenty of natural sunlight and a computerised misting system. Behind the check-in desk is a 20,000-gallon coral reef aquarium that is home to sharks, puffer fish and angel fish, which swim among buildings of a sunken city. The forest is also home to one of the Mirage's top-notch restaurants, Kokomo's, where steaks and seafood are served in the delightfully exotic setting.

Opened in 1989, the Mirage's theme of a Polynesian island oasis was a taste of the big things to come in Las Vegas, but has itself stood the test of time. It is also home to one of the biggest shows in the city – the *Siegfried and Roy* magical show of illusions featuring tigers, lions, leopards and other animals, and the animal habitats for both the dolphins and the tigers are attractions in themselves. The new Secret Garden, where you can see white lions, and the 2.5-million-gallon Dolphin Habitat have been built to create public awareness of the plight of endangered animals.

Accommodation ranges from luxurious standard rooms to opulent bungalows with their own private garden and pools, and eight two- and three-bedroom private residences.

★ ★ ★ ★ **INSIDE TRACK** ★ ★ ★
★   ★
★   ★
★ Don't miss the Secret Garden for ★
★ a real close-up encounter with   ★
★ the white tigers that perfom in   ★
★ Siegfried and Roy's show at the   ★
★   Mirage.   ★
★ ★ ★ ★ ★ ★ ★ ★ ★ ★ ★ ★ ★ ★ ★ ★ ★ ★

Monte Carlo

Posh-but-worth-it hotel with great chilling-out facilities.
Location: The Strip just north of West Tropicana
Theme: Re-creation of the Place du Casino in Monte Carlo
Cost: $344 million
Rooms: 3,261
Shows: *Lance Burton, Master Magician*
Restaurants: Six plus a 210-seat food court
Chilling out: 21,000-square-foot pool area with waterfalls, a pool, spa, children's pool, wave pool and rafting down the Easy River
Shopping: Street of Dreams promenade
Wedding chapels: One
Other facilities: Health spa and exercise room

Room rates: From $60 Monday to Thursday; from $100 Friday to Sunday
Reservations: 702-730 7000

This elegant, upmarket resort hotel is so popular that it is hard for British travel agents to book you a room here. After its opening at the beginning of 1996, the 32-storey resort was fully booked for the rest of the year by the end of July. Modelled on the famous Place du Casino in Monaco, the emphasis is definitely on providing an elegant and refined atmosphere in which to part with wads of cash in the casino. Massive chandeliers, marble flooring, ornate fountains and gas-lit promenades all go towards setting the elegant tone. After a hard day seeing the sights, make sure you get back in time to make full use of the water facilities, which include a heated spa, children's pool and wave pool that re-creates both the sound and feel of ocean surf waves. Resident entertainier Lance Burton is one of the top magicians in America and, along with Siegfried and Roy at the Mirage, produces some of the most spectacular illusions in the world.

★ ★ ★ ★ **INSIDE TRACK** ★ ★ ★
★   ★
★   ★
★ Skip the expensive buffet at the ★
★   Monte Carlo and go for one of   ★
★ the gourmet restaurants instead. ★
★ ★ ★ ★ ★ ★ ★ ★ ★ ★ ★ ★ ★ ★ ★ ★

New York-New York

For live-wire, 24-hour action this is the place to be!
Location: The Strip at West Tropicana
Theme: The Big Apple – doh!
Cost: $460 million
Rooms: 2,033
Shows: Michael Flatley's *Lord of the Dance*
Entertainments: Coney Island Emporium
Restaurants: Six
Chilling out: Outdoor pool
Shopping: Gift shops

Wedding chapels: One
Other facilities: Spa and fitness centre
Room rates: From $89 Monday to Thursday; from $129 Friday to Sunday
Reservations: 702-740 6969

Dubbed the Greatest City in Las Vegas, the resort's façade recreates the Manhattan skyline with 12 of its most famous skyscrapers from the Empire State Building to the Statue of Liberty, along with a 300-foot-long replica of Brooklyn Bridge and a Coney Island-style roller coaster called Manhattan Express™. From the food to the architecture to the sights and sounds of America's capital city, this Las Vegas resort recreates the energy and vibrancy of New York – then adds the Central Park casino! Its current show, Michael Flatley's *Lord of the Dance*, has been playing to great reviews since the summer of 1998. The 28,000-square-foot amusement park recreates Coney Island as it was at the turn of the century (without the gangs!) and is home to the Manhattan Express roller coaster, the world's first heartline twist and dive roller coaster which loops its way around the perimeter of the resort, plus carnival games, bumper cars, shooting galleries and interactive driving simulators.

★ ★ ★ ★ **INSIDE TRACK** ★ ★ ★
★   ★
★   ★
★   It's a good 10-minute walk   ★
★ through shops and casinos to get ★
★ to the New York's roller coaster ★
★ ride, but it's well worth the trek! ★
★ ★ ★ ★ ★ ★ ★ ★ ★ ★ ★ ★ ★ ★ ★ ★

Paris Las Vegas

Sophisticated chic with all the ambience of the French capital
Location: The Strip, south of East Flamingo
Theme: Capital of France!
Cost: $760 million
Rooms: 2,916
Entertainments: Observation deck on

the Eiffel Tower, plus five lounges, two featuring live entertainment.
Restaurants: 13
Chilling out: Roof-top swimming pool in a manicured French garden and tennis courts.
Shopping: French shops in the resort's Rue de la Paix district
Wedding Chapels: Two
Room rates: From $125 Sunday to Thursday; from $230 Friday and Saturday
Reservations: 702-739 4111

Bringing to life the ambience and spirit of France's capital, this new theme resort opened in the autumn of 1999 with replicas of the Eiffel Tower, Arc de Triomphe, Paris Opera House and the Louvre. The 34-storey hotel tower is fashioned after the famous Hôtel de Ville. Like its sister hotels, the Mandalay Bay and Venice, the new Paris aims at the more sophisticated traveller with prices – by Las Vegas standards, at least – to match.

To get you in the mood, each of the guestrooms comes with a stately armoire, rich French fabrics, crown mouldings and spacious marble bathrooms that have separate bathtubs and showers. You can also wander around the quaint, cobblestone streets and winding alleyways of the Rue de la Paix district to find an array of French boutiques, including a garden shop, wine and cheese shop and clothes shops, all with façades that represent different districts in Paris.

The pièce de resistance, though, has to be a trip up the Eiffel Tower for stunning views – only now you remember you're not in France, as you see Las Vegas' Strip and Valley. Here you can dine at the Eiffel Tower Restaurant in a softly-lit restaurant, sampling classic gourmet French food. If you don't want the full dining experience, you can sip on a glass of champagne in the piano bar while inspecting the breathtaking views. Once you get back down on terra firma, stroll through the casino, where the 40-foot ceiling that encloses

cobblestone pathways, ornate street signs and a replica of the Pont Alexandre III bridge is painted to emulate the Parisian sky.

Rio Suite Hotel

Proving there is life beyond the Strip, the Rio truly is an entertainment city in its own right.
Location: 3700 West Flamingo
Theme: Tropical paradise
Cost: $200-million expansion
Rooms: 2,563 suites
Shows: Impressionist/comedian Danny Gans and RioBamba Cabaret
Enertainments: Masquerade Show in the Sky and Club Rio
Restaurants: 14, many of which are consistently ranked among the top of their kind by the Zagat survey
Chilling out: Sand beach and outdoor recreational area
Shopping: Masquerade Village
Wedding Chapels: Two
Room rates: From $65 Sunday to Thursday; from $139 Friday and Saturday
Reservations: 702-252 7777

The Rio is consistently voted the best value hotel in America and has some of the finest restaurants – Buzio's, Fiore Rotisserie, Napa and The VooDoo Café – in the city. It is also home to the first Wine Cellar Tasting Room in the city, which has the world's largest collection of fine and rare wines, along with an array of tasting accessories.

Since the major expansion project, it now has the Masquerade Show in the Sky, in which guests can take a ride aboard fantasy floats as they glide above the crowds in a Mardi Gras-style fiesta of music and dance. Danny Gans, an unknown to us Brits, is a big draw to Americans and has been voted Entertainer of the Year in Las Vegas. His comedy drag show opens an evening of 90s-style fun in the music and video nightclub in the Copacabana Showroom.

Outside, a sand beach lies at the edge of a tropical lagoon, complete with waterfalls and four nautical-shaped swimming pools and five jacuzzi-style spas. You can also eat and drink al fresco at the entertainment centre. When it comes to weddings, the Rio does it in style. An entire floor of the Masquerade Tower has been given over to wedding facilities including two chapels and two themed, 1,200-square-foot honeymoon suites and reception areas.

★ ★ ★ ★ **INSIDE TRACK** ★ ★ ★
★   ★
★   ★
★   Never use the phone in your ★
★   hotel room – you'll be charged ★
★   a small fortune. Instead, get an ★
★   international phone card from   ★
★   BT before you go.   ★
★ ★ ★ ★ ★ ★ ★ ★ ★ ★ ★ ★ ★ ★ ★ ★ ★

Stratosphere

Extremely good value for money hotel and best gambling odds in town!
Location: At the north end of the Strip
Theme: Tallest building west of the Mississippi
Cost: $550 million
Rooms: 1,500
Shows: *American Superstars* and *Viva Las Vegas*
Entertainments: Highest observation tower in America, world's highest roller coaster and world's highest thrill ride, the Big Shot.
Restaurants: Four including the revolving Top of the World Restaurant on the 106th floor
Shopping: The Tower Shops
Wedding chapel: One
Other facilities: State-of-the-art video arcade
Room rates: From $39 Monday to Thursday; from $99 Friday to Sunday
Reservations: 702-380 7777

At first glance, the Stratosphere may seem like a one-theme wonder – a place where you take the 30-second, high-speed elevator to the observation deck for dramatic views of Las Vegas, have a drink in the bar, allow the world to go round and

round (literally) and then return to earth. But that would be to miss out on the 1,149-foot tower's hidden depths – two of the most amazing thrill rides in the city and one of the best restaurants in town, the Top of the World. Then there are the competitively-priced rooms – among the cheapest on the Strip – and the amazing odds available in the casino that make it the best place to try out your new-found skills on the tables (see Chapter 4)! If it's night-time and you're not inside the Stratosphere, then watch out for its spectacular nightshow of dancing lights that can be seen throughout the Las Vegas Valley.

Treasure Island

A fun, comfortable resort that's good value for money for young families.
Location: The Strip at Spring Mountain Road
Theme: Robert Louis Stevenson's novel *Treasure Island*
Rooms: 2,891
Shows: Cirque du Soleil's *Mystère*, plus live music in two lounges and the Buccaneer Bay pirate sea battle
Entertainments: Mutiny Bay entertainment centre, filled with computer video games, pinball and electronic games
Restaurants: Seven
Chilling out: Tropical paradise pool with private cabanas
Shopping: The Pirate's Walk shopping promenade
Wedding chapels: Two
Other facilities: Spa and beauty salon
Room rates: From $70 Monday to Thursday; from $250 Friday to Sunday
Reservations: 702-894 7444

Owned by the Mirage, the same attention to detail that is the hallmark of that establishment has been given to this re-creation of the Robert Louis Stevenson book – and an elevated tram connects the hotel to its Mirage sister next door. The 'signature' of the resort is the battle between a British frigate and an eighteenth-century pirate ship, which culminates in huge masts snapping and plunging into the sea, buildings exploding into flames and sailors being catapulted into the air. It certainly draws the crowds at its showtimes (4pm, 5.30pm, 7pm, 8.30pm and 10pm daily, depending on the weather).

You arrive at the hotel by crossing the long wooden deck across the waters of Buccaneer Bay and are transported to the bustling, eighteenth-century pirate town in Buccaneer Bay Village. The village serves as the town plaza and the hub of the resort's attractions, and the theme of a pirate city is extended throughout the resort.

Treasure Island recently underwent a $25-million redesign, which included a spectacular new lobby and registration desk overlooking a tropical pool and an Italian restaurant that features celebrity artwork. Mutiny Bay is filled with state-of-the-art video games, pinball and electronically-simulated games. But central to the resort's thrilling entertainments are the twice-nightly shows by Cirque du Soleil, who created a spectacle specifically to complement the resort's pirate town theme.

★ ★ ★ ★ ★ ★ ★ ★ ★ ★ ★ ★ ★ ★ ★ ★ ★
★   ★
★   If you plan to see the pirate   ★
★   battle at Treasure Island,   ★
★   arrive early to grab a prime   ★
★   viewing spot as the crowds   ★
★   build up quickly.   ★
★ ★ ★ ★ ★ ★ ★ ★ ★ ★ ★ ★ ★ ★ ★ ★ ★

Tropicana

Fabulously exotic chilling-out environment for grown-ups.
Location: The Strip at Tropicana
Theme: Tropical island of paradise
Rooms: 1,875
Shows: *Folies Bergère* and *Comedy Stop*
Entertainments: Live poolside entertainment and Wildlife Walk
Restaurants: Eight
Chilling out: Water park

Wedding chapels: One
Other facilities: The world's only swim-up blackjack table!
Room rates: From $59 Monday to Thursday; from $119 Friday to Sunday
Reservations: 702-739 2222

The Tropicana has spent millions upgrading to create a colourful Caribbean Village façade and new main entrance to the Paradise Island, while its 'signature' is a spectacular laser light show on its Outer Island.

Inside, Wildlife Walk, in the covered walkway between the resort's two towers, is a wildlife habitat for tropical creatures from toucans to pygmy marmosets, cockatoos to Amazonian parrots. From here you can also see down to the five-acre waterpark, which is home to peacocks, flamingos, Mandarin ducks, African crown cranes and black swans, plus lagoons, spas, waterfalls, a giant waterslide and the world's largest indoor–outdoor swimming pool. Here, live poolside entertainment will have you tapping your toes and moving your body to the beat of everything from rock to reggae as you gently sip a cocktail or two.

★ ★ ★ ★ ★ ★ ★ ★ ★ ★ ★ ★ ★ ★ ★ ★ ★
★   ★
★   Pay a bit extra to get a room in   ★
★   the Tropicana's new tower with   ★
★   stunning views of the Strip – the   ★
★   older garden section is in dire   ★
★   need of an overhaul.   ★
★ ★ ★ ★ ★ ★ ★ ★ ★ ★ ★ ★ ★ ★ ★ ★ ★

The Venetian

All-out sophisticated luxury.
Location: The Strip at East Spring Mountain Road
Theme: Renaissance Venice
Cost: $1.2 billion
Rooms: 3,036 suites
Attraction: Madame Tussaud's
Entertainment: Headliners at the four-level music venue

Restaurants: 12, mostly celebrity-chef restaurants
Chilling out: Pool deck with private cabanas and Canyon Ranch SpaClub
Shopping: Grand Canal Shoppes
Room rates: From $139 Sunday to Thursday; from $199 Friday and Saturday
Reservations: 702-414 4100

Here you will find replicas of everything that Venice stands for, from the Doge's Palace to St Mark's Square, the Grand Canal and Rialto Bridge, all recreated to the finest details by sculptors with the help of two historians to 'ensure the integrity of the design and architecture'.

All the rooms are suites and at least double the size of a standard Las Vegas hotel room. The premium standard rooms feature a private bed chamber with draped canopies, a 130-square-foot bathroom finished in Italian marble and a sunken living room area with a sofa, two chairs, a desk and game table. All rooms have a safe, mini bar, fax machine and copier, computer printer, three telephones with dual lines and dataport access and two colour televisions.

You will want to step out of your room though, as this resort has some of the finest dining in all of Las Vegas. The selection includes Wolfgang Puck's Postrio, Joachim Splichal's Pinot, Emeril Lagasse's Delmonico Steakhouse and Stephan Pyle's Star Canyon. To get to any of these, take a stroll through the first-ever Madame Tussaud's Wax Museum outside London or check out the acts in the four-level musical venue.

If you get a little tired, try the Canyon Ranch SpaClub, operated by the world-renowned spa. Next to the five-acre pool deck with its private cabanas and modelled on a Venetian-style garden, the state-of-the-art SpaClub features massage and treatments, a 40-foot rock-climbing wall, Pilates studio, spinning gym, therapeutic Watsu pools and Canyon Ranch Café.

The centrepiece of the main shopping mall, known as the Grand Canal Shoppes, is the reproduction of Venice's majestic Grand Canal and St Mark's Square. Beneath a dramatic 70-foot ceiling, you will find almost 100 shops along the cobbled walkways of Venetian streets.

The Future

The New Aladdin

Location: The Strip at Harmon Avenue
Theme: Middle Eastern
Cost: $1.3 billion
Rooms: 3,600
Entertainments: 7,000-seater Aladdin Theatre for the Performing Arts
Shopping: A complex of shops in a Middle Eastern setting

The original Aladdin Hotel was imploded in 1998 to make way for a brand new Aladdin on a Middle Eastern theme, which is due to be completed in 2000. Early plans to team up with Planet Hollywood to produce a music hotel have fallen by the wayside, but the owners are looking for new partners to build a separate 1,000-room music hotel on the same site. By November 1998 there were at least 40 hotel-building projects in the pipeline, though the rush was put down to the introduction of new state laws at the end of the year, which imposed more stringent requirements on casino developers. How many will make it beyond the drawing board is unknown, but plans include a wrestling theme resort on the site of the old Debbie Reynolds hotel casino, which closed down due to bankruptcy. Andrew Lloyd Webber is also reported to be planning a hotel-casino with a musicals theme. Many feel that the current boom in Las Vegas may have reached its peak, though, as 32 million visitors a year are needed just to fill the current 120,000 rooms. But it is a crazy, crazy city that seems only to be happiest when building new properties, so who knows?

THE BELLAGIO

THE VENETTIAN

HOTEL PARIS

LUXOR

HOTELS

EXCALIBUR

DESERT INN

RAINFOREST ATRIUM AT THE MIRAGE

FIREWORKS AT THE STRATOSPHERE

ATRIUM AT THE DESERT INN

NEW YORK-NEW YORK

HOTELS

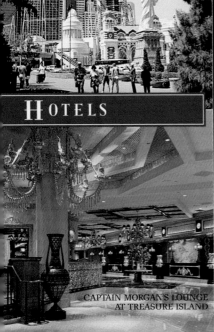

CAPTAIN MORGAN'S LOUNGE AT TREASURE ISLAND

3 SHOWTIME
How to find your way around the
entertainment capital of the world

One of the cornerstones of Las Vegas' early success was its policy of paying big bucks for big name entertainers who could pull in big crowds. Entertainment is even more important now as a whole raft of top-notch musicals, plus magical and circus-led extravaganzas, have elevated the Strip to the second Broadway of America. And, like everything else in the city, it's available at excellent value-for-money prices. It may cost $100 to see a headliner in action, but $51.50 to see a $45-million extravaganza like *EFX*? You'll be sorry if you miss out!

The City of Entertainment is also cram-packed with shows, revues, adult revues, live music and music venues and is also fast becoming one of the best places to see top comedy acts. The choice is endless, but if you have only a few days in town, I'd recommend trying to get in to one of the top shows, checking out the local papers and fun books for free and two-for-one deals and then trying any of the smaller shows. You'd be hard-pressed to find something that is not good value for money.

The major shows

I have stuck to the major, long-running spectacles, but you may find locals raving about a production that has not been booked for a long run, and which is worth a visit. Some prices include local sales tax, but if not specified, add 7% to the prices given. **Guide to ratings:** * * * * * pure brilliance; * * * * fantastic; * * * a great show; * * poor value for money.

O

At the Bellagio on the Strip, 702-693 7722. If you've ever been lucky enough to see the Cirque du Soleil troupe in action, you'll know what makes these artists so special. The 70-odd cast of dancers, acrobats, actors, clowns, comedians and musicians may represent age-old talents of an old-style circus (without the animals), but that is where any similarities with the past comes to an end. *O*, like all the shows performed by the troupe, is a surrealist celebration of trapeze, dance, high-flying acrobatics and humour. In this case, though, every act is performed in, on and above water in a $70-million theatre that was developed specifically for the fabulous Bellagio resort and Cirque du Soleil.

O takes its title from the phonetic pronunciation of the French word for water – *eau*. The story takes you on a 90-minute voyage of the history of theatre in the trademark Cirque style. There are daring displays of aerial gymnastics, high-flying trapeze numbers, synchronised swimming, fire-eating, mind-boggling contortions, clowns and high-diving stunts.
Rating: * * * * * Breathtakingly brilliant.
Shows: Friday to Tuesday at 7.30pm and 10.30pm.
Prices: Main floor $100, balcony $90 including tax.

Mystère

At Treasure Island on the Strip, 702-894 7111. You're taken on a journey through time that allows the supreme athletes to show off their extraordinary flexibility and strength with a mesmerising aerial bungee ballet, a precision performance based around Chinese poles and an awe-inspiring trapeze act. This truly is state-of-the-art theatre. The show originally cost $20 million to stage and is rivalled only by its new sister show at the Bellagio. Along with *Siegfried and Roy*, it should definitely be on your must-see list.

Rating: ***** You'll want to go back again and again.
Shows: Wednesday to Sunday at 7.30pm and 10.30pm.
Prices: $69.85 including tax.

Siegfried and Roy

Theater Mirage, the Mirage on the Strip, 702-792 7777. World-renowned or not, Siegfried and Roy are not necessarily names that strike an immediate chord with us Brits. But don't allow that lack of knowledge to let you miss out on one of the biggest and best shows in Las Vegas. The two illusionists appear in an extraordinary extravaganza that has been choreographed by a top impresario and will appeal to all ages. Central to the production are rare white tigers, two-ton elephants and a host of other rare and exotic animals that are made to disappear in a mystifying series of tricks. It is worth noting that the two illusionists have taken a great deal of trouble to create special habitats for their animals and in particular house the tigers in a 'Secret Garden' that is designed to educate onlookers about this rare and endangered species.
Rating: ***** One of the best shows in town. Mesmerising.
Shows: 7.30pm and 11pm every day except Wednesday and Thursday.
Prices: $89.35 including two drinks, tax and tip.

EFX

MGM Grand Theater, the MGM Grand on the Strip, 702-891 7777. Nine-time Tony Award-winning singer and dancer Tommy Tune has replaced David Cassidy who previously replaced Michael Crawford as the star of this $45-million Broadway spectacular. The 70-strong cast go on a surrealist, high-tech journey through space and time in an adventure that calls for singing, dancing and amazing pyrotechnics and visual effects. Central to it all is Tune's quest to regain the powers of magic, laughter and imagination to win the heart of his true love. When Cassidy took over from Crawford, the plot was altered to include a filmed intro by the EFX Master, James Earl Jones. This is regarded in the industry as the technical masterpiece of theatre productions and put Las Vegas on the map in entertainment terms when it first arrived here. The plot may be a bit thin but the brilliant costumes, singing and dancing make up for it. During rest periods, the 1,700-seater Grand Theater is used as a venue for major entertainers such as Liza Minnelli, Rodney Dangerfield and Stevie Wonder.
Rating: ***** Spectacular effects and show-stoppers.
Shows: 7.30pm and 10.30pm, Tuesday to Saturday.
Prices: Adults $51.50 and $72, children $37 including tax and programme.

★★★★ **INSIDE TRACK** ★★★
★   ★
★   ★
★ Try not to sit close to the side at ★
★ the front at *EFX* as you may end   ★
★ up seeing the machinery rather   ★
★ than enjoying the effects!   ★
★★★★★★★★★★★★★★★★★★★★★★

Chicago

Mandalay Bay on the Strip, 702-632 7580. The award-winning musical is the first full-length Broadway show to make it to Las Vegas. Marilu Henner stars as the nightclub dancer who shoots her boyfriend but escapes the death penalty and even jail, thanks to a devious lawyer (some tortology there!). Based on a true story, it shocked America when it happened in the 1920s.
Rating: ***** Sheer class and style.
Shows: Saturday at 7pm and 10.30pm. Sunday and Tuesday to Friday at 7.30pm.
Prices: $82.50, $71.50 or $60.50 including taxes.

Jubilee!

Jubilee Theater at Bally's on the Strip, 702-739 4567. A lavish, seven-act tribute to American music, with topless showgirls and scantily-clad guys. From the roaring 20s to the rock 'n' roll era of Elvis, it also features a seductive Sampson and Delilah sequence, a master magician who makes a 26-foot-long helicopter appear, and a spectacular sinking of the *Titanic* in which 2,000 gallons of water flood on to the stage. Just to give you some idea of the scale of its lavishness, more than 1,000 costumes are worn by the cast of 100 dancers and singers, while 70 different sets and backdrops and about 100,000 light bulbs are required to create the enchanting spectacles.
Rating: **** Lavish, wonderful over-the-top production numbers.
Shows: Tuesday and Sunday, 7.30pm, Saturday, Monday, Wednesday and Thursday 7.30pm and 10.30pm. Adults only.
Price: $49.50 to $66 including tax.

Danny Gans: Man of Many Voices

Rio Suite Hotel, 702-252 7776. Fresh from his hit one-man show on Broadway, impressionist and comedian Danny Gans portrays everyone from Prince to Sinatra. He wows locals and tourists alike with his range of 300 voices and is consistently a sell-out.
Rating: **** Sure-fire winner.
Shows: Wednesday to Sunday at 7.30pm.
Price: $83 including tax, tip and two drinks.

The Best of the *Folies Bergère* … Sexier Than Ever

Tiffany Theater in the Tropicana on the Strip, 702-739 2414. A turn-of-the-century Parisian music hall is the scene for the opening and final acts of the longest-running show in Las Vegas. The *Folies* made their début in town just two years after the Tropicana opened in 1957 in their tribute to France's early nightclubs and have been entertaining crowds almost non-stop since. This latest version combines award-winning production numbers from past *Folies* shows with new production sequences, dazzling costumes and scenery and, of course, the famous *Folies* showgirls, who perform amazing feats in their high-kicking can-can and chorus-line numbers.
Rating: *** Well done, but more old-style revue than new spectacle.
Shows: 8pm and 10.30pm every night except Thursday.
Prices: $49.75 for table seating, $59.75 for booth seating.

★ ★ ★ **INSIDE TRACK** ★ ★ ★
★   ★
★   Choose your seat with care at   ★
★   *Folies* – it can be hard to see   ★
★ from some of the long tables and ★
★   the plastic seats get uncomfy   ★
★   after a while.   ★
★ ★ ★ ★ ★ ★ ★ ★ ★ ★ ★ ★ ★ ★ ★ ★ ★

Spellbound

Spellbound Theater, Harrah's Hotel, 702-369 5000. A comedian, jungle animals and human displays of acrobatic strength and skill make this a truly spellbinding show. Magician Mark Kalin and his assistant, Jinger, tackle some death-defying stunts to bring you thrilling illusions in a celebration of magic and music. The show is updated every year.
Rating: **** Action-packed, high-energy entertainment.
Shows: 7.30pm and 10pm nightly except Sunday.
Price: $34.95.

Lance Burton: Master Magician

Lance Burton Theater, the Monte Carlo, 702-730 7160. Another great illusionist demonstrates his powers to mystify and entertain in his own show at a theatre especially created for him. After finishing a run at the now defunct Hacienda, Burton spent a whole year putting together show-stoppers for his new routine at the Monte Carlo. Once described by Johnny Carson as 'the best magician I've ever seen', Burton's show involves classic feats of levitation, Houdini-style escapes and mysterious disappearing acts, all done with the flair and pizzazz expected of modern-day magicians. The man himself is seen as the late 1990s answer to David Copperfield.

Rating: **** Two hours of awe-inspiring, rib-tickling entertainment.
Shows: 7.30pm and 10.30pm Tuesday to Saturday.
Prices: $34.95 to $39.95 including tax.

Splash: Voyage of a Lifetime

Splash Theater, Riviera Hotel, 702-477 5276. Another big-time crowd-puller aimed specifically at grown-ups and, as the name suggests, there are plenty of water-based show-stoppers in this magical extravaganza. You are taken deep beneath the ocean waves in *Splash's* 'virtual submarine' on a nautical voyage of discovery around the North Pole, the Bermuda Triangle and the lost city of Atlantis. A 20,000-gallon on-stage water tank provides a perfect setting for the synchronised swimmers, divers and mermaids.

Rating: *** Past its heyday, but still great fun.
Shows: 7.30pm and 10.30pm every night. Adults only.
Prices: $39.50 for reserved seating, $49.50 for VIP reserved seating.

Imagine: A Theatrical Odyssey

Luxor Theater, Luxor Hotel, 702-262 4400. A mixture of aerial acts, choreography and illusions that seems to be inspired by many of the other resort shows. You are taken on an adventure to a mysterious lost world, then an undersea garden and finally a cyberworld in what is largely a plotless show. The three-act show leaves no time for intermissions, but stunning dancing and aerobatics, high-flying strap and bungee acts and

some magical moments will have you glued to your seats for the 90-minute performance.

Rating: *** Great choreography and fine spectacles.
Shows: 7.30pm nightly except Thursday plus 10pm Monday, Wednesday, Friday and Sunday.
Price: $39.95 including tax.

Legends in Concert

Imperial Theater, Imperial Palace, 702-794 3261. Here's a neat way to see all your favourite music stars from Elton John to Madonna, Michael Jackson to Elvis, the Beatles to Liberace. The look- and sound-alikes truly have *Stars in Their Eyes* and together put on one of the most highly rated and popular shows in town. *Legends in Concert*, which has been going strong since 1983, is also the first Las Vegas show to appear on Broadway, reinforcing the growing recognition of the Strip as the second Broadway of America.

Rating: *** Great impersonations let down a bit by a lack of exciting choreography.
Shows: 7.30pm and 10.30pm every night except Sunday.
Prices: $29.50 for adults including tax and two drinks and $14.75 for under 12s.

An Evening at La Cage

Mardi Gras Plaza on the third floor of the Riviera. Frank Marino stars in the quicksilver world of lipstick, high heels, nine-button evening gloves and put-down lines to die for in this upmarket drag show that wins over the hearts of even the most conservative theatre-goers.

Rating: *** Great fun and good value for money.
Shows: 7.30pm and 9.30pm every night except Tuesday.
Price: $21.95 to include two drinks but not tax.

★ ★ ★ **INSIDE TRACK** ★ ★ ★

Arrive early for *La Cage* to get good seats and get your free drinks before you go in as no drinks are served inside the showroom.

Forever Plaid

At Bugsy's Celebrity Theater, the Flamingo Hilton, 702-733 3333. The smash-hit off-Broadway spoof of musicals celebrates the mood of the 1950s with music, comedy and some great characters. The Plaids are a mediocre harmony group, who return from the dead in a quest for one great gig.
Rating: ★★★★ Two hours of pure entertainment.
Shows: 7.30pm and 10pm every night except Monday.
Price: $19.95 plus tax.

Enter the Night

Stardust Theater, Stardust Hotel, 702-732 6325. Las Vegas revue meets Broadway style and Hollywood hi-tech in a mysterious and exciting celebration of the world of entertainment. It includes great music, great ensemble dancing, a topless fashion parade, plus the hilarious Gauchos and a duo of robotic dancers.
Rating: ★★★ Great fun entertainment.
Shows: 7.30pm and 10.30pm Tuesday to Saturday, 8pm on Sunday and Monday. Adults only.
Price: $29.85, $35 and $45 to include tax, tip and two drinks.

★ ★ ★ ★ **INSIDE TRACK** ★ ★ ★

Follow the locals and eat elsewhere before or after the show – the Stardust is not famed for its good food or service!

American Superstars

Broadway Showroom, the Stratosphere on the Strip, 702-380 7711. Another testimony to the huge success of the long-running *Legends in Concert* is this celebrity-tribute extravaganza. Here you can see stars such as *Men in Black*'s Will Smith strut his stuff *Big Willi*-style and a full line-up of the Spice Girls, alongside impressionist favourites Michael Jackson, Madonna and Gloria Estefan.
Rating: ★★★ Fun, but not as good as *Legends*, this is for real fans of *Stars in Their Eyes*!
Shows: 7pm every night except Thursday, plus 10pm Wednesday, Friday and Saturday.
Prices: Adults $22.95 plus tax and 5–12s $16.95 plus tax.

Michael Flatley's *Lord of the Dance*

New York-New York on the Strip, 702-740 6815. A great show, with the dazzling dance sequences and gifted cast we have come to expect of a Flatley show. And that's the problem – you may feel you've seen it all before.
Rating: ★★★ Polished, but nothing new.
Shows: Tuesday, Wednesday and Saturday at 7.30pm and 10.30pm, Thursday and Friday at 9pm.
Price: $57 Tuesday to Thursday, $68 Friday and Saturday including tax.

Dinner shows

King Arthur's Tournament

King Arthur's Arena at the Excalibur, 702-597 7600. Central to this recreation of a knight's battle are the laser lights, fireworks and clouds of billowing water vapour that give the production an air of mystery and magic. The musical begins when Merlin grants a young boy's wish to be a knight by transporting him back to the Middle Ages and transforming him into the White Knight of Kent. Along the way he meets King Arthur and Queen Guinevere and battles

3

39

with the treacherous Dark Knight to win a princess's hand in marriage. The trick to seeing this show is to finish off your dinner before you become engulfed in water vapour!
Rating: **** One of the top shows – good for horses, feasts and magic!
Shows: 6pm and 8.30pm.
Price: $34.95 plus tax.

Caesars Magical Empire

At Caesars Palace, 702-731 7333. Caesars Magical Empire is an elaborately-themed, multi-chambered restaurant/theatre where dinner is combined with illusions and magic. A centurion guides you to one of ten dining chambers where you'll be entertained by a wizard during your meal. Afterwards you are guided through misty catacombs for the series of 'shows' and you can take a brief break at the Grotto Bar, which nestles in a dragon's mouth cave, or at the Spirit Bar, which is haunted by a mysterious poltergeist who enjoys spooking unwary guests. Each show in the Secret Pagoda lasts 18 minutes with performances every 25 minutes, starting at 6.15pm. The Sultan's Palace has a 35-minute stage show every 50 minutes, starting at 7.10pm.
Rating: ** Great idea but basically an over-priced Disney-style ride.
Shows: For over 12s only. Dinner and shows held from 4.30pm to 10pm.
Prices: $75. $15 discounts for early (4.30–6pm) and late (9–10pm) dinner seatings. Drinks in the bars are charged separately. Free tours Friday to Tuesday from 10.45am to 3.45pm (probably your best bet!).

★ ★ ★ ★ **INSIDE TRACK** ★ ★ ★
★ Prepare for long waits to see the ★
★ different shows that make up the ★
★ dining experience at Caesars ★
★ Magical Empire. ★
★ ★ ★ ★ ★ ★ ★ ★ ★ ★ ★ ★ ★ ★ ★ ★ ★

The Great Radio City Spectacular

Flamingo Showroom, Flamingo Hilton on the Strip, 702-733 3333. Starring the Radio City Rockettes, the high-kicking, precision chorus-line routines which have been a hallmark of American musicals since the 1930s are at the core of a ten-scene showcase for America's most famous dance troupe. Glamorous, yet suitable for all ages, the travelling Rockettes have made the Flamingo their home since they opened in 1995, and were recently awarded the Liberace Legend Award in honour of their contribution to Las Vegas and the world of entertainment.

★ ★ ★ ★ **INSIDE TRACK** ★ ★ ★
★ ★
★ Get to the *Great Radio City* ★
★ *Spectacular* early as the queues ★
★ are long and wind back into the ★
★ casino (wonder why?). That way ★
★ you'll get a good seat, too. ★
★ ★ ★ ★ ★ ★ ★ ★ ★ ★ ★ ★ ★ ★ ★ ★ ★

Rating: *** Good, but overpriced.
Shows: Dinner shows nightly (except Friday) at 7.45pm, cocktail shows at 10.30pm.
Prices: Dinner shows from $52.50 including tax and tip. Cocktail shows $42.50 including tax.

Copacabana Dinner Show

At the Rio Suite Hotel in Flamingo Road, 702-252 7777. Enter a bygone era and enjoy the ambience and style of a classic supper club in a beautiful, theatre-in-the-round setting. You can dance after dining before the show based on the Latin Copacabana musical. And in the grand old style, the singers and dancers move through the audience to create a truly intimate experience.
Rating: *** A fun night of old-style entertainment.
Shows: 6pm and 8.30pm Tuesday to Saturday.
Prices: Vary – call ahead.

Afternoon shows

Viva Las Vegas

At the Broadway Showroom of the Stratosphere on the Strip, 702-380 7711. Combining lively dance numbers, singing, comedy and displays of magic, this is a revue in the old style of variety acts. The highlight is Golden Joe Baker's hilarious avant garde rendition of Elvis classics.

Rating: **** A belter of a show at a great price!

Shows: 2pm and 4pm Monday to Saturday.

Price: $10 plus tax.

★ ★ ★ INSIDE TRACK ★ ★ ★
★ ★
★ ★
★ Viva Las Vegas is not only a great ★
★ afternoon show, but you're ★
★ bound to find free tickets for it – ★
★ or 'win' them at the Stratosphere ★
★ casino! ★
★ ★ ★ ★ ★ ★ ★ ★ ★ ★ ★ ★ ★ ★ ★ ★ ★

Comedy Magic

Maxim Showroom, Maxim Hotel in Flamingo Road, 702-734 8550. Lunchtime comedy from Nick Lewin.

Rating: *** A fun way to pass a couple of hours.

Shows: 1pm and 3pm every day except Sunday.

Prices: $9.95 to include one drink, tax and tip or $12.95 to include tax, tip, two drinks and the Brunch Buffet.

Star-name venues

Grand Garden Arena: MGM Grand on the Strip, 702-891 7777. The biggest venue in Las Vegas regularly hosts major concerts and sporting events. This is where Holyfield met Tyson for their heavyweight champion title clash and where top-notch performers like Sting, Elton John, Bette Midler, Gloria Estefan, Phil Collins and Billy Joel play when they're in town. The 16,325-seat venue has also hosted the Professional Bull Riders Championships and national league

hockey. Tickets are likely to cost anything from $100 up depending on who you go to see.

Hollywood Theater: MGM Grand, 702-891 7777. The MGM's more intimate venue (a mere 650 seats) is still big enough to attract such names at Wayne Newton, Smokey Robinson, Gladys Knight, Tom Jones and the Righteous Brothers.

Circus Maximus Showroom: Caesars Palace, 702-731 7333. Since its gala opening in 1966, Judy Garland, Frank Sinatra, Diana Ross and Liberace have headlined here. More recent stars include David Copperfield, Liza Minnelli, Julio Iglesias and Celine Dion.

Crystal Room: The Desert Inn, 702-733 4566. Recent headliners include Sheena Easton and Hall and Oates.

Hilton Theater: Las Vegas Hilton, 702-732 5111 for show information. Headliners include Johnny Mathis.

Celebrity Room: Bally's, 702-739 4567 for information, times and reservations. Headliners include Liza Minnelli and Penn and Teller.

Circus Maximus: Caesars Palace, 702-731 7333 for show times, prices and reservations. Recent acts include Huey Lewis and the News, Earth, Wind and Fire and Tony Bennett.

Orleans Showroom: The Orleans, 702-365 7075. Recent headliners include the Everly Brothers, Air Supply and Frankie Avalon.

Congo Room: Sahara on the Strip, 702-737 2515 for information and reservations. Recent headliners include the Drifters, the Platters and the Coasters.

Comedy

Catch a Rising Star: MGM Center Stage Cabaret, the MGM Grand Hotel on the Strip, 702-891 5551. The 'Catch' chain of American comedy venues has helped shape the careers of many of the best-known and best-loved comedians of America – from Robin Williams to Billy Crystal, Jerry Seinfeld and more. Las Vegas now has a growing crop of comedy

Booking tickets in advance

By and large you should have no problem getting tickets to see most of the shows, and you can usually buy tickets in advance by phone or in person at the hotel's theatre box office. Just bear in mind that getting show tickets in Las Vegas depends on the time of year, the day of the week and whether there is a huge convention in town. For details of the best times to visit see Seasons (page 147) in Chapter 9. In all cases, phone ahead to confirm showtimes, dates and prices as these are subject to change without notice. You can find out exactly who will be performing – including the big 'headline' stars during your visit to Las Vegas – by phoning the Las Vegas Convention and Visitors' Authority on 702-892 0711 to request a free copy of *Showguide*. Many of the major tour operators will also be able to book tickets in advance for the major shows or you can try attraction specialists Keith Prowse (01232 232425). A cheapter alternative for advance booking is to look at the Las Vegas Host Shows web page on www.lasvegashost.com/lvhshows.htm. You can even ask questions by emailing them at: lasvegashosts@mltvacations.com or by phoning 702-798 5246.

spots, but this remains by far the best with top comedians headlining nightly at 7.30pm and 10pm. Price: $14.

The Comedy Stop: Comedy Stop Theater in the Tropicana on the Strip, 702-739 2714. Shows at 8pm (non-smoking) and 10.30pm. Price: $16 including tax, tips and two drinks.

The Improv at Harrah's: Harrah's, 702-369 5000. Stand-up routines by up-and-coming stars of comedy at 8pm and 10.30pm Tuesday to Saturday. Price: $14.95 plus tax.

Comedy Fixx: MGM Center Stage. Friday and Saturday only at midnight. Price: $14.95 plus tax.

Comedy Max: Maxim Showroom, Maxim Hotel in Flamingo Road, 702-734 8550. Shows 7pm and 9pm every night. Prices: $16.25 including tax, tip and two drinks.

The Riviera Comedy Club: Mardi Gras Plaza on the second floor of the Riviera Hotel on the Strip, 702-477

5274. Shows 8pm and 10pm nightly, plus 11.45pm on Friday and Saturday. Price: $14.95 including two drinks but not tax.

Other venues: You'll also find comedy at **Coconuts** (3246 East Desert Inn Rd, 702-733 9147); **Courtyard Bar and Grill** (3055 East Flamingo, 702-454 2545); **Hoops Lounge** (6851 West Flamingo, 702-873 7224) and **Johnnie's Underground** (32 Fremont Street, Downtown, 702-225 5894). Call in advance for nights and show schedules.

Cinema

Omnimax® Movie Theater: Caesars Palace. No ordinary cinema, this theatre is a spectacular experience of sight and sound and showcases large-format movies on a giant, dome-shaped screen that immerses you in the movie. The seats recline 27 degrees to give a panoramic view of the screen while a nine-channel 'sensuround' sound system engulfs the audience with 89 speakers from ten speaker banks. Movies are shown every 70 minutes from 2pm until 10.10pm from Sunday to Thursday and from 11.40am to 11.20pm on Friday and Saturday. Adults $7, under 12s and hotel guests $5.

Free shows

Lumineria: Show at Caesars Magical Empire, daily from 11am to 4.30pm, for fiery illusion stunts.

Circus Circus: See free circus acts in the Main Arena from 11am until midnight every day.

Fremont Street Experience: It's worth making the trip downtown if only to see the spectacular, computer-driven light and sound show in which the entire ceiling of the recently-enclosed shopping precinct is brought to life with one of three shows – *Odyssey: An Illuminating Journey, Viva Las Vegas* and *Country Western Nights*. The 10-minute spectacle can be seen on the hour every hour from 8pm to midnight every night of the week. Afterwards, head on to the Downtown casinos, which offer great value and friendly environments (see Chapter 4).

House of Blues

Mandalay Bay on the Strip, 702-632 777. The legendary chain of restaurants-cum-nightclubs has arrived in Las Vegas with its eclectic mix of music to serve all tastes. The live music venue for 1,500 people plays host to everything from rock to R&B, reggae, hip-hop, country, jazz and, of course, blues. The 500-seater restaurant serves everything from the casual to the sublime including the classic Elwood sandwich (named after Dan Aykroyd's character in *The Blues Brothers*), Memphis-style ribs with Jack Daniels sauce, Cedar Plank Salmon with Watercress-Jicama Salad and Voodoo Shrimp served with Rosemary Cornbread.

Live music and nightclubs

The growth of a younger, more upwardly mobile local population and type of visitor is reflected in a recent surge towards state-of-the-art nightclubs that are frequented by locals and visitors alike. These are the biggest and most popular.

Studio 54: MGM Grand, 702-891 1111, 10pm to 5am Monday to Saturday. *The* place to be seen in Las Vegas! Following in the footsteps of the original 1970s New York nightclub, the MGM Grand version, which opened in 1997, is a high-energy nightclub with state-of-the-art sound, video and lighting along with a troupe of live dancers. There are four separate dance floors and bars, an exclusive area for invited guests, plus the **Rainforest Café**, a giant show bar with video screens and music.

Ra: Luxor, 702-262 4000, 10pm to 6am Wednesday to Saturday. Another all-nighter where you most definitely dress to impress! In keeping with the Luxor's Egyptian theme, it has been named after the Egyptian sun god and boasts two massive bars with a central dance floor surrounded by tables and booths for more privacy, while VIPs get their own special area. Other features of the club, which opened in 1997, include two cigar lounges, a sushi and oyster bar and a valet parking service at the southern entrance of the hotel. It also has a Ladies' Night on Wednesday when out-of-town women pay half the normal $10 entrance and locals get in free.

Club Rio: Rio Hotel, 702-252 7777, 10pm till late Wednesday to Saturday. A strict no-jeans policy, with collared shirts for men. Its outstanding features are a video wall surrounding the circular room and a misting system to keep you cool when things get hot! A real experience and one of the top establishments for trendy young things.

The Beach: 365 Convention Center Drive, 702-731 1925, 24 hours a

3

day, seven days a week. One of the most happening venues in town. Maybe it has something to do with the bikini-wearing waitresses and muscle-bound bartenders. Rock 'n' roll fans will enjoy Wednesday's special night.
Drink and Eat Too: 200 East Harmon Avenue, 702-796 5519, Tuesday to Saturday. The place to go for a fun, party atmosphere. Full of trendy, young locals and tourists, it's a friendly place where you can dance, drink and eat too!
The Joint: Hard Rock Hotel, Harmon Avenue, 702-226 4650 for music updates. The place to go for cracking live music in a great rock 'n' roll environment.
The Nightclub: Las Vegas Hilton, 702-732 5111, Thursday to Saturday. Showcases up-and-coming singers, while top resident DJs provide the kind of music that make this another of the best nightspots in town. Dressing up to the nines is a must!
Club ThirtySomething: 71 North Rancho Drive, 702-631 9399, Wednesday to Monday. Aims specifically at the over 30s who like to dress up and dance the night away.
Utopia: 3765 South Las Vegas Boulevard, southern end of the Strip, 702-740 4646. Another of the hot nightspots for young trendies, with a different theme every night of the week. Tuesday is Ladies' Night, Thursday and Saturday Techno, and Hip-Hip on Sundays. Saturday is the main night for those into electronica.
Cleopatra's Barge: Caesars Palace, 702-731 7110, Tuesday to Sunday. Another theme offering, this time from the Greco-Roman resorts. Statues and centurions abound in the beautiful setting where live contemporary dance music is served up.
L'Isles Bar: Stratosphere, 702-380 7777, Tuesday to Sunday. An intimate, tropical-theme lounge setting for Caribbean and reggae music, with shows at 9pm and 1.45am.
The Bomb: 3015 Boulder Highway, 702-384 2655, Friday and Saturday.

Filled with locals who enjoy listening to live music in the relaxed atmosphere. Dress is casual.
Dylan's Dance Hall and Saloon: 4660 Boulder Highway, 702-451 4006, Thursday to Saturday. A must for country fans and lovers of everything from line dancing to the two-step and ten-step. You'll get plenty of stomping action to the latest country tunes.
Moose McGillycuddy's: 4770 South Maryland Parkway, 702-798 8337, Wednesday to Saturday. Filled with college students, who give it a high-energy, fun atmosphere.
The Attic: 1350 South Main Street, downtown, 702-390 8488, Friday and Saturday. A more casual place where you'll find a fun crowd who are not worried about whom they impress.

Other live music clubs

Also see under Bars in the Eating and Drinking chapter.
Jazz: Jazz can be found at the **Bank Club** (1930 East Fremont, 702-474 9262); **Favorites** (4110 South Maryland Parkway, 702-796 1776); **Kiefer's Atop the Carriage House** (105 East Harmon Avenue, 702-736 8000); **Mad Dogs and Englishmen** (515 South Las Vegas Boulevard, 702-382 5075); **Pepper's Lounge** (2929 East Desert Inn Road, 702-731 3234); **Play It Again Sam** (4120 Spring Mountain Road, 702-876 1550); **Pogo's Tavern** (2103 North Decatur Boulevard, 702-646 9735); **Shifty's Cocktail Lounge** (3805 West Sahara Avenue, 702-871 4952); and at **Sit 'N' Bull Lounge** (3220 North Jones, 702-645 0066).
R and B: The best places for this style of music are: **Beers and Cheers** (713 Ogden Avenue, 702-474 9060); the **Bluenote Lounge** (1000 East Sahara, 702-732 7326); **Metz Night Club** (3765 South Las Vegas Boulevard, 702-739 8855); and **Sand Dollar Lounge** (3355 Spring Mountain Road, 702-871 6651).
Pop: Find this at **Brewed Awakening** (2305 Sahara at Eastern, 702-457

7050); **Casablanca's** (6320 East
Charleston, 702-438 6200); **Ellis
Island** (4178 Koval Lane, 702-733
8901); and the **Sports Pub** (4440
South Maryland Parkway, 702-796
8870).
Rock: If you are a rock fan, try the
Clubhouse Tavern (4001 North Las
Vegas Boulevard, 702-643 2337);
On the Roxx (5740 West Charleston,
702-878 0001); and **Tommy Rocker's**
(4275 South Industrial Road, 702-
261 6688).
Country and Western: Your venues
are **Gold Coast Dance Hall** (4000
West Flamingo, 702-367 7111); **Idle
Spurs Tavern** (1113 Rainbow
Boulevard, 702-363 7718); **Saddle
'N' Spurs Saloon** (2329 North Jones,
702-646 6292); **Sam's Town Western
Dance Hall** (5111 Boulder Highway,
702-456 7777), with free dance
lessons; and **Silverado Dance Hall**
(5255 Boulder Highway, 702-458
8810).

Strip joints

Almost all are open 24 hours a day.
Showgirl Video (631 South Las Vegas
Boulevard, 702-385 4554); **Can-Can
Room** (3155 Industrial Road, 702-
737 1161); **Centerfold Lounge**
(1024 North Boulder Highway, 702-
564 7865); **Cheetahs** (2112 Western
Avenue, 702-384 0074); **Club Exotic**
(call for free limo, 702-252 8559);
Crazy Horse (4034 Paradise Road,
702-732 1116); **Girls of Glitter Gulch**
(Fremont Street Experience, between
1st and Main Street, 702-385 4774);
Little Darlings (3247 Industrial Road,
702-893 3409); **Olympic Garden**
(1531 Las Vegas Boulevard, 702-385
8987) male and female dancers;
Palomino Club (1848 North Las
Vegas Boulevard, 702-385 8987);
Talk of the Town (1238 South Las
Vegas Boulevard, 702-385 1800);
and **Wild J's** (2923 South Industrial
Road, 702-892 0416).

Gay and Lesbian Las Vegas

Surprisingly, for a city that claims to be so adult, there is relatively little available
for gays and you have the Mormon history of Las Vegas to thank for that.
Nevadan anti-sodomy laws were only repealed in 1995 and many local gays
still prefer to stay in the closet. Yet the annual **Gay Pride Parade** in April or May
(call 702-733 9800 for details) is testimony to the presence of a gay community.
A good place to start is probably the **Gay & Lesbian Center** at 912 East
Sahara Avenue between Sixth Street and Maryland Parkway, 702-733 9800.
It is a relatively new building and a new meeting point for gays. Open from
10am to 7.30pm Monday to Friday, call ahead for schedules. The Center also
has a useful website: **www.gayvegas.com** you may want to check out.
Get Booked at the Paradise Plaza, 4640 Paradise at Naples Drive, 702-
737 7780, is a bookstore at the heart of the **Gay Triangle** at the corner of
Naples Drive and Paradise Road, just south of Hard Rock Café. It is open 10am
to midnight Monday to Thursday, 10am to 2am Friday, noon to 2am Saturday
and noon to midnight Sunday. The Gay Triangle area has several bars, Get
Booked and the **Mariposa** coffee house. You'll be able to pick up copies of the
two free monthly gay papers – Las Vegas Bugle and Q-Tribe – at any of those
locations.

Accommodation

Riviera, 2901 The Strip at Riviera Boulevard, 702-734 5110. The most openly
gay hotel on the Strip, it is the home of La Cage, a top drag show starring Frank
Marino as Joan Rivers.
The Ranch, 1110 Ralston Drive, near Martin Luther King Boulevard, 702-631
7708. It's expensive and doesn't take credit cards, but is run by lesbians.

Lucky You, 702-384 1129. An exclusively gay B&B just two blocks from the Strip within walking distance of gay bars. Well priced but no credit cards accepted.

Clubs and Bars

All are open 24 hours daily.

Angles & Lace, 4633 Paradise Road at Naples, 702-733 9677. Consists of two bars – Angles for men and Lace for women. Usually the crowd starts here and migrates across the street to the Gipsy.

Backdoor Lounge, 1415 East Charleston Boulevard, 702-385 2018. Has a happy hour every night from 5pm to 7pm. Monday night a free poker party starts at 7pm and there is a free barbecue on Saturday nights at 6pm.

Backstreet Bar & Grill, 5012 South Arville Road, about one mile west of the Strip on Tropicana, 702-876 1844. Home of the Gay Rodeo Association and probably the friendliest bar in town, the best times to visit are Sunday around 4pm and Tuesday and Thursdays around 7pm when the line dance classes get going.

Badlands Saloon, 953 East Sahara Avenue, inside the Commercial Center, 702-792 9262. A country and western bar. Wear a cowboy hat after 9pm!

The Buffalo, 4640 Paradise Road, opposite Angles, 702-733 8355. A Levi and leather club and home of the Satyricons Motorcycle Club.

The Eagle, 3430 East Tropicana, about four miles east of the Strip, 702-458 8662. Another Levis and leather club, famous for its Underwear Night on Wednesdays.

Flex Lounge, 4371 West Charleston Boulevard, 702-385 3539. A great mixed club with drink specials, dancing and live music.

The Freezone, 610 East Naples, 702-794 2300. All-round bar with restaurant.

Gipsy, 4605 Paradise Road opposite Angles, 702-733 9677. A dance club popular with the younger crowd and considered the centre of gay action. Sundays free otherwise there is a $5 entrance.

Good Time Bar & Grill, 1775 East Tropicana, 702-736 9494. Has happy hours from 5am to 7am and 5pm to 7pm. Monday is the most popular night. No credit cards.

Keys, 100 East Sahara Avenue, 702-731 2200. Las Vegas's first piano bar featuring sing-along entertainment – considered to be the hottest little piano bar in town.

Inferno, 3340 Highland Drive at West Desert Inn Road, 702-734 7336. A mixed club with sizzling go-go boys and a Latino night every Thursday. Entrance $5 after 10pm.

The Spotlight, Commercial Center, 957 East Sahara Avenue, 702-696 0202. Eclectic working class bar.

Snick's Place, 1402 South Fourth Street, 702-385 9298. For the mature crowd. Sunday morning from 9am to noon is time for a Bloody Mary special.

Tropical Island, 3430 East Tropicana, 702-456 5525. A recently renovated ladies bar.

Cafés

Garlic Café, Decatur Twain Shopping Center, 3650 South Decatur Boulevard, 702-221 0266. The only openly gay-owned café in town, you get to choose the strength of garlic you eat. It's always busy and serves great food. Open 5pm to 10pm daily.

Mariposa, Paradise Plaza, 4643 Paradise Road, at Naples Drive, 702-650 9009. A fun and friendly place with patio seating and great food. Also located in the heart of the Gay Triangle. Open 3pm to 3am daily.

4 GAMBLING

Everything you need to know about having a flutter without blowing all your holiday money

Y ou've seen the erupting volcano, watched the pirate battle and witnessed amazing circus acts – all in the most opulent, best-that-money-can-buy settings. Now you've hit the nitty gritty, the *raison d'être* of the city – the casinos. And it won't have taken you long. Most of the Strip resorts have their casinos laid out in such a way that you can't fail to notice them even before you've got to your room. It's no surprise really: you have to accept that there is one reason and one reason alone for the glamour and razzmatazz – the making of money, and absolutely tons of it at that. In 1998 casino takings stood at $8.1 BILLION a year in Nevada, with Las Vegas casinos taking a lion's share of $6.3 billion. All this from 198,065 slot machines and 6,141 live tables state-wide.

The resorts of the 1990s – the Luxor, the MGM Grand, Treasure Island, New York-New York and the Bellagio and the new Mandalay Bay, Paris and Venetian hotels – and the billions spent on their creation, were triggered by a massive growth in casino income at the beginning of the decade. A location on the Strip is considered so important that an acre of land there is now worth a cool $10 million.

High-roller baccarat players, the very latest slot machines, state-of-the-art video gambling machines and sports betting are the big money-spinners, and you'll also find everything else from roulette to craps and poker to blackjack.

But it's not all been plain sailing for the casino bosses of Las Vegas. An increase in competition from Atlantic City and the fact that 22 American states have now legalised gambling has meant the city has had to work hard to position itself as an entertainment destination in its own

right, while providing the most sophisticated games and facilities – and all at the most incredible prices.

Then there has been the massive anti-gambling lobby from politicians, federal bureaucrats and religious organisations to deal with, while Congress intends to set up a two-year study on the effects of gambling on states and cities. As a result, the American Gaming Association (gaming being the Las Vegas euphemism for gambling!) put $200,000 million into a new foundation to study compulsive gambling and develop treatment. The casinos know that the hard-luck stories of desperate gamblers are bad for business. They want people to win, they want people to have fun and to know when to walk away because they want them to come back again and again and again. That way, they know, the odds are they'll always get their money back – and more on top!

★ ★ ★ **INSIDE TRACK** ★ ★ ★
★   ★
★   ★
★ Remember the golden rules of ★
★ gambling: stick to your own limits ★
★   and always, always quit while ★
★   you're ahead!   ★
★ ★ ★ ★ ★ ★ ★ ★ ★ ★ ★ ★ ★ ★ ★ ★

To this end, the industry has been working hard to make casinos more user-friendly by providing free lessons in easy-to-find locations. A move to put 'comps' (see page 59) on a more straightforward footing has led to the creation of loyalty cards by many casinos where the amount of money you spend and time you spend gambling generates points to put towards free meals, free rooms and free shows. Whether you intend to spend $20 or $2,000 gambling, or just sit in one of the myriad of bars and watch the action, all these factors mean you can have a fantastic time in Las Vegas without parting with huge amounts of dosh – as long as you follow the rules: **stick to your own limits and always, always quit while you're ahead!**

★ ★ ★ ★ ★ ★ ★

★ Money raised from gambling was
★ used to buy uniforms, provisions
★ and bullets for troops fighting us
★ Brits during America's fight for
★ independence.

★ ★ ★ ★ ★ ★ ★ ★ ★ ★ ★ ★ ★ ★ ★ ★ ★

High rollers

The casinos like to keep all their customers happy, but they go to extraordinary lengths to accommodate high rollers – and I mean HIGH! The game they tend to play, baccarat, accounts for a massive 13% of casino takings. The Las Vegas Hilton has spent $40 million building three high-roller suites called Sky Villas. The massive apartments come with marble floors, chandeliers, five bathrooms, gold-plated bathroom fixtures, their own swimming pool, putting green, 24-hour butler, chef, maid and limo service, workout facilities, media room and state-of-the-art entertainment and video equipment. They were built on part of what used to be Elvis Presley's 5,000-square-foot penthouse suite and will be offered free of charge – but only to people with a gambling purse starting at $2 million! To complement the suites, there is an exclusive $12-million VIP baccarat facility.

Baccarat, with its high-bet limits and liberal odds, is worth a cool $1 billion in gambling income world-wide and other Las Vegas casinos have been working hard to cash in. Bally's casino on the Strip has hired a high-roller expert to weed out the big fish

– gamblers willing to bet $300,000 to $1 million – from the 'whales', who only bet around $250,000 a hand! Big baccarat players tend to be Asians, Latin and South American gamblers, and Asians in particular have been targetted by the Tropicana, which recently opened a room specifically for them, called the Jade Palace. The normal limits are $10,000 a hand in games of pai gow, pai gow poker and mini-baccarat.

★ ★ ★ ★ ★ ★ ★

★ You cannot bet on the
★ presidential elections in Las
★ Vegas, nor on University of
★ Nevada sporting events or the
★ local Las Vegas Stars professional
★ baseball team.

★ ★ ★ ★ ★ ★ ★ ★ ★ ★ ★ ★ ★ ★ ★ ★ ★

High-stakes poker is big business, too, and Binion's Horseshoe casino in downtown Las Vegas has been home to the World Series of Poker title for the last two decades. Thousands of players from all around the world pay a fee to take part in the poker extravaganza that lasts 24 days. Then each May, more than 300 players pay $10,000 each to buy into the four-day World Championship No-limit Texas Hold 'Em competition. The winner is guaranteed $1 million and walks away with the champion poker player of the world crown.

The law

You must be over 21 to gamble in Las Vegas and under 18s are not allowed in arcades from 10pm to 5am during the week and from midnight to 5am at weekends. And in a further move to appease the anti-gambling lobby, the city has passed a new law that bans under 18s from walking down or cruising the Strip after 9pm without a parent or guardian.

Fun books and other freebie sources

Whether or not you intend to do any gambling, always check the casino cages for their free fun books. These will give free goes on slot machines, may entitle you to double a bet at the blackjack table or increase the value of a keno ticket. They will also be full of bargains on food and drink or offer discounts on souvenirs such as T-shirts. You can also find these books at car rental agencies, hotels, motels and other locations in the city. Some tour operators – most notably Funway – have put together their own fun books, which include fantastic deals on excursions and attractions.

In addition, the monthly *Las Vegas Advisor* gives subscribers lots of information on deals and freebies available in Las Vegas and sometimes includes valuable coupons or arranges special deals for subscribers. Write to the *Las Vegas Advisor*, Huntington Press, PO Box 28401, Las Vegas, Nevada 89126. Subscriptions are $54 a year, but you'll generally get back that cost in money-saving coupons, let alone all the other tips!

How to get in on the action

I remember the first time I visited Las Vegas, the bright lights were so overwhelming and the sheer scale of everything so overpowering that it seemed far too daunting to go into the casinos and play a game or two. Removing some of the mystique surrounding these games of chance is not to remove the magic of the setting, but it will give you the right kind of edge.

When it comes to a weekend gambling spree, the average American will allow a budget of between $200 and $500. When a touring Brit arrives in town, their budget of between $20 and $50 is usually simply there to fritter away while downing complimentary drinks. If you do want to have a go, though, here is a guide to the different games, the rules, and the best ways to place your bets so that even if you don't win, you won't blow your entire budget in the first ten minutes. The

aim of the game is to make your spending money last as long as possible while having fun – and, who knows, you may even come out a winner! Bear in mind that these tips are aimed at those people who are new to gambling as opposed to those looking for more detailed and advanced information. But I have included details of where you can go for further information and more in-depth advice.

★ ★ ★ INSIDE TRACK ★ ★ ★

When in a casino always remember Big Brother is watching you! Mirrors or dark glass in the ceilings hide people watching casino action to stop cheating by players or dealers. And there are cameras behind the decorative-looking glass to record action at the tables.

★ ★ ★ ★ ★ ★ ★ ★ ★ ★ ★ ★ ★ ★ ★ ★

Gambling lingo

Acorn	Player who is generous with tips
Ante	Money you bet in card games
Bank	Inventory of coins and chips on all table games
Big digger	Ace of spades
Book	Place where bets are made on sporting events
Boxcars	Term used when a gambler rolls two sixes for a point of 12
Boxman	Craps table dealer who sits over the drop box and supervises bets and payoffs
Bumble puppy	Careless or inexperienced card player
Bust	Exceed the maximum score allowed, for instance 21 in blackjack
Buster	Term used for illegally-altered dice
Casino cage	Secure area within the casino for banking services and casino operations
Casino boss	Person who oversees the entire casino
Comp	Free meal, gift, etc. (short for complimentary)
Coupons	Redeemable for nearly everything from a free meal to a free pull on a slot machine
Crossroaders	Card cheats who travel across America in search of card games
Dealer	Person who conducts table games
Drop box	Locked box on 'live' gaming tables where dealers deposit your cash
Eye in the sky	One-way mirror used for surveillance of the casino area
Flat top	Slot machine with a fixed jackpot, as opposed to a progressive slot machine where the jackpot increases according to the amount of play
Frog skin	Old-time gamblers' name for paper money
Gaming	Las Vegas euphemism for gambling
Green	Gambling chip worth $25, also known as a quarter
High roller	Someone who bets large sums of money

Hit me	What you say when you want another card from the dealer in a blackjack game
In red	If you get a free meal, your name will appear in red on the maître d's reservation list
Ladderman	The person who supervises baccarat games and has the final say over any disputes
Limit	Minimum and maximum bet, as decided by the casino
Loose	Term used to describe slot machines that pay out at the best percentages
Maître d'	I know this is technically not a gambling term, but you'll hear it so often in casinos that it's worth mentioning that this is the head waiter
Marker	IOU
Nevada lettuce	$1,000 bill
Pit	Area of the casino containing gambling tables
Pit boss	Person who oversees a number of table dealers
Red	Gambling chip worth $5, also known as a nickel
RFB comp	If the casino is impressed with someone's credit rating, they will arrange a free room, food or drink during a hotel stay
Shoe	Contains the packs of playing cards used in blackjack and baccarat
Shooter	Person rolling the dice in craps
Snake eyes	Craps term used when the dice holder rolls a point of two
Soft hand	When you have at least one ace in your blackjack hand. It is counted as either one or 11 so you have two possible totals
Spoon	One device used by slot machine cheats
Stand	To refuse any more cards in blackjack
Stickman	Dealer who moves the dice around on a craps table with a hook-shaped stick
Table games	Everything from blackjack and baccarat to roulette
Toke or gratuity	Tip
Whale	Gambler who is willing to bet $250,000 a hand
Whip shot	In craps, the way of rolling the dice to hit the table in a flat spin so the desired numbers are on top when the dice stop rolling

4

The odds

There are two aspects to every game you play – the odds inherent in each game on you winning (the odds) and rules designed to favour the house, including payoffs at less than actual odds or predetermined payoffs, as in slot machines (the edge). It is because of this edge that, no matter how well you are playing or how much luck you seem to be having, the odds will **always** favour the casinos, who'll win everything back in the long run. That's why when you've come to the end of a winning streak you should always walk away.

Table games with the best odds on winning or on reducing your losses are baccarat and blackjack. Craps is seriously not good, roulette not a lot better and in keno you have about as much chance of winning as you do with our National Lottery, though the cost of the bet is usually lower than $1, so you may not care.

As a general rule, the smaller casinos away from the Strip are what are known as the 'loosest' – they will offer the best returns on slot machines. For some time the Downtown casinos have been rated as the 'loosest slots in America' by the *Casino Player* Magazine. For instance, slot machines will give anywhere from a 95% to a 99% return on your play. That means if you bet $1, you'll get between 95 and 99 cents back if you win. Downtown, you have more chance of finding machines with a 98% and 99% return. The exception on the Strip is the Stratosphere, which has made a corporate decision to lure in punters with the promise of the best returns in town. Their deals include 100 times odds on craps, single-zero roulette, hand-dealt double-deck blackjack, double-exposure blackjack (where you see both the dealer's cards), 98% return on 100 $1 slots and more than 100% return on 100 video poker machines. But do bear in mind that there are only a certain number of the high-paying machines, so always

check the returns on a particular machine before you play.

Limits

The table limits are an important consideration because the higher the minimum bet, the quicker you'll get through your money. Unless you're a serious gambler, you'll steer clear of baccarat. The minimums at most Strip resorts are $100! Cheapest, though, is New York-New York, which has games with minimum bets of $10. You can also play mini-baccarat at the Stratosphere with minimum bets of $5 per hand.

Most Strip resorts have minimums of $5 on blackjack. The cheapest are Circus Circus ($2), Excalibur ($2), Luxor ($2), Monte Carlo ($3), Treasure Island ($3) and Stratosphere ($3). In comparison, you'll find $2 blackjack tables aplenty and $1 roulette at casinos away from the Strip.

★ ★ ★ **INSIDE TRACK** ★ ★ ★
★   ★
★   Limits fluctuate. Minimum bets
★   tend to be higher in the evening, ★
★   at weekends and during special   ★
★   events. The Strip hotels all have   ★
★   higher minimums than   ★
★   Downtown casinos.   ★
★ ★ ★ ★ ★ ★ ★ ★ ★ ★ ★ ★ ★ ★ ★ ★ ★ ★

Table games

Baccarat

There is normally an aura of glamour surrounding this game as it tends to attract high rollers and is usually played in a separate, often more refined area, cordoned off and staffed by croupiers in posh tuxedos. But don't be put off by the glamour of it all. The mega-bucks, high-roller games will be played in special VIP rooms, so the areas you see really are for mere mortals! What's more, it is an easy game to play and offers the best chance of you beating the casino.

Card counters

You will probably have heard of *card counters*. These are people who basically keep a track of the low and high cards that are being played in blackjack to try to determine the likelihood of drawing a high or low card at a crucial moment – eg when you've got a 15, which is unlikely to be enough to win but you can't guarantee you'll get a six or under. There are many different forms of card counting, but the most simple is the one used with single-deck blackjack. Basically, ten, J, Q and K are worth minus two, everything else is worth one. Starting from minus four, you count in your head upwards and down according to the cards dealt. Generally you should bet low when the score is negative (you're more likely to bust) and high when the count is positive or above minus two. It is not illegal to count cards but the casinos in Las Vegas frown on this misguided attempt by players to cheat them out of money and tend to refuse to let card counters into their casinos. This is why it's best to practise your technique in advance so you're not too obvious in your attempts at counting!

4

Generally up to 15 players sit around a table where two cards from an eight-deck shoe are dealt to each of the players and to the bank. You can bet either on you winning, the bank winning or there being a tie, but you are only playing against the bank, not the other players. Each time you win, the casino takes a commission, though not if you lose. The idea is simple: you're aiming to get to a total of either eight or nine and the value of the cards are: ace to nine – face value; tens and face cards – zero. If the cards add up to more than ten, only the second digit is counted. For instance, if your hand contains a nine and a four, it is worth three as you drop the first digit from the total. In this case you'd ask the dealer for another card. The house edge in baccarat is very low, which is why it is such an attractive proposition. The edge when betting on a bank hand is 1.17% (though that is increased by the fact that a commission is always paid to the

house on with-bank bets) and the edge on a player is 1.36%.

Blackjack or 21

After baccarat, this is one of the easiest games to play and the rows of blackjack tables in casinos reflect the huge number of gamblers who play the game. The object is to get as close to 21 as possible without 'busting'. There can be up to six people around a table, all playing against the dealer. Bets are placed first, then the dealer gives two cards to each player and himself, the first face down (known as the hole card), the second showing (upcard). Numbered cards count as their face value, face cards count as ten and aces are worth either one or 11. You can either decide to stand with the two cards you received or take a hit (another card from the dealer) until you're happy with your hand or you go bust. When all the players have finished, the dealer turns over his hole card and takes hits until his total

★ ★ ★ INSIDE TRACK ★ ★ ★
★   ★
★   ★
★   In blackjack, avoid high   ★
★   minimum/low maximum tables   ★
★   like the plague – they'll eat up   ★
★   your bankroll in a very short   ★
★   space of time.   ★
★ ★ ★ ★ ★ ★ ★ ★ ★ ★ ★ ★ ★ ★ ★ ★

exceeds 17. If the dealer busts, everyone around the table wins, otherwise only those whose hands are higher than the dealer's win. If the first two cards you are dealt total 21, then you've got what is known as a natural, ie a blackjack, and you automatically win. If both you and the dealer are dealt a blackjack then it is a stand-off and no one wins. As a general rule, if you have a hand without an ace against the dealer's seven or higher, you should take hits until you reach at least 17. Against the dealer's four, five or six, you can stand on a 12 or higher; if against the dealer's two or three, hit a 12. With a soft hand (which includes an ace), hit all totals of 17 or lower. Against the dealer's nine or ten, hit 18.

What gives the house the edge is that you have to play your hand first so even if the dealer busts after you have, you're still a loser. But there are two ways to help you even the odds – you can double down or split pairs. If you feel you may have a good hand and will only need one more card, you double down – this is where you double your initial bet and accept one extra card to complete your hand. If you are dealt a pair of cards you can opt to split them, thereby increasing your chances of winning. You separate the cards to create two hands, thereby doubling your bet, and draw extra cards for each hand. If splitting aces you are only allowed to take one extra card for each ace. If the next card is an ace, though, you can split again. The rule is always to split aces and eights.

A word about **'insurance'**. When the dealer's 'show' card is an ace, you will be offered the chance to insure yourself against the dealer getting a blackjack to win 2–1 if the dealer holds a blackjack, so you break even. But it is not a good bet to make because even if you end up with a blackjack, you'll only get 2–1 on a bet that should pay 9–4.

Another way the casino gets an edge is by using a shoe containing six packs of playing cards. This makes busts less likely, which helps the dealer, who is forced by the rules to take more hits than the player. And blackjacks are also less frequent, another drawback as you get paid 3–2 for those.

If you want to learn more, call into the **Gambler's Book Club** (630 South 11th Street, 800 634 6243) where you'll find copies of just about every book ever written about blackjack, and experts on the game – including card counters – who are happy to answer questions.

★ ★ ★ INSIDE TRACK ★ ★ ★
★   ★
★   ★
★   Carry a sweater – the air con is   ★
★   deliberately chilly to put you off   ★
★   facing the desert heat outside.   ★
★   And, be warned, people have   ★
★   been known to crack a rib when   ★
★   going from freezing-cold casinos   ★
★   straight out into the desert heat!   ★
★ ★ ★ ★ ★ ★ ★ ★ ★ ★ ★ ★ ★ ★ ★ ★

Craps

We've all seen this game played down New York alleyways in gangster movies, now here's your chance to give it a go! Sadly it is one of the most complicated table games on offer, but it is also the one that seems to produce the most excitement as players crowd around the table waiting for the shooter to roll the dice. You join in a game by standing anywhere around the table where there's room, start betting any time and wait for your turn to shoot. When rolling the dice you have to do so hard enough for them to bounce off the far wall of the table to ensure a random bounce. Basically, the shooter rolls a pair of dice that determine the outcome of everyone's bets. The first roll is called the 'come-out roll'. If it is a seven or an 11, the shooter and all those who bet with him or her win. If the shooter rolls a two, three or 12, that is craps and the shooter and all those betting with him or her lose. If the shooter rolls a four, five, six, seven, eight, nine or ten, he or she must roll the same number again to win. If the shooter rolls a seven before that number, he or she 'sevens out' and loses.

There is a whole series of bets that can be made – with the most bizarre titles you could imagine – from 'pass lines' to 'don't pass', 'come' and 'don't come', 'field', 'big six' or 'eight', 'any craps', 'hard ways', 'bet the horn', 'any seven' and 'under or over seven'. The odds on winning and payouts vary wildly:
Best bets: The **Pass Line**, where you are betting with the shooter, and the **Don't Pass Line**, where you are betting against, pay even money. **Come** and **Don't Come** bets are the same as the **Pass** and **Don't Pass** bets, with the same odds, but can only be placed after the first roll of the dice. Best bet of all is the **Free Odds**, which is only available to the above betters, but is not even indicated on the table. Once the point has been established by the first roll of the dice, you can make a bet equal to your original and get true odds (2–1 on the four and ten, 3–2 on the five and nine and 6–5 on the six and eight) rather than even money.
Poor bets: The **Field**, where you bet that any number in the Field, ie not five, six, seven or eight, will be rolled. If the numbers mentioned come up you lose. **Place Bets**, where you bet the four, five, six, seven, eight, nine or ten will be thrown before a seven, sound like a good idea but the casino edge is so great that you should not consider any bets other than placing the six and eight.

The downright daft!: Big Six and **Big Eight** bets on either the six or eight or both can be made at any time and either must appear before a seven is thrown to win. But the bet only pays even money so the casino advantage is high. Worst bets of all, though, are the **Proposition Bets**, which include the **Hard Ways** and **One-roll Bets**. The casino advantage is so great that you shouldn't even consider these.

Roulette

This game has been growing in popularity in America since Europeans started visiting the city in greater numbers, but generally it does not have very good odds of you winning. Also, the American roulette table has 36 numbers, plus a green zero and a green double zero – as opposed to the European wheel, which does not have the extra double zero (the only Strip exception is at the Stratosphere). You place chips on the game board, gambling that either a single number, any of a dozen numbers, a column of numbers, corner of four numbers, red or black, or odd or even comes up on the wheel. After all the chips are down, the dealer sends a small metal ball spinning around the roulette wheel, which spins in the opposite direction. When the ball drops into one of the slots, the winner(s) collect(s). The lure is that if your number comes up you're paid at the rate of 35–1, which is great. But what makes roulette a poor game for strategists is that it basically involves blind luck.
Best way to reduce the chance of losing is to stick to betting that the

ball will drop on either a red or black number; and odd or even number of numbers 1–18 or 19–36. **Worst bet** is any one number. Other bets include groups of 12 numbers (2–1), groups of six numbers (5–1), groups of four numbers (8–1), groups of three numbers (11–1), groups of two numbers (17–1) and a group of 0, 00, 1, 2 and 3 (6–1).

★ ★ ★ ★ ★ ★ ★

★   ★

★   ★

★ Exits from casinos are hard to ★

★ find and even if you do see a ★

★ signpost it won't be plain sailing ★

★ getting there, as you way will be ★

★ blocked by a maze-like ★

★ arrangement of slot machines! ★

★ ★ ★ ★ ★ ★ ★ ★ ★ ★ ★ ★ ★ ★ ★ ★

Card games

Poker

For the real Wild West experience, this is a must! There are many variations, but most follow the same principles: all players play for themselves, paying a certain sum of money per hour of play to the casino, and a regular deck of cards is used. Before joining a game, always check with the dealer to find out the specific game being played.

Seven Card Stud Poker: The easiest poker game in the world. You are dealt two cards face down, then a third face up. The player with the lowest card makes the first bet, other players can match the bet, raise it or withdraw. Then another card is dealt face up and the player with the highest hand showing starts the betting. This is repeated until four cards have been dealt face up. The seventh and final card is dealt face down to those players still in the game and the final round of betting begins. This is showdown time and players may raise bets up to three times. When the last bet is covered or called, the dealer calls for the

showing of hands and the highest one wins.

Poker is a game which requires nerves of steel and the skill to know when to cut your losses and drop out. Professional poker players reckon that you'll have a pretty good idea of your chances by the time the first three cards have been dealt, and there are basic combinations that you need to have if you are going to continue.

The odds on getting three of a kind are about 400–1 and it indicates you've more than likely got a winning hand. But don't overplay your bets or you'll scare off other players, just keep covering the bets until the sixth card is dealt to allow the pot to build and then you can up the ante. A pair of aces or kings is another good start but keep an eye on what cards appear on the table – if something that you really need for your hand turns up elsewhere and your cards haven't improved by card five you should drop out. The same goes for a pair of queens or jacks. Three cards to a straight flush is a good start but if you haven't improved your hand by card five, drop out.

Texas Hold 'Em: This is the game of the high-stakes World Series of Poker and is similar to Seven Card Stud except that only two of the seven cards are dealt to the player, the other five are dealt face up and used collectively by all the players. Obviously the first two cards you're dealt are the most important and need to be either a pair of aces, kings, queens or jacks or two high-value cards.

Pai Gow Poker: Played with a deck of 52 playing cards plus one joker, which can be used only as an ace to complete a straight, a flush or a straight flush. Players are dealt seven cards which they arrange to make two hands – a low hand of two cards and a high hand of five. The cards are arranged according to high-draw poker rankings, ie the highest two-card hand is two aces and the highest five-card hand is a royal flush.

The object is for both hands to beat the banker's hands.

Caribbean Stud Poker™: Played with a standard 52-card deck and no joker, it is the first casino table game to offer a progressive jackpot. You start by placing your bet in the box marked 'ante' and then have the option to bet $1 to enter the progressive jackpot, after which all the players and the dealer are dealt five cards. None of your cards is exposed, though one of the dealer's is, but you cannot draw any more cards. Now you have to decide whether to play or fold; in the latter case your ante is lost. To carry on playing, you have to wager double your ante in the box marked 'bet' to see the dealer's hand. If the dealer's hand is less than ace-king high, then he folds and automatically pays the ante bets at even money. The bet wagers are considered 'no action' and returned to the player regardless of their hand. If the dealer's hand is ace-king high or higher, then he calls all bet wagers. If the dealer's hand is higher than yours, he takes both the ante and the bet. If it's lower than yours, he pays the ante at even money and the bet according to the signposted rates, based on your hand. Regardless of the dealer's hand, if your hand qualifies for the progressive jackpot, you will win the appropriate amount for your hand (shared if there is more than one winner).

Let It Ride Poker™: In this game, you are not playing against the dealer or the other players but simply trying to get a good poker hand. To play, you place three equal bets as indicated on the table layout and then get three cards. After looking at your cards you can ask for your first bet back or 'let it ride'. The dealer then exposes one of his cards, which becomes all of the players' fourth card. At this point you can either ask for your second bet back or again let it ride, after which the dealer exposes another card to complete the five-card hand. Winning

hands are then paid according to the payout schedule.

Pai Gow

In this ancient Chinese game, 32 dominoes are shuffled by the dealer and then placed in eight stacks of four each. Up to eight players are dealt one stack. The object of the game is to set the four dominoes into two pairs for the best ranking combinations – most casinos have charts to show the rankings. The house banks the first hand and throws three dice to determine which player gets the first stack of dominoes. The rest are then dealt in rotation. On every winning hand the house keeps 5% of the winnings.

Keno

This game originated in China more than 2,000 years ago but is basically a form of our Lottery. You mark anywhere between one and 15 of the 80 numbers on the keno ticket, then place your bet with the keno writer. You then keep a duplicate ticket to match against the 20 numbers drawn by the casino at a set time. All the casinos have their own rules about winning combinations, so check before playing. The alternative to this game is throwing your money in a bin, but the lure of it all is the massive payouts.

Slots

If your idea of slot machines is an old one-armed bandit in an amusement arcade, then think again. Las Vegas is home to the most sophisticated, state-of-the-art machinery in the world and gamblers get so mesmerised by the idea of their winning line coming up that they spend hours feeding money into these machines. But slot machines are such big business now that they account for around 60% of total casino earnings – and so fill a staggering amount of floor space in the casinos.

Mechanical penny and nickel slot machines that took one coin at a time have been replaced by **computerised dollar slot machines** that can accept multiple coins simultaneously and now feature poker, keno, blackjack, bingo and craps. Some even accept credit card-style gambling and the linking up of machines has led to massive $10-million-and-more jackpots. You can still play for as little as a nickel a go, but some slots now allow you to use $500-dollar tokens – usually in special VIP slot areas!

★ ★ ★ ★ **INSIDE TRACK** ★ ★ ★
★   ★
★   ★
★   Only play on machines that tell   ★
★   you the return and look for a   ★
★   99% return on $1 slots.   ★
★   ★
★ ★ ★ ★ ★ ★ ★ ★ ★ ★ ★ ★ ★ ★ ★ ★ ★

Progressive slots are machines that are computer-linked to other machines throughout the States and pay out incredible jackpots. One of the progressive slots is known as **Megabucks**, which is computer-linked to other machines in the state of Nevada. The **CircusBucks** progressives start the jackpot climbing at $500,000, but that is nothing compared to the most recent **Super Megabucks**, where the jackpot starts climbing at $10 million! What's more, gamblers can now phone a toll-free number to find out the current jackpot total on Megabucks and seven other progressive slot networks run by International Game Technology. The number is: 888-448 2946.

Video games

These are basically **interactive slot machines** aimed directly at the new generation who grew up with computers and computer games. Multiple-use videos can offer up to ten games with anything from poker to keno and blackjack, plus regular slot machines and are activated simply by touching the screen. Some machines even allow you to play for a $1 million poker payout with a 25-cent

bet! Another reason for the increase in popularity of video games is that you can play at your own pace, without pressure from dealers, croupiers or other players. The returns that you should be looking for on all the different games are listed below.

All-American Poker: Also known as Gator Bonus Poker, go for machines that pay 8–1 on full houses, a flush and a straight.

Bonus Deuces: Best machines are those paying 20–1 for a wild royal flush, 10–1 on five of a kind and straight flush and 4–1 on four of a kind and a full house.

Deuces Wild: Look for a 5–1 payout on four of a kind, which is considerably better than 4–1 for four of a kind that you'll find on many of these video machines.

Double Bonus Poker: Find a 10/7 machine – one that pays 10–1 on a full house and 7–1 on a flush.

Flush Attack: Do not play on a machine that needs more than three flushes to go into Attack Mode, then look for one that pays 8–1 for a full house and 5–1 on flushes (known as an 8/5 machine).

Jack or Better: Look for 9/6 machines, which pay 9–1 for a full house and 6–1 on flushes.

Joker Wild: Kings or better. Look for a machine that pays 20–1 for four of a kind, 7–1 for a full house and 5–1 on a flush.

★ ★ ★ ★ **INSIDE TRACK** ★ ★ ★
★   ★
★   ★
★ There are no windows, no clocks ★
★ and few information desks inside ★
★   casinos to remind you of the   ★
★   outside world.   ★
★ ★ ★ ★ ★ ★ ★ ★ ★ ★ ★ ★ ★ ★ ★ ★ ★

Sports betting

The **Race and Sports Book,** as it is known, gives you the chance to bet on horse races and major sporting events. For horse races you can bet on a win (first place only), a place (first or second) and a show (first, second or third). Further bets include naming the first two horses in any order, naming the first two horses in correct order or the horses that will win any two specified races. Details of races, the horses and odds are displayed or you can read local newspapers, racing sheets and other publications before making your mind up. Then watch the action on closed-circuit broadcasts live from race tracks across America. The latest innovation in sports betting are proposals for a progressive prize MegaSports jackpot where the final payout is determined by the amount of betting action over a certain period of time. The prize pools would start at $1 million.

The surge in televised coverage of sporting events in America has also created a surge in sports gambling. During one Super Bowl weekend (held every February), nearly 200,000 visitors flocked to the city to bet more than $50 million on their favourite team and spent a further $50 million in the city in the process! At Caesars Palace Race and Sports Book – the first to open in Las Vegas – they have a total of 50 different ways to part with your cash, including betting on the number of quarterback sacks or the total field goals.

The Internet

World Wide Web Casinos predict they will make $100 million a year with their new Internet casino. Around 200 players an hour vie for jackpots worth as much as $10 million, climbing to a potential $200 million. The casino will offer home access to gambling on blackjack, craps, video poker, roulette, worldwide bingo and three-dimensional, interactive slot machines.

Classes

Many hotels are linked to the **Players Network**, which you can access through the TV for tips on how to play different games, table etiquette and sports betting. For 'live' classes, try

Caesars Palace, where you can get classes and low-bet table play in a beautiful setting. Craps is taught at 11am and 5pm, roulette at 12 noon, blackjack at 12.15pm and 3.15pm, pai gow poker at 2pm and mini-baccarat at 4pm. You can also ask for lessons in Let It Ride and Caribbean Stud, and all lessons are available Monday to Friday. The **Tropicana** runs free craps lessons at noon and free Caribbean Stud lessons at 11am, both Monday to Friday. The **Imperial Palace School of Gaming** offers free blackjack and craps lessons twice a day, seven days a week. **Circus Circus** runs free blackjack classes at 10.30am and 3pm, roulette classes at 11am and craps classes at 11.30am Monday to Friday in the main casino. For tips on how to play all the different video poker machines including Deuces Wild, Double Bonus Poker and Jacks or Better, then it is worth taking the trip to north-west Las Vegas for **Bob Dancer's** weekly lessons at the **Fiesta Casino Hotel** (2400 North Rancho Drive, 702-631 7000). Circus Circus offers free poker lessons at noon Monday to Friday in the poker room and along with the Tropicana, offers low-bet games that are perfect for beginners! The Tropicana also offers baccarat games for beginners in a youthful yet sophisticated environment.

★ ★ ★ ★ **INSIDE TRACK** ★ ★ ★
★ ★
★ Floral fragrances are pumped ★
★ around selected slot machines, ★
★ which increases play by up to ★
★ 50 per cent. ★
★ ★ ★ ★ ★ ★ ★ ★ ★ ★ ★ ★ ★ ★ ★ ★

Comps

The days of casinos just liberally handing out free drinks have gone, though you'll still get one or two if you find the right coupons in the casino's fun book. But you can still get comps on everything from free rooms to food, show tickets, front-row seats and limos, without being a high roller. It's all a question of having the right kind of nerve to demonstrate to the right person – the pit boss – that you are betting enough and playing for long enough to deserve a freebie. The amount you bet will automatically place you in different categories – 'black-action' players, for instance, usually bet $100 a go and 'quarters' $25, which will 'earn' you different comps.

First of all you'll need a **player's card**, which you can request from the casino as soon as you arrive. A game of blackjack is your best bet and as soon as you sit down at a table ask to be 'rated', presenting your player's card to the pit boss. This effectively starts the clock on your play and the idea from this point is to make it look as if you're placing good bets for as long a period of time as possible, while reducing your risk of losing money by playing as little as possible. In blackjack you have a 50–50 chance of winning your first hand, so bet $25 – which will give you a decent rating with the pit boss. Once the floorperson has walked away, bet as little as you can, depending on the table's minimum. Also, don't play every hand. If the dealer is on a winning streak, tell him or her you're going to sit things out until they've busted a couple of times. A natural break in a game is provided when the dealer starts to shuffle and at this point you can whizz off (not forgetting your chips!) to another table out of your pit boss's jurisdiction, though you must always tell them where you're going. Then

lay your chips on the table and chat to the dealer, making it look as if you're playing without actually making one bet. After an hour of 'play', take a break, asking the dealer to mark your seat. It's a pleasant enough way of spending a few hours, but always remember the golden rule of never going beyond the amount of money you have given yourself to play with. Obviously you'll need to walk around the casino for a while before you start playing so you know which pit bosses cover which tables. Thereafter it will be down to your ability to act in a natural way!

Deception and subterfuge are not always necessary when it comes to earning freebies, though. Many of the casinos are so determined to foster good relationships with their customers that they have introduced **loyalty cards,** where the amount of play gives you points that can be put towards meals, rooms, shows or even getting cash back. Always ask at your hotel, but here are a few of the best around.

The **Island Winners' Club** at the Tropicana rewards slot, video poker and table-game players. Slot and video poker players can earn both comps and cash by inserting their club card into the slot machine. On average, about two hours of play on a dollar slot with maximum coins played on each 'pull' will earn about $10 cash back. Table game players present their card to a floorperson to earn comp credits at blackjack, craps or roulette tables. Credits are based on the average bets and length of time you play.

The **Play Rio Card** at the Rio Suite Hotel and Casino in Valley View Boulevard at Flamingo Road, will allow you to earn points during both slot and table play towards reduced-price or comp suites, comp dining or tickets for the *Copacabana* Dinner Show. You sign up at the Play Rio Center.

The **Emperor's Club** at Caesars Palace awards points based on the amount of play on slot and video poker machines above 25 cents per play, which are redeemable for cash. In addition, members of the club get discounts at selected shops in Appian Way and Forum Shops and invitations to hotel getaway weekends, themed parties, cocktail receptions with celebrities and free draws for cash prizes. You can sign up at either of the two Emperor's Club booths.

With **Total Gold** at Harrah's you build up points not only at the Las Vegas casino, but also at all Harrah's resorts including those at Tahoe and Atlantic City.

Slot players can join **Club Magic** at the Las Vegas Hilton, to win cash, comps and merchandise based on the amount of play. By joining the **Gold Chamber** slot and table club at the Luxor you can get a 98.4% return on slot games, plus other comps. The **Ringmaster Players' Club** at Circus Circus allows you to build up points through playing slot machines and table games, which can be redeemed for cash. The Ringmaster VIP club allows you to build up credits for free meals and free rooms. In addition, being a member of the club (ask any of the Ringmaster staff for a form) gives you access to excellent room rates, as well as invitations to special events.

The casinos

As much imagination has gone into the décor of the casinos as in every other part of the resort hotels. At the Luxor you'll find a sumptuous setting surrounded by the Nile, the plush Caesars Palace Casino continues to be the favourite of regular American gamblers and the Las Vegas Hilton continues its *Star Trek: The Experience* theme into its SpaceQuest Casino, where you can part with your cash in a fabulous sci-fi setting. The largest race and sports book is also to be found at the Hilton and if you're having trouble parking, then you can always place your bets at the new drive-up sports book at the **Imperial Palace**!

You can beat the heat of the summer months at the **Tropicana** by swimming up to the blackjack table, open daily from 9.30am to 5pm. In the indoor area of the resort's indoor–outdoor swimming pool, up to 14 players sit on marble stools up to their hips in water. They play with plastic cards and use either chips or cash. The paper money is kept in mint condition by specially-heated rotating drop boxes that dry the cash in less than 60 seconds!

If you want to see how the other half live, take a sneak look in the VIP high-limit area at the **MGM Grand**. Here high rollers rub cheeks with celebrities in a setting based on the elegance and style of the grand old casinos of Monte Carlo. Tall, classic columns, rich, rose-coloured curtains and fine cherry wood and suede tables embroidered with the gold MGM Grand monograms are a sight to behold.

At **Caesars Palace Forum Casino** you can take a break from gambling and have your photo taken with Caesar and Cleopatra as they stroll around with their royal entourage, while the west corridor is home to animatronic Atlantis statues!

The **Excalibur** casino continues its theme with staff dressed in medieval costume and trumpet players blowing on horns straight out of Robin Hood movies.

The **Las Vegas Hilton Casino** is one of the most beautifully decorated, with marble, rich woods and tier after tier of crystal chandeliers, while the **Race and Sports SuperBook** is the biggest in the city with an impressive array of more than 40 video monitors to screen nearly every major sporting event and race being televised in America at any one time. The new *pièce de resistance* is the **SpaceQuest Casino** where gamblers board a futuristic space station that orbits the earth, with specially created space windows that create the illusion of circling the globe from sunrise to sunset.

4

Downtown casinos

Now home to the last neon signs of what used to be Glitter Gulch city, the Downtown casinos are generally more friendly and relaxed, have cheaper-play slot machines, better returns and more comps. Regular visitors to Las Vegas may like staying at the ritzy, glamorous Strip hotels, but often enjoy a trip downtown to play on the nickel slot machines. **Binion's Horseshoe**, home to the world poker championships, is famous for its single-deck blackjack and liberal rules, single-zero roulette, great odds-on crap, loose nickel and quarter machines and loads of comps. Binion's is also known for its friendly atmosphere, while the **Golden Gate**, another friendly establishment, still serves up its famous 99-cent shrimp (ie huge prawn) cocktail. And you'll find the world's largest regular slot machine at the **Four Queens Hotel** in Downtown Las Vegas. It is the size of a small motorhome and allows six people to play at the same time! The old

Copper Mine at the **Gold Spike** has many old-time penny slots that are just perfect for people who hate to waste money and the karaoke bar at the **Gold Coast** is excellent for entertainment (locals dressed as their favourite stars, such as Roy Orbison, Dean Martin and Elvis) and cheap drinks.

★ ★ ★ **INSIDE TRACK** ★ ★ ★
★   ★
★   ★
★ If someone tries to entice you ★
★ into Sassy Sally's with the promise ★
★   of a drink – forget it. The slots   ★
★   are not loose and you'll never   ★
★ find a drinks waitress to get your ★
★   freebie!   ★
★ ★ ★ ★ ★ ★ ★ ★ ★ ★ ★ ★ ★ ★ ★ ★ ★

The favoured haunt of locals, though, is **Sam's Town** on Boulder Highway (going out towards the Hoover Dam). The free light and laser show is excellent and you'll find great odds on slots and video machines, and good comps.

Smoking

The chances of Nevada following California's lead and banning smoking in all indoor public places where food or drink is served is slim to negligible. When one casino adopted a non-smoking policy, it saw a dramatic downturn in business. After three years of lacklustre business, the Silver City Casino gave up. After lifting the ban in 1995, it saw an immediate and 'healthy' increase in business!

EATING AND DRINKING

Your choice of the best restaurants and eating places in town

There was a time when Las Vegas was most famous for its 99-cent shrimp (ie giant prawn) cocktails and the amazing all-you-can-eat buffets – and not a lot else in the dining department. But, like every other aspect of the city, things have changed as a result of the massive influx of bright young professionals from California and a surge in sophisticated visitors looking for something more than a bit of casino action. Now you cannot walk more than 100 yards down the Strip without coming across one of the many recently opened theme restaurants, trendy diners, celebrity-chef eateries or any of the staggering number of smart restaurants that serve delicious food in elegant settings.

Seriously upscale restaurants from New York and California have been clambering over each other to open new outlets in Las Vegas, while a whole raft of celebrity chefs have been lured to the recent clutch of sophisticated hotels that have opened including the Bellagio, Mandalay Bay, Paris and Venetian. While there are still plenty of cheap dining options, it is now possible to part with much larger wads of cash at Charlie Palmer's Aureole (Mandalay Bay), New York's Le Cirque (Bellagio), Mark Miller's Coyote Café, Julian Serrano's Picasso (Bellagio) and Wolfgang Puck's five outlets – Chinois, Postrio, Spago, Trattoria del Lupa and his Wofgang Puck's Café.

In addition, there are two new entertainment-orientated restaurants at the Mandalay Bay – the House of Blues and Rum Jungle – that promise a feast as well as plenty of fun. Whatever you want to eat – caviar and smoked salmon, French, Caribbean, Japanese, dim sum, noodles or Mexican – it is all here in Las Vegas.

But, be warned, although this is the city that never sleeps, most of the top-notch restaurants close by 11pm, though there is no shortage of 24-hour cafés and diners.

Obviously, space dictates that I cannot list all the restaurants on offer, so I have simply provided information on what are considered to be the finest restaurants in each category. They're all popular, though, so book a table in advance.

Price codes

$	=	under $25
$$	=	$26 to $50
$$$	=	$51 and up!

Theme restaurants

Allstar Café

3785 The Strip between Harmon and Tropicana, 702-795 8326. Cashing in on the trend of being rich and famous and then opening a restaurant are the tennis stars André Agassi and Monica Seles – and who can blame them? The food might not be brilliant, but it's a fun setting. Open 11am to 11pm Sunday to Thursday and till midnight at weekends. **$**

Bacchanal

Caesars Palace on the Strip, 702-731 7731. If it's a **Roman feast** you want, then this is the place to go! The Roman garden and fountains, vistas of ancient Roman countryside and costumed staff provide the right setting, while a sound system with special effects of thunder and lightning allow the ancient gods of Zeus and Venus to talk to you during dinner. It's a set-price ($69.50 including wine), six-course meal consisting of crudités, pasta, soup, salad, main course and dessert. Wine

Craig Road

Chevenne Ave

95

Jones Blvd

Rancho Dr.

M.L.King Hwy.

Las Vegas Blvd

Pecos Road

Lamb Blvd

Nellis Blvd

Lake Mead Blvd
Vegas Drive

Tonopah Ave
OWENS

Washington Ave

Westcliff Dr
Alta Dr
W. Charleston Blvd

Rancho Dr

11st

Main St

Fremont

Boulder Hwy

Bonanza Rd

E. Charleston Blvd

W. Sahara Ave

Jones Blvd

Spring Mtn Rd

Las Vegas Blvd

Desert Inn

W. Flamingo Rd

Twain

E. Flamingo Road

Decatur Blvd

Valley View

W. Tropicana Ave

15

Las Vegas Blvd

Paradise Road

Maryland Pkwy

Eastern Ave

Sandhill Road

Durango Rd

Rainbow Dr

W. Sunset Rd

N
W ✦ E
S

E. Sunset Rd

Mtn Vista

Stephanie St

Boulder Hwy

Major St

Palo Verde Dr

**LAS VEGAS
TOWN PLAN**

Mead Blvd

Pecos Road

Green Valley Pkwy

Henderson NV

BOULDER CITY

Here is a general overview of Las Vegas so you can familiarise yourself with the grid plan. It does not contain all the roads, but does have most of those referred to in this chapter. Remember Las Vegas Boulevard is The Strip and any roads to the right are East, while any to the left are West. The map in the hotels chapter (see page 23) shows you where the major resort hotels are located.

is served by exotically clad wine godesses. Caesar and Cleopatra put in an appearance during your meal, while you'll also be entertained by belly dancers. Open Tuesday to Saturday with seating at 6pm, 6.30pm, 9pm and 9.30pm. $$$

Dive!

On the Strip at the Fashion Show Mall, 702-369 3483. The second **submarine restaurant** opened by Steven Spielberg and his partners – the first is in Los Angeles. A replica of a sub and 64 video monitors are

used to create the underwater environment, while every hour the computer-controlled light and sound system sets off flashing lights, a surging water wall, bubbles through the portholes and steam through the overhead pipes to simulate a 'dive'. The food from the galley includes hot and cold gourmet subs, wood-oven-roasted chicken, barbecue ribs, burgers, salads, fresh pasta and fries. Miss it and miss out! Open Sunday to Thursday 11.30am to 10pm and until 11pm on Friday and Saturday. $

Top 40 restaurants

(In alphabetical order)

André's (South 6th Street and Monte Carlo)

Aqua (Bellagio)

Aureole (Mandalay Bay)

Bamboo Garden (West Flamingo Road)

Brown Derby (MGM Grand)

Buccaneer Bay Club (Treasure Island)

Búzios (Rio Suite Hotel)

Cheesecake Factory (Forum Shops)

Chinois (Forum Shops)

Coyote Café (MGM Grand)

Drai's (Barbary Coast)

Eiffel Tower Restaurant (Paris)

Emeril's Delmonico Steakhouse (The Venetian)

Emeril's New Orleans Fish House (MGM Grand)

Fiore Rotisserie and Grille (Rio Suite Hotel)

Frogeez on 4th (Downtown)

House of Blues (Mandalay Bay)

Hyakumi Japanese Restaurant and Sushi Bar (Caesars Palace)

Il Fornaio (New York-New York)

Isis (Luxor)

Le Cirque (Bellagio)

Mamounia (South Maryland Parkway)

Mayflower Cuisinier (West Sahara Avenue)

Millennium (Luxor)

Morton's (Fashion Show Mall)

Mr Lucky's 24/7 (Hard Rock Hotel)

Napa (Rio Suite)

Olives (Bellagio)

Papyrus (Luxor)

The Palm (Forum Shops)

Picasso (Bellagio)

Pinot (The Venetian)

Postrio (The Venetian)

Sergio's Italian Gardens (East Tropicana)

Sir Galahad's (Excalibur)

Smith & Wollensky (The Strip opposite MGM Grand)

Spago (Forum Shops)

The Steak House (Circus Circus)

VooDoo Café (Rio Suite)

Wolfgang Puck's Trattoria del Lupa (Mandalay Bay)

5

Drink & Eat Too

9200 East Harmon Avenue, 702-769 5519. More of a **live music venue** with five different bars than a restaurant, but its selection of pizzas, pastas and salads, served until all hours in the Dining Room, keep it in the restaurant theme section. It is co-owned by Michael Morton, brother of Hard Rock's Peter Morton and son of the owner of Morton's of Chicago, and was intended as a place to have fun, fun, fun. Other foods include daily speciality dishes, sandwiches, appetisers and a selection of cheesecakes and coffees. Open 11.30am to 4.30am daily. **$**

Hard Rock Café

4475 Paradise Road, 702-733 8400. Another **chain theme restaurant** that won't let you down in the memorabilia and food departments. You can even pick up a Hard Rock T-shirt or other souvenir to prove you've been there! **$**

Harley Davidson® Café

On the Strip at Harmon Avenue, 702-740 4555. The second outlet that pays homage to the **100-year-old motorbike** and is hard to miss with its 28-foot-high, 15,000-pound $500,000 Harley Davidson Heritage Softail Classic bike outside! Inside the 20,000-square-foot, two-storey café is a celebration of the free-spirit lifestyle of Harley Davidson motorbikes. And the food and drink lives up to it, too! You can sip on a range of cocktails with names such as Hill Climber, Rockin' Rita and Flat Tracker or cordials in a take-home glass from a Shock Absorber (that's a vodka, rum, triple-sec, melon, sour mix and 7-Up, so one should have you flat out!) to a Wheelie, Kickstart or Red Line. Soak up the alcohol with some of the delicious dishes that include fajitas, hamburgers, barbecue chicken, chillis, pasta and hot dogs. **$**

Mortoni's

Hard Rock Hotel, 702-693 5000. Offers straightforward **Italian cuisine** in a setting that pays homage to **Hollywood of old** with vintage photos of legendary stars such as James Dean, Grace Kelly, Marilyn Monroe, Clark Gable, Frank Sinatra, Dean Martin and Peter Lawford among others. Only natural ingredients are used in the dishes that include delicious salads, pizzas, steaks, veal and pasta. Open for dinner every night from 6pm to 11pm. **$$**

Motown Café

New York-New York, 702-740 6440. One of the better theme cafés comes complete with **R&B** music to reflect the roots of Motown music. The food is rich and the ambience richer. Open 7.30 to 11.30pm Sunday to Thursday and till 2am at weekends. **$$**

The Nitro Grill

Excalibur, 702-597 7777. The first-ever wrestling theme grill is a mixture of wrestling shows, live music, shopping and dining and features scheduled and impromptu wrestling celeb appearances. Open daily. **$$**

★★★ **INSIDE TRACK** ★★★
★ ★
★ Don't forget to check out your ★
★ fun books and local magazines ★
★ for great two-for-one deals. ★
★★★★★★★★★★★★★★★★★★

Planet Hollywood

The Forum Shops at Caesars Palace, 702-791 7827. California comes to Las Vegas with the kind of cuisine you'd expect on the other Strip – **Sunset Boulevard!** Gourmet pizzas, pastas, fish, burgers and more are served in the usual Planet Hollywood settings of stunning memorabilia with great sounds. **$**

Race Rock International

Fremont Street on the corner with The Strip, 702-382 7223. The award-winning **'supercharged'** dishes include gourmet pizzas, burgers, pastas, salads, Nitro Wings, BBQ chicken and ribs, steak and salmon, while the tractor trailers sell everything on a Supercharged Race Rock theme from T-shirts to jackets.

The Rainforest Café

MGM Grand on the Strip, 1-800 929 1111. A real-life simulation of a **rainforest** complete with tropical rainstorms featuring thunder and lightning that boom and spark across the entire restaurant. It's an untamed paradise brimming with exotic tropical birds, animated elephants, leopards and gorillas and tropical trees. You enter the dining area by

EFX AT THE MGM GRAND

SHOWS

STUDIO 54

KING ARTHUR'S
TOURNAMENT AT EXCALIBUR

LEGENDS IN CONCERT AT THE IMPERIAL THEATER

JUBILEE!

CIRQUE DU SOLEIL'S
'O' AT TREASURE ISLAND

S H O W S

JUBILEE!

CEASAR'S MAGICAL EMPI

ABOVE: SPORTS BOOK AT THE
LAS VEGAS HILTON

RIGHT: CASINO AT
THE DESERT INN

ABOVE: MAJESTIC STATUES AT
CAESARS PALACE

BELOW: EGYPTIAN SPLENDOUR
AT THE LUXOR

GAMBLING

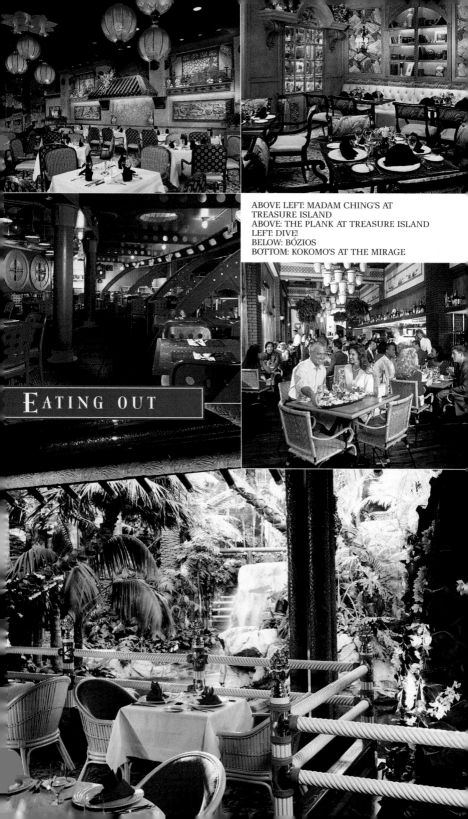

ABOVE LEFT: MADAM CHING'S AT
TREASURE ISLAND
ABOVE: THE PLANK AT TREASURE ISLAND
LEFT: DIVE!
BELOW: BÚZIOS
BOTTOM: KOKOMO'S AT THE MIRAGE

EATING OUT

walking under a 10,000-gallon double archway aquarium filled with marine fish from around the world. The food consists of pastas, salads, sandwiches and delectable desserts. Open 11am to 11pm daily. **$**

Seafood and steakhouses

Aqua   Choice
Bellagio, 702-693 7111. Michael Mina and Charles Candy's smart San Francisco seafood restaurant is brought to delightful life in Las Vegas by award-winning chef Mark Lo Russo. The five-course, $70 **tasting menu** includes Dungeness crab cakes on chopped tomatoes, ahi tuna medallion with seared foie gras, spinach, potato cake and portabello mushrooms in a pinot noir sauce. There is also an elaborate caviar service. **$$$**

Burgundy Room
Lady Luck, 206 North Third Street, 702-477 3000. If you want to get away from expensive gourmet rooms, then the Burgundy serves up **classics** like beef Wellington and steak au poivre in an attractive setting at reasonable prices. Open 5 to 10pm daily. **$$**

Búzio's   Choice
Rio Suite Hotel, 702-252 7697. Probably one of the best seafood restaurants in town – not just because of its extraordinary selection of **seafood dishes**, but also because of its **pricing policy** – dinner will cost around $24 per person. This is another fine restaurant based at the Rio Suite Hotel and well deserves its appearance in the annual Zagat survey of top restaurants in Las Vegas. Dishes include New Zealand mussels in garlic butter, seafood pastas, cioppina, bouillabaisse and chowders all with fresh baked crackers, bread and breadsticks. Open 11am to 11pm daily. **$$**

Emeril's Delmonico Steakhouse   Choice
The Venetian, 702-733 5000. Emeril Lagasse's second outlet in Las Vegas, it has already won the Ivy Award from Restaurants and Institutions, and features the **food surprises** that have made Emeril famous. Open 5.30 to 10.30pm daily. **$$$**

First Floor Grill
Four Seasons, 702-632 5000. Four Seasons' chef since 1986, Wolfgang von Wieser, brings a contemporary approach to the **traditional grill** concept. The menu includes caviar, goose liver, sashimi and tartar plus a huge selection of fresh seafood and charcoal grill dishes such as dry aged prime beef, filet mignon and rack of lamb. Open 5.30 to 10.30pm daily. **$$$**

Hugo's Cellar
Four Queen's, 202 Fremont Street, Downtown, 702-385 4011. A popular choice with locals and visitors alike, so book ahead to get a table. Famous for its **excellent wine list.** Open 5.30 to 10.30pm daily. **$$**

Michael's
Barbary Coast, 3595 The Strip at East Flamingo, 702-737 7111. Despite its unprepossessing setting, this is the choice of Las Vegas high-flyers so tables are hard to get. The food is superb, but the prices match. **For real foodies** only. Open 6 to 9.30pm daily. **$$$**

Morton's   Choice
The Fashion Show Mall on the Strip, 702-893 0703. A branch of the Chicago-based steakhouse, Morton's serves huge piles of **excellent food at good prices**. Try the broiled sea scallops wrapped in bacon for starters before heading on to a huge selection of massive steaks from Porterhouse steak to New York sirloin steak, rib-eye steak and double filet mignon. For an alternative you can also tuck into whole Maine lobster,

5

shrimps or swordfish steak. Open Monday to Saturday from 5pm to 11pm and Sundays until 10pm. **$$**

The Palm　　　　Choice

Forum Shops at Caesars Palace, 702-732 7256. Following on from the success of the New York restaurant, the Las Vegas version also appears in the Zagat top 40. Famous for crab cakes, lobster, prime rib and the house speciality, **charcoal-burnt steak**. Open 5 to 11pm daily. **$$**

The Plank

Treasure Island, 702-894 7223. The Plank is an intimate **pirate's library** serving seafood and mesquite-grilled specialities. Open from 5.30pm to 11pm Thursday to Monday. **$$**

Prime

The Bellagio, 702-693 7223. Award-winning chef Jean-Georges Vongerichten uses only the highest quality meats, seafood and chops to create a **fine dining** experience. Open 5.30 to 10.30pm daily. **$$**

Ruth's Chris Steakhouse

3900 Paradise Road, 702-791 7011 and 4561 West Flamingo Road, 702-248 7011. A chain of franchised steakhouses which started in New Orleans, these places have a reputation for serving **prime meat on a sizzling-hot platter** with butter. Other offerings includes lamb, chicken and fish with delicious vegetables from sautéed mushrooms to creamed spinach. Open daily from 4.30pm to 10.30pm. **$$**

Smith & Wollensky　　Choice

3767 on The Strip opposite the Monte Carlo next to the MGM Grand, 702-862 4100. Alan Stillman's New York **steakhouse** group's $10 million, free-standing, three-storey restaurant seats up to 600 diners in a catacomb-like series of rooms, niches and chambers. Open daily 11.30am to 11pm. **$$**

Star Canyon

The Venetian, 702-414 4100. Dallas-based chef Stephan Pyles brings his new **Texas cuisine** to Las Vegas and has won Best New Restaurant by Esquire, Bon Appetit and Town & Country. **$$**

The Steak House　　Choice

Circus Circus, 702-794 3767. An exception to every other rule at the family-friendly Circus Circus, this is definitely **adult-friendly** (the kids are running around the lobby outside) and serves some of the best steaks and seafood in town, making it one of the finest in its price range. Here you'll find generously-portioned steaks, shrimps, crab and lobster plus a delicious Caesar salad, chicken and black bean soup. Open for dinner at 5pm daily. **$$**

Tillerman

2245 East Flamingo Road, 702-731 4036. One of the best places in town to get a fabulously **fresh seafood** dinner – and not at sky-high prices. The huge ficus tree in the centre of the room creates a beautiful, romantic garden setting, while the skylight is opened on hot desert nights. Pacific salmon, Chilean sea bass and Florida snapper are some of the seafood platters on offer, while you'll also find steaks and pasta. Open daily from 5pm to 11pm. **$$**

The Top of the World

Stratosphere, 702-380 7711. The name says it all! More than 800 feet up the **tallest free-standing building** in America, the Top of the World revolving restaurant makes a full 360-degree revolution every 70 minutes. Awarded the Best Gourmet Room award by the Las Vegas Review-Journal, the **top-notch food** includes sizzling steaks and fresh fish and seafood, tasty salads and flaming desserts. Open from 5pm to 11pm Sunday to Thursday and until midnight on Friday and Saturday. **$$**

American restaurants

America

New York-New York, 702-740 6451.
A large, open restaurant with a few
booths, serves **classic casual
American food** such as roast turkey,
meatloaf, pastas, salads and burgers.
If all else fails to capture your
imagination, try the all-day breakfast.
Open 24 hours daily. **$**

Aureole   Choice

Mandalay Bay, 702-632 7777.
Charlie Palmer, famous for his New
York Aureole, has been enticed to
open a second outlet, this time in Las
Vegas. The New York restaurant is
consistently voted number one for
American cuisine by the Zagat survey
and Charlie was awarded Best Chef
by the James Beard Foundation in
1997. For this restaurant, a **four-
storey wine tower** has been created
and wine stewards strap on harnesses
to be hoisted up the tower to make
their wine selections from the Cellar in
the Sky. Charlie has also bought a
huge collection of rare French and
American wines from a private
collector to add to his comprehensive
wine list. Open 5.30 to 10.30pm
daily. **$$$**

Brown Derby   Choice

MGM Grand, 702-891 1111. A
recreation of the **Hollywood landmark
restaurant** that has been a meeting
place for celebs and movie movers
and shakers. The MGM has created
the Brown Derby in its Studio Walk,
complete with the signature Cobb
salad and grapefruit cake made
famous by the original. You'll also get
massive portions of steak, beef,
chicken, lamb and seafood. Open
daily from 6pm to 11pm. **$$**

Buccaneer Bay Club   Choice

Treasure Island, 702-894 7111. One
of the choicest **American** restaurants
around with a series of nooks and
crannies that give a bird's-eye view of
the **spectacular pirate show** outside.

You can tuck into lobster bisque,
salads, duckling and shrimp. There
are specials every night and the chef
is happy to prepare special orders.
The soufflé afters are the 'signature'
desserts of the restaurant. Open from
5pm to 10.30pm. **$$$**

Cheesecake Factory   Choice

The Forum Shops, 702-731 7110.
Famous for its **extensive menu** – there
are more than 250 items plus nearly
30 specials – this is more of a place to
people-watch than expect gourment
cuisine. It's in a perfect location and
something is bound to appeal. **$**

Grand Lux Café

The Venetian, 702-414 4100. A
second outlet in Las Vegas for the
wildly successful Cheesecake Factory
complete with all the choices. **$**

Green Shack

2504 East Fremont at Charleston
Boulevard, 702-383 0007. The city's
oldest restaurant and a good place to
get a **slice of Las Vegas history**. The
first customers were the men who built
the Hoover Dam and it's seen plenty
of action since. Open 5 to 10pm
daily. **$**

Millennium   Choice

Luxor Hotel, 702-262 4773. Fun,
hi-tech restaurant decorated in bold
patterns and colours with neon and
faux-industrial finishes. Here you'll
find trendy cuisine with specialities
including Astral Appetisers, Photonic
Pizzas and Hyper-Space Salads. The
open ceiling looks up to the top of the
world's largest atrium. Open daily. **$**

Nero's

Caesars Palace, 702-731 7731.
Nero's specialises in dry-aged prime
beef, tender chops and fresh seafood
– all artistically presented. **House
specials** include grilled lamb chops
on crispy polenta with baby greens
and garlic, grilled swordfish with
sweet potato purée, herb-roasted
onion, pea shoots and lemon aioli,

5

and halibut pan-roasted in lobster oil with braised baby artichokes, steamed clams and saffron couscous. The menu changes according to the season but perennials include crab cake, carpaccio of beef with shaved Parmesan, salad of frisée, fennel, roasted red peppers and truffle aioli. Open daily from 5.30pm to 11pm. **$$$**

Pegasus

Alexis Park Hotel, 375 East Harmon, 702-796 3353. Pegasus offers **gourmet dining** in a classy environment. Dishes include freshly made pastas, beef, pork and fresh fish that come with delicious vegetables. Open for dinner between 6pm and 11pm. **$$**

Best views in town

Eiffel Tower Restaurant (Paris)

Kiefer's Atop the Carriage House (East Harmon Avenue)

The Top of the World (Stratosphere)

VooDoo Café (Rio Suite Hotel)

Asian restaurants

Bamboo Garden   Choice

4850 West Flamingo Road, 702-871 3262. Popular spot for locals who love the delicious range of **unusual** (for Las Vegas) **dishes** at the very **reasonable prices.** It looks modest enough, but the friendly staff provide excellent service and dishes include cream of seafood soup, Mongolian lamb, firecracker beef, emerald shrimp and Peking duck with Mandarin pancakes. Open for lunch every day except Sunday 11am to 3pm and for dinner 11am to 10.30pm, Sunday 5pm to 10pm. **$$**

Benihana Village

Las Vegas Hilton, 702-732 5821. **Japanese fantasyland** in an enchanting garden setting complete

with thunder and lightning storms, lush flowers, flowing ponds and an authentic Torii Arch. There are two restaurants to choose from – the Hibachi where skilled chefs chop, slice and grill your food tableside and the Seafood Grille, where delicious delicacies are the order of the day. You can enjoy drinks and Oriental hors d'oeuvres in the **Kabuki Lounge** while your table is prepared. Open 5pm to 11pm daily. **$$$**

Chin's

In front of the Fashion Show Mall on the Strip, 702-733 8899. Another favourite frequented by locals and tourists alike. It specialises in **Hong Kong** cuisine with dishes like deep-fried chicken in strawberry sauce, steamed scallops with black beans on baby abalone shells, shredded chicken salad and shrimp puffs. For lunch you can get a plate of **dim sum** or tuck into a soup. Open Monday to Saturday 11am to 11pm, Sunday noon to 10pm. **$$**

Chinois   Choice

Forum Shops, Caesars Palace, 702-369 6300. Celebrity chef Wolfgang Puck's second outlet in Las Vegas provides dream cuisine from **China, Japan** and **Thailand**. The menu features sushi, sashimi, wok-fried and grilled seafood, poultry and meats with fresh, high-quality ingredients and home-made desserts. You have a choice of settings, too – you can dine at the **sushi bar**, in the **'outdoor' café** or the dramatic dining room. There are even **private dining rooms**. Open 11am to midnight. **$$**

Empress Court

Caesars Palace, 702-731 7110. Empress Court has a watery theme with a large, salt-water **aquarium** at the entrance to reflect the waters of its cuisine – the more unusual **Hong Kong** dishes.Chinese furniture such as chow tables, tea tables and altar tables in ebonised wood or aged silver leaf add an authentic feel to the room. Like most of the dining establishments at Caesars Palace, this is a lot more pricey than your average Chinese, but then you will get silver service and some amazing dishes such as bird's nest, shark's fin and fresh lobster broths, a vegetarian feast and freshly prepared noodles. Open Thursday to Monday from 6pm to 11pm. **$$$**

HoWan

3145 Las Vegas Boulevard South, 702-733 4547. Beautifully decorated with **tapestries and antiques**, with a **fish and seafood tank** to delight the mostly high-roller and tourist customers that frequent this establishment. That should give you some idea about the prices – definitely the upper end of the scale, while the costumed staff provide an excellent service. Many Asians eat here and enjoy tucking into **house specialities** such as minced squab and crackling shrimp, steamed fish, lobster and seaweed with cabbage and bean curd soup. Open every day from 6pm to 11pm. **$$$**

Hyakumi Japanese Restaurant and Sushi Bar   Choice

Caesars Palace, 702-734 6116. Home to award-winning executive chef Hiroji Obayashi. For dinner you have a choice of three **set-price menus** that include a four-course feast of appetisers, miso soup, salad and main course from $54 to $64 or à la carte dishes that include beef, chicken or fish teriyaki, yakitori, shrimp and vegetable tempura. The **sushi bar** also has a fabulously large selection of delicacies including fresh yellow tail, salmon egg, squid and abalone. This may be pricey but, if you love Japanese food as much as I do, then every cent will be money well spent. The main restaurant is open Tuesday to Sunday from 6pm to 11pm and the sushi bar stays open until midnight on Friday and Saturday. **$$$**

Lillie Langtry's

Golden Nugget Hotel, 129 Fremont Street, 702-385 7111. Provides Downtown gamblers with delicious and exotic **Cantonese** dishes in a brightly decorated setting with great service. The **Great Combination Plate** is a favourite starter, before moving on to black-pepper steak, stir-fried shrimp or lemon chicken among other main courses. Open from 5pm to 10.30pm. **$**

Madam Ching's

Treasure Island, 702-894 7223. One of the classier Chinese restaurants. Here you will find a mouthwatering selection of **Szechwan** and **Cantonese** cuisine in a traditional Chinese setting. Open from 5.30pm to 11pm Wednesday to Sunday. **$$**

The Mandarin Court

1510 East Flamingo Road, 702-737 1234. Designed as a replica of a Peking palace, this is something of a landmark locally. Despite that, it is an excellent place to go to get far from the madding crowds and enjoy delicious **traditional Chinese** food at good prices. It is also one of the best places to go to fill up in the middle of the night as it serves its trademark sweet and sour dishes **until 4am! $$**

Moongate

Mirage, 702-791 7111. Moongate is housed in a series of connected buildings of classical Chinese architecture surrounding an open courtyard filled with beautiful cherry blossom trees. The romantic setting is just right for mouthwatering classics from **Szechwan** and **Canton**. Open 5.30pm to 11pm. **$$**

Papyrus   Choice

Luxor Hotel, 702-262 4774. This is the place for romantics to go, with its cosy atmosphere and intimate grass-hut booths. Here you enter the Pacific Basin and dine on **Polynesian, Szechwan, Cantonese** and other Oriental food that includes such

5

mouthwatering delights as ahi tuna tartare in soy-chilli sauce, Papyrus eight-treasure fried rice, pork loin with Mandarin sauce, Korean-style shortribs with basil mashed potatoes and tempura vegetables. Open daily from 6pm to 11pm. **$$**

Thai Spice

4433 West Flamingo Road, 702-362 5308. A friendly restaurant that attracts a lot of the local Asians and tourists alike. Tuck into traditional **Thai** food from fish cakes to noodles, Thai-spiced beef and pepper-garlic pork. Open 11.30am to 10pm Monday to Thursday and until 11pm on Friday and Saturday. **$**

Cajun/creole restaurants

Big Mama's Soul Food Kitchen

Utopia Center, opposite Rue de Monte Carlo, 702-597 1616. Good, **honest food** at **rock-bottom prices.** Known for its gumbo, fried catfish and BBQ dishes. For a slice of real New Orleans food, try a piece of delicious pecan pie. **$**

Emeril's New Orleans Fish House   Choice

MGM Grand, 702-891 1111. A real must-visit restaurant if you want to experience celebrity chef Emeril Lagasse's New Orleans blend of modern **creole/Cajun cooking**. Tuck into seared Atlantic salmon served on a wild mushroom potato hash with herb meat juices and a spicy onion crust or grilled fillet of beef with creole oyster dressing and home-made hollandaise sauce. Open from 11.30am to 2.30pm and 6pm to 11pm. Next door is the seafood bar, a **walk-up-style eatery** featuring fresh shellfish and other seafood specials. **$$**

Kiefer's Atop the Carriage House

105 East Harmon Avenue, 702-739 8000. This place has one of the best **views of the Strip**, which you can look down at while you dine on

delicious **creole** food from Louisiana at reasonable prices. **$$**

The VooDoo Café   Choice

Rio Suite Hotel, 702-252 7777. The Voo Doo provides superb **Cajun and creole** dishes in an elegant New Orleans setting, while the view of the Strip is one of the best in town. **$$**

Caribbean restaurants

Rum Jungle

Mandalay Bay, 702-632 7777. Here food and drink become the artistic environment with a **dancing firewall** of food that turns into a soothing wall of water, and volcanic mountains of rum and spirits rise up behind the illuminated bar. The menu is tropically-inspired and many of the dishes are cooked over a giant open fire pit. Follow your meal by **dancing** to Latin, Caribbean and African beats until the wee small hours. Open 5pm to 4am. **$$$**

Caviar restaurants

Caviarteria

Forum Shops, 702-792 8560. The setting is perfect for one of the most heavenly experiences in the world as the Caviarteria has done all that is needed to recreate a small but **elegant New York-style** restaurant. Here you tuck in to top-quality caviar and smoked salmon and wash it all down with some fine champagne. Enjoy! **$$**

The Petrossian Bar

The Bellagio, 702-693 7111. A lavish bar next to the resort's dramatic entrance with its ballustraded walkway overhung by beautiful Cypress trees, it specialises in everything from **afternoon tea** to **caviar, champagne** and smoked salmon. **$$$**

Red Square

Mandalay Bay, 702-632 7777. Check out the extensive caviar selection or try out the menu of

Celebrity chef restaurants

Aqua – Michael Mina and Charles Candy

Aureole – Charlie Palmer

Border Grill – Mary Sue Milliken and Susan Feniger, the duo known as Too Hot Tamales

Coyote Café – Mark Miller

Drai's – Victor Drai

Emeril Lagassé's Delmonico Steakhouse

Emeril Lagassé's New Orleans Fish House

Il Fornaio – Luigi Bomparolo

Le Cirque – Elizabeth Blau

Napa – Jean-Louis Palladin

Olives – Todd English

Picasso – Julian Serrano

Pinot – Joachim Splichal

Wolfgang Puck's Trattoria del Lupa
Wolfgang also owns Chinois, Postrio, Spago and Wolfgang Puck's Café

5

updated Russian classics at the frozen ice bar, where you can choose from a selection of more than 100 frozen vodkas and infusions, martinis and Russian-inspired cocktails. **$$$**

English restaurants

Sir Galahad's   Choice
The Excalibur, 702-597 7777. This place serves up **traditional English** roast beef and Yorkshire pudding in its English castle setting with staff in dress reminiscent of King Arthur's day. The house speciality is basically prime rib, but you'll also find chicken and fish on the menu if you don't fancy tucking into the main meal, which is served from a large, copper cart. Open Sunday to Thursday 5pm to 10pm and Friday, Saturday and holidays 5pm to midnight. **$**

French restaurants

André's   Choice
401 South 6th Street, 702-385 5016. André's is one of the most well respected French restaurants and has been serving up delicious **gourmet food** to locals and tourists alike for nearly two decades. Just one block off the Strip, the restaurant is housed in one of the early homes of Las Vegas – dating all the way back to 1930! Owner/chef André Rochat converted the home into a French country chateau and has a myriad of dining rooms in addition to the main dining area. André is such a well respected figure of gastronomy and his restaurant so much of an institution in the city that he was invited to open an outlet at the **Monte Carlo Hotel** (702-798 7151). The menu changes all the time, but mouthwatering offerings include chartreuse of

Muscovy duck stewed in Merlot with portabella mushrooms and spring vegetables, sautéed prime fillet of beef with green peppercorn and cognac cream sauce, baked zucchini, gratin dauphinois and baby carrots anglaise and Maine lobster. Open every night from 6pm to 10pm. **$$$**

Aristocrat

850 South Rancho Drive, 702-870 1977. Another well established and fine French restaurant which is filled with locals and tourists. Tuck into classics such as mussels in white wine, beef Wellington, filet mignon or any of the **fresh fish specialities** that are changed daily. Open for lunch weekdays from 11.30am to 2pm and dinner daily from 6pm to 11pm. **$$**

Camelot

Excalibur 702-597 7777. Gourmet cuisine served in the Excalibur castle overlooking make-believe English countryside makes for a truly wonderful eating experience. Epicureans will find everything they are looking for from a fine **wine cellar** to a **cigar room**, lounge and **private dining chambers**, while the casual ambience makes it a friendly place for anyone to enjoy a meal. **$$**

Le Cirque   Choice

The Bellagio, 702-693 7111. Elizabeth Blau, who has been with the Maccioni family's famous flagship restaurant in New York for more than a decade, recreates its **gourmet French** dishes with great aplomb, while the views of the Bellagio's famous fountains lend it more than a touch of ambiance. **$$$**

Eiffel Tower Restaurant
Choice

Paris, 702-739 4111. The 'signature' dining experience of the new resort hotel is set 17 storeys up on the Eiffel Tower replica and has **stunning views** of Las Vegas' glittering golden mile. The softly-lit ambience includes a romantic **piano bar** where you can

enjoy a glass of champagne or an entire meal while absorbing the views, or try the full gourmet experience in the restaurant. **$$$**

Frogeez on 4th   Choice

Bank of America Center, 300 S Fourth St, 702-380 1122. André Rochat and Mary Jane Jarvis of André's fame provide another fine dining experience in Downtown Las Vegas. The menu and wine lists are short but sweet, while the ambience – particularly with live music at weekends – is always good and the bar is jumping on a Friday night. Open 11am to 11pm daily. **$**

Isis   Choice

Luxor Hotel, 702-262 4773. Consistently voted one of the top ten gourmet restaurants in America by the *Best of the Best Restaurant Guide*. You enter the elegant establishment by walking along the intimate colonnade walk of caryatid statues to the glass doors embossed with gold-leaf wings of Isis. Inside there are displays of reproduction Egyptian artefacts, many based on those found inside King Tutankhamun's tomb, and the vaulted ceiling is decorated with gold. It certainly is a grand setting in which to dine on house specialities inspired by **gourmet French cuisine** and the finest seasonal dishes money can buy. Open daily from 6pm to 11pm. **$$$**

Le Montrachet Bistro

Las Vegas Hilton, 702-732 5651. Offers delicious French food in an **elegant and luxurious setting** and elaborate fresh flower arrangements on each of the tables. The menu changes with the seasons. Open from 6pm to 11pm every night except Tuesday. **$$$**

Monte Carlo

Desert Inn, 702-733 4524. This is the posh resort's award-winning 'signature' restaurant overseen by top French chef Arnauld Briand. The setting is inspired by France's beautiful Côte d'Azur and mouthwatering dishes include Dover sole with Chardonnay sauce, beef Wellington with pommes pailles and truffle sauce plus escargots in garlic butter, sautéed veal sweetbreads with porcini mushrooms and warm asparagus laced with truffle dressing. Open from 6pm to 11pm. $$$

Napa   Choice

Rio Suite Hotel, 702-252 7737. Inspired by the **Californian wine** region, it serves gourmet food by world-renowned chef Jean-Louis Palladin. Open from 6pm to midnight, Wednesday to Sunday. $$

Palace Court

Caesars Palace, 702-731 7731. Another fine dining experience at Caesars Palace – with prices to match! The setting is beautiful – shades of terracotta, tan and pink adorn the walls and balloon-shaped curtains are draped along the two-story, circular glass wall, while there is a 45- by 20-foot **mural of a French garden** and courtyard. You'll be offered delicious dishes from pan-seared liver and confit turnips served with aged port wine sauce to roasted rack of lamb with smoked flageolet beans, goats' cheese and baby artichokes and the perfect Dover sole. Open for dinner every night from 6pm to 11pm. $$$

Pamplemousse

400 East Sahara Avenue, 702-733 2066. Like all the top French restaurants, this small but elegant restaurant is **pricey – but it's worth it.** House specialities include roast duckling in red wine and banana rum sauce and veal medallions in cream sauce, plus a huge selection of fresh seafood according to the season from mussels to monkfish and salmon. Open for dinner daily except Monday from 6pm to 11pm. $$$

Pinot Brasserie   Choice

The Venetian, 702-414 4100. Famous Los Angeles chef Joachim

Splichal brings his **Pinot concept** to the city. Open 11am to 11pm daily. $$

La Rotisserie

Paris, 702-739 4111. A wide choice of **gourmet dishes** include the 'signature' Scottish pheasant brushed with tarragon mustard sauce and served with red-bliss potatoes, and lime oil-brushed swordfish with basil garlic mashed potatoes. Desserts include classics like crème brulée and raspberry clafoutis. $$$

Fusion restaurants

Fiore Rotisserie and Grille   Choice

Rio Suite Hotel, 702-252 7702. One of the best restaurants in town, with great food, service and prices that won't break the bank! It has an eclectic range of dishes from chilled, roasted eggplant (aubergine) with balsamic vinaigrette and pesto to spaghettini with pastrami duck breast and cabbage for starters and Black Forest ham with shiitake mushrooms to Gulf red snapper sautéed with fennel and mushrooms. Cigar lovers will be pleased to note that the restaurant has an excellent selection on offer for after your meal and a **special cigar patio** where you can imbibe coffee and cognac to your heart's content. Open for lunch weekdays only from 11.30am to 2pm and dinner nightly from 6pm to midnight. $$

Fog City Diner

Hughes Center, 325 Hughes Center Drive, 702-737 0200. Simple diner food given a twist with **Japanese-inspired** mu shu burritos, first class seafood and shellfish, plus soups and sandwiches. Open 11.30am to 10pm. $

Gatsby's

MGM Grand on the Strip, 1-800 929 1111. Gatsby's offers a blend of **French** and eclectic **Californian** cuisine

5

in an intimate setting. Specialities include farm-raised ostrich, pâté de foie gras and ahi tuna (the 'signature' dish of executive chef Terry Fong) for starters. Main courses include rack of lamb, prime meat, fish and game, plus vegetarian specialities. Open daily from 6pm to 11pm. $$$

Jerome's

Rio Suite Hotel, 702-792 3772. Another Rio hotel winner with **Italian, French** and **American** dishes. Specialities include fresh fish and lobster, filet mignon and pasta dishes. Open for lunch weekdays from 11am to 2pm and for dinner every day from 5pm to 11pm. $$

La Provence

Paris, 702-739 4111. Waiters and waitresses dressed in traditional French peasant outfits will sing as they serve up **French-Italian cuisine** from the region of Provence. Classics include tapanade, bouillabaisse, estoufad and roasted rack of lamb with feta cheese and garlic crust. $$$

Mayflower Cuisinier   Choice

Sahara Pavilion, 4750 West Sahara at Decatur Boulevard, 702-870 8432. One of the most highly-rated restaurants in Las Vegas and consistently comes in the Zagat Top Ten. Here you will find **Mongolian/ Chinese cuisine** served Californian-style in a casual, but elegant environment. Book ahead for a table at weekends. Monday to Saturday 5 to 10pm and weekdays only from 11am to 3pm. $$

Spago   Choice

The Forum, 702-369 6300. This is celebrity chef Wolfgang Puck's famous outlet in Las Vegas and as with all his other establishments in Los Angeles, is a popular place for celebs and local movers and shakers. You'll find everything from pastas to salads and seafood. Open for dinner from 6pm to 10pm Monday to Thursday and until 10.30pm Friday to Sunday.

The **separate café** is open for lunch Sunday to Thursday from 11am to 11pm and until 1am Friday and Saturday. $$

Wolfgang Puck's Café

MGM Grand Hotel, 1-800 929 1111. A brightly decorated café with mosaic-tiled booths around the open kitchenette – another of celebrity chef Wolfgang's five outlets in Las Vegas Tuck into the usual eccentric array of **Italian nosh** and pizzas. Open daily from 11am to 11pm. $

Italian restaurants

Andiamo

Las Vegas Hilton, 702-732 5664. Andiamo specialises in fine northern Italian specialities in a beautiful setting. The **exhibition kitchen** gives customers the chance to watch chefs preparing the fresh pastas, pastries and sauces. Open 6pm to 11pm. $$

Antonio's

Rio Suite Hotel, 3700 West Flamingo Road, 702-252 7777. This, like all the Rio restaurants, makes an excellent choice – this time for those in search of a delicious Italian meal. Dishes include osso bucco, pork loin, lobster and chicken. Open daily from 5pm to 11pm. $$

Battista's Hole in the Wall

4041 Audrie Lane, 702-732 1424. This restaurant serves classic Italian fare in a **fun and friendly** atmosphere that makes it a great eating place for locals and tourists alike. Open for dinner only from 6pm to 11pm. $$

Bertolini's

Forum Shops at Caesars Palace on the Strip, 702-735 4663. A **sidewalk-style café** inside the exquisite Forum Shops in the piazza surrounding the Fountain of Gods. Outside you can watch the world go by, but inside there are quieter seats to be found. Pastas and rice dishes, pizzas, soups and salads, chicken and fish. $

California Pizza Kitchen

3400 Las Vegas Boulevard South, 702-791 7353. Part of a growing **national chain** which serves mostly delicious pizzas with mouthwatering selections of fresh ingredients. Open 11am to midnight Monday to Thursday and until 2am on Friday and Saturday. **$**

Canaletto

The Venetian, 702-414 4100. Based on a new concept by Il Fornaio's Larry Mindel. Classics include **home-made ravioli** filled with fresh Maine lobster in a lobster cream sauce topped with shrimp. **$$**

Chicago Joe's

820 South 4th Street, 702-382 5637. Chicago Joe's has been around for more than 20 years and is famous for its **Italian sauces.** Try the cream garlic dressing with one of the many delicious salads, Mexican Gulf shrimp and Maine lobster. Open for lunch and dinner. **$**

Il Fornaio   Choice

New York-New York Hotel on the Strip, 702-740 6969. Superb recreation of an Italian restaurant from New York's Little Italy. Here you'll find classic Italian cuisine and 'signature' breads, rolls and pastries from the **in-house bakery.** By the way, most of the waiters migrated to Las Vegas from New York when the hotel opened, so the accents are real! **$$**

Francesco's

Treasure Island, 702-894 7111. Filled with **artwork by celebrities** including crooner Tony Bennett, the menu here includes fresh pastas, antipasti, Mediterranean-style seafood and 'signature' freshly-baked breads. Open from 5.30pm to 11pm daily. **$**

Mortoni's

Hard Rock Hotel, 4455 Paradise Road, 702-693 5047. A real hip joint, good for celebrity watching, while pictures of the 'Rat Pack' line

the walls. The food's pretty good too, though go for the **fish specialities** to get a truly tasty meal. Open 6 to 11pm daily. **$$**

Portofino

Desert Inn on the Strip, 702-634 6909. Portofino overlooks the casino and is reached by climbing the grand, sweeping staircase or glass-encased lift. Here the favourites include zuppa di cavolo, minestra Basilica, seafood pescatore, scaloppini alla francese and tiramisu in a **romantic, candle-lit atmosphere.** Open every day from 6pm to 11pm. **$$**

Postrio   Choice

The Venetian, 702-414 4100. Based on Wolfgang Puck's San Francisco **bistro. $$**

Sergio's Italian Gardens
Choice

1955 East Tropicana Avenue, 702-739 1544. Consistently rated as one of the best Italian restaurants in town, Sergio's has a **delightful garden** with Roman columns. Dishes include calamari, Belgium endive salad, sautéed veal and filet mignon Rossini. Open 11.30am to 2.30pm Monday to Friday, 5.30pm to 11pm daily. **$$**

Terrazza

Caesars Palace on the Strip, 702-731 7731. Set in an ornate rotunda overlooking the Garden of the Gods swimming pools and gardens, Terrazza is open for **lunch, brunch and dinner.** A la carte choices include risotti, antipasti, soups, fresh fish and seafood, meats, pastas and freshly-baked pizza and focaccia breads. Lunch from Wednesday to Saturday from 11.30am to 2.30pm, brunch on Sunday from 10.30am to 3pm and dinner is daily from 5.30pm to 11pm (last seating at 10pm). **$$**

TreVisi

MGM Grand, 702-891 7777. There are two Italian restaurants at the MGM – La Scala and TreVisi. But the

5

former is very pricey and lacking in good service, while the TreVisi is a more **informal café,** which serves up good honest pizzas, pastas and breads at reasonable prices. $$

Venetian

3713 West Sahara Avenue, 702-876 4190. No, not the hotel, but it still stands out a mile due to the **exterior and interior murals.** When it opened in 1955 it was the first place to serve pizza in Las Vegas! It still does a roaring trade serving everything from pizza to pasta and plenty of other delightful dishes in between – all at great prices. Open for dinner only. $

Wolfgang Puck's Trattoria del Lupa   Choice

Mandalay Bay, 702-632 7777. The most recent of celebrity chef Wolfgang Puck's five eating outlets in Las Vegas, this one is pure Italian with **traditional recipes** cooked in pizza ovens and **wood-burning rotisseries.** The interior was designed by Adam Tihany, who has created a typical small, secluded piazza in Milan with views of pasta, meats and bakery production areas. Open 5.30 to 11pm. $$

Good for people-watching
Bertolini
Gordon Biersch
Mortoni's
Mr Lucky's 24/7
Red Square
VooDoo Café

Mediterranean restaurants

Drai's   Choice

Barbary Coast, The Strip at East Flamingo, 702-737 7111. Run by ex-Hollywood producer Victor Drai, this is one of the most popular

venues in town among the locals. Tuck into a fusion of French and Mediterranean food to the background sounds of **live jazz and blues.** Winning dishes include seared jumbo scallops with citrus ginger sauce, crispy duck confit and seven-hour leg of lamb. Open 5.30pm to 1am daily. $$

Olives   Choice

Bellagio, 702-693 7111. Todd and Olivia English bring their famous Boston Olives to Las Vegas with Mediterranean-style dishes in a **lively café setting.** Open 11.30am to 11pm. $$

Picasso   Choice

Bellagio, 702-693 7111. Julian Serano, who dazzled diners at San Francisco's Masa, brings his trademark Spanish-tinged French cuisine to one of the world's most opulent settings for a restaurant – dine here and you'll be surrounded by **$52-million-worth of Picasso originals** and even some of the artist's ceramics. The menu changes nightly but usually includes Julian's foie gras in Madeira sauce or warm lobster salad with mangoes or potatoes. The views of the Bellagio's dancing fountains finish off a superb dining experience. $$$

Mexican restaurants

Bamboleo

4949 North Rancho Drive, 702-658 4900. Traditional dishes from not just Mexico but **Brazil** and **Argentina** too – and all in a fun and friendly atmosphere. Open 11am to 11pm Sunday to Thursday and until midnight on Friday and Saturday. $

Border Grill

Mandalay Bay, 702-632 7777. Mary Sue Milliken and Susan Feniger, the duo known on American TV as Too Hot Tamales, are renowned for their Border Grill in Los Angeles and have now opened an outlet in the new all-jumping hotel, Mandalay Bay. Their **bold and tasty** Mexican dishes are served in a vibrant beach-side setting. **$$**

Cozymel's

Hughes Center, 355 Hughes Center Drive, 702-732 4833. An upscale franchise restaurant serving **spectacular seafood specials** and delicious fajitas. Open 11am to 10pm Monday to Thursday and to midnight on Friday and Saturday. **$**

Guadalajara Bar and Grille

Palace Station Hotel, 2411 West Sahara Avenue, 702-367 2411. A 24-hour joint, which is open from 11am to 5pm for lunch and from 5pm to 11am for dinner, and is famous for its **99-cent margaritas.** It may be a little off the beaten track, but you'll still need to make a reservation! **$**

Margaritagrille

Las Vegas Hilton, 702-732 5111. One of the best Mexican restaurants in town. Specialities include enchiladas, spicy burritos, chimichangas, crispy tostadas and tacos as well as the chef's own sizzling fajitas. You can also get delicious fresh fruit margaritas from the **salsa bar.** Open daily 11.30am to 3pm and 5pm to 11pm. **$**

Margarita's Mexican Cantina

Frontier Hotel on the Strip, 702-794 8200. **Classic Tex-Mex** food from burritos to tacos, enchiladas and chimichangas. The tortillas are freshly prepared and come with the usual salsa, guacamole and bean dips. **$**

Ricardo's Mexican Restaurant

MGM Grand Hotel on the Strip, 1-800 929 1111. Fun place to go for entertainment and food. Based in the resort's **Studio Walk,** you'll find a walk-up margarita bar, taco bar and a gift shop (another essential ingredient, it seems, of themed restaurants in Las Vegas!) and classic Mexican dishes. **$**

Viva Mercado's

6182 West Flamingo Road, 702-871 8826. Regularly wins the local daily paper's poll for best Mexican restaurant in town. That is due to declicious food including chile relleno, carnitas and Mexican-style steak at great prices. **$**

Moroccan restaurants

Mamounia   Choice

4632 South Maryland Parkway, 702-597 0092. Mamounia provides delicious **Moroccan** dishes in a simulated Middle Eastern **desert tent setting** complete with low benches or pillows, costumed waiters and belly dancers. House specialities include all the Moroccan classics such as hummus, kefta, tabbouleh, briouats, cacik yogurt dip, shish kebabs and couscous. Delicious food at great prices. Open daily from 5.30pm to 11.30pm. **$$**

Marrakech Restaurant

3900 Paradise Road, 702-737 5611. The oldest **Moroccan** restaurant in town and takes the whole desert-eating thing one stage further than Mamounia by expecting diners to eat with their hands! The house specialities include Moroccan-style chicken in a light lemon sauce and flambé lamb brochette. Dinner includes a **belly-dancing show**. Open daily from 5.30pm to 11pm. **$$**

Southern restaurants

House of Blues   Choice

Mandalay Bay, 702-632 7777. Dan Akroyd's famous House of Blues on Los Angeles' Strip arrives in Las Vegas at the majestic Mandalay Bay, and promises to be one of the hottest places in town. You'll find every kind of dish from Southern to creole and Cajun staples as well as wood-fired pizza and burgers. Gospel lovers will enjoy the **Gospel Brunch**, which features live music and an all-you-can-eat Southern-style buffet. At other times of the week expect blues-inspired and other live music. Open 11am to 3pm daily. **$$**

South-western restaurants

Coyote Café   Choice

MGM Grand Hotel, 1-800 929 1111. Just about the best South-western **coffee-shop-style restaurant** in town and serves one of the meanest breakfasts around. Mark Miller's dishes include black beans, blue-corn enchiladas and chicken burritos topped with home-made guacamole and sweetened mild salsas. Margaritas and custom-blended pineapple rum provide delicious afters! Open daily from 6pm to 11pm. **$$**

Chili's Grill and Bar

There are three restaurants in this chain: at 2590 South Maryland Parkway, 702-733 6462; 2520 South Decatur Boulevard, 702-871 0500; and 2751 North Green Valley Parkway, 702-433 3333.

Cafés and Diners

Binion's Coffee Shop

Binion's Horseshoe Hotel, 128 Fremont Street, 702-382 1600. Binion's gets cram-packed with downtown gamblers so you have to pick your time to avoid long queues. Specialities include **Benny Binion's Natural**, considered to be one of the best-priced, most delicious breakfasts in town, and **Binion's Delight**, a hamburger platter with chips. Late-nighters won't go far wrong with the famous **$3 steak dinner**, which is served from 10pm to 5.45am. **$**

Bugsy's Diner

Flamingo Hilton, 702-733 3111. The gangster who created the Flamingo is remembered by the Hilton, who have given the hotel a complete overhaul in the last few years. This **cafeteria-style coffee shop** and diner serves up

eggs, hamburgers and roast beef sandwiches to your specifications, plus delicious piping-hot waffles. Good at any time of the day, but a great stop for breakfast. **$**

Café Michelle

1350 East Flamingo Road, inside the local mall, 702-735 8686. The place to go for plenty of **cheap grub** far from the madding crowds. The red-and-white checked tableclothes and Cinzano umbrellas over tables in the plaza create a **European ambience**, while you tuck into omelettes, crêpes, salads and seafood. **$**

Café Roma

Caesars Palace on the Strip, 702-731 7547. One of the least expensive of all the Caesars Palace dining options, though it continues the hotel's Greco-Roman theme with large columns and golden walls. There is a **full American menu** 24 hours a day and a **Chinese menu** after 5pm. **$**

China Grill's Café and Zen Sum

Mandalay Bay, 702-632 7777. Set in the environs of the stupendous new Mandalay Bay, the Zen bar café sits right next door to the China Grill and offers some of the same dishes but at much lower prices. The focus is on preparing every dish in woks or on grills with sauces used strictly for flavour. The speciality of the house is the **conveyor dim sum bar. $**

Cyber City Café

Target Shopping Center, 3945 Maryland Parkway at East Flamingo, 702-732 2001. **Internet addicts** will want to make the trip out to the University District on the east side of town. Once you arrive you can flake out in the overstuffed sofas, drink copious amounts of coffee and check out your email for next to nothing.

Jazzed Café

Napoli Plaza, 2055 East Tropicana in the University District, 702-798 5995.

It's worth making the trek out to the east side of town to see how the locals live it up at the hippest café for miles. Check out one of the best **wine lists and coffee selections** in town, surrounded by dancers, who go for the dark ambience.

Jitters

2457 East Tropicana, 702-898 0056. Jitters specialises in providing one of the biggest and best selections of **coffees** in town and even roasts its own beans on the premises! Apart from the coffee you'll also get yourself a decent breakfast, lunch or dinner for under $10. **$**

Mr Lucky's

Hard Rock Hotel, 702-693 5000. The second of only two restaurants at the **world's first rock and roll hotel**, this is a fun setting for a fun meal. You'll find excellent choices for breakfast, lunch and dinner, while afterwards you can check out the rock 'n' roll memorabilia in the hotel casino, including items once owned by stars such as the Supremes, Elvis and James Brown. **$**

Ralph's Diner

Stardust Hotel on the Strip, 702-732 6330. This place has **juke boxes** on the tables, 1950s music and other paraphernalia from the original American diner era including black-and-white checkerboard lino and an old-fashioned **soda fountain**. Blue Plate specials start at $3.95. **$**

Roxy's Diner

Stratosphere on the Strip, 702-380 7711. A fun place to go to experience a piece of **1950s America** – everything from the décor to the uniforms and music pay homage to the rock and roll era. Food includes chicken, fried steak with home-made gravy and Mom's meat loaf with fresh vegetables and real mashed potatoes. Drinks include thick, cold milkshakes in tall, frosty glasses. Open 12 noon to 10pm daily. **$**

Live Music
House of Blues
Rum Jumgle
Frogeez on 4th
Drai's
Drink & Eat Too
The Nitro Grill

Hotel restaurants

Many of the best restaurants reviewed and listed above are in the top resort hotels. To make life easier I have listed all the eating places at the main resort hotels in town. Those marked with an * are a Choice. Take it as read that the hotels also have their own buffets!

Bellagio

702-693 7111. When the Bellagio opened at the end of 1998 it set a new standard both for hotels and restaurants and deliberately went out of its way to attract top celebrity chefs including Elizabeth Blau, Julian Serrano and Todd English.

Le Cirque*	French
Picasso*	Spanish/French
Aqua*	Seafood
Olives*	Mediterranean
Osteria del Circo	Tuscany
Prime	Steakhouse
Jasmine	Chinese
Shintaro	Sushi bar
Noodles	Asian
Sam's American	American
Café Bellagio	24-hour dining
The Petrossian Bar	Caviar

Caesars Palace

702-731 7110. The resort is posh and the restaurants reflect that – serving top-notch and largely pricey meals. If you're feeling flush, you can do no wrong by trying any of the following establishments.

Palace Court	A la carte French
Empress Court	Gourmet Chinese

Hyakumi*	Japanese sushi bar
Bacchanal	Roman feast with dancers
Neros	Contemporary American
Terrazza	Italian
Café Roma	24-hour snacks
La Piazza Food Court and Lounge	Restaurant/late-night lounge

Circus Circus

702-734 0410. The Steak House is one of the finest of its kind in town and is regularly honoured by local newspaper polls as the Number One steakhouse of Las Vegas.

Steak House*	American
Stivali	Italian

Desert Inn

702-733 4444. When Desert Inn decided to go upmarket and spent $200 million on renovations and expansions, they also upgraded their restaurants and staff. To this end they lured award-winning chef Arnauld Briand from New York's famous Rainbow Room to oversee all their restaurants. The proof of the excellent results are literally in the pudding!

Monte Carlo	Gourmet French
Portofino	Gourmet Italian
HoWan	Gourmet Chinese
Terrace Pointe	24-hour bistro

Excalibur

702-597 7777. Themes abound at the eating establishments of this resort that pays tribute to King Arthur's day. Sir Galahad's is a Tudor-style rib house, there's Italian cuisine in an Italian setting at Lance-A-Lotta Pasta and live music and country dancing at Wild Bill's Saloon.

Camelot	Gourmet dining overlooking the English countryside!
Sir Galahad's*	American ribs
Lance-A-Lotta Pasta	Italian
Wild Bill's Saloon and Steakhouse	Chargrilled steaks/ American food

Sherwood Forest Café	24-hour bistro

Hard Rock Hotel

702-693 5000. The rock 'n' roll memorabilia that adorn the first-ever hotel on this theme make a visit to the casino a must – and while you're there you won't be disappointed by either of the two dining establishments.

Mortoni's	Italian
Mr Lucky's 24/7	Coffee shop

Las Vegas Hilton

702-732 5111. The elegant resort hotel has some fine restaurants. The prices are on the high side but then you are getting some of the best ingredients cooked to perfection and served in delightful settings.

Benihana Village	Japanese
Le Montrachet Bistro	French
Andiamo	Italian
Hilton Steakhouse	Steaks
Barronshire	English
Garden of the Dragon	Chinese
Margaritagrille*	Mexican
The Coffee Shop	Snacks
Buffet of Champions	All-you-can-eat buffet!

Luxor

702-262 4000. Isis, the gourmet French restaurant, is consistently ranked among the top ten restaurants in all of America, while the Sacred Sea Room and Papyrus are also excellent choices for fine dining.

Isis*	Gourmet French
Sacred Sea Room	Casual American
Millennium*	Trendy American food
Papyrus*	Polynesian
Pyramid Café	American

Mandalay Bay

702-632 7777. The hotel is in the top-end bracket and aims directly at the more sophisticated traveller in search of fun. To this end they have two cracking live music venues – House of Blues and Rum Jungle –

among a selection of celebrity chef restaurants.

Aureole*	American
Wolfgang Puck's	
Trattoria del Lupa*	Italian
Shanghai Lilly	Cantonese
China Grill	Chinese
Four Seasons	French
Border Grill	Mexican
China Grill's Café	Chinese and
and Zen Sum	dim sum
Rum Jungle	Caribbean
Red Square	Caviar
House of Blues*	Southern
Raffles Café	24-hour dining
The Noodle Shop	Chinese
Four Seasons Café	Casual French

MGM Grand

702-891 7777. Celebrity chefs Wolfgang Puck and Emeril Lagasse both have restaurants here, while the Brown Derby is a faithful recreation of the original Hollywood haunt of celebs and movie moguls. Some people complain about the size of the MGM, but if you get lost in any of the eateries you'll simply feel you've found paradise on earth!

Gatsby's	Gourmet Californian
Dragon Court	Mandarin and
	Cantonese
Brown Derby*	American
Puck Café	Celebrity chef
	Italian restaurant
Ricardo's Mexican	Mexican
Restaurant	
Mark Miller's	
Coyote Café*	South-western
Emeril Lagasse's	
New Orleans	
Fish House*	Creole/Cajun
Franco Nuschese's	
TreVisi and La Scala	Italian
The Rainforest Café	Bistro
Studio Café	24 hours
Stage Deli	New York deli
Food Court	Hamada Express,
	McDonald's,
	Nathan's Famous,
	Mamma Ilardo's Pizza
	and Häagen Dazs

Mirage

702-791 7111. You won't go wrong dining at any of the eateries, and many offer fine food at mostly reasonable prices.

Mélange	French
Kokomo's	Seafood
Mikado	Japanese
Moongate	Chinese
Ristorante Riva	Italian
California	Californian
Pizza Kitchen	
Caribe Café	24-hour
	coffee shop
The Noodle Kitchen	Casual Chinese

Monte Carlo

702-730 7777. Here you will find one of the best restaurants in town – André's – and three run by top Californian restaurateurs, Salvator Casola, his son Sal and Chipper Pastron. Their Market City Caffe is an Italian eatery featuring fresh home-made bread and pasta dishes. The Dragon Noodle company features the Tea Bar with a range of exotic teas and the Golden Bagel is a replica of a classic New York deli.

André's*	Gourmet French
Blackstone's	American
Café	Casual
Pub & Brewery	Microbrews
Market City Caffe	Italian
Dragon Noodle Co	Asian

New York-New York

702-740 6969. Each of the hotel's restaurants provides a themed dining experience based on the New York areas including Little Italy, Chinatown and Manhattan. The quality is good and the prices are reasonable.

Gallagher's	Steaks and stuff
Steakhouse	
Il Fornaio	Italian
Chin Chin	Chinese
America	24-hour bistro
Nathan's Hot Dogs	New York
	street food
The Village Eateries	Fast food outlets

5

Paris

702-739 4111. The Paris-inspired resort keeps the French theme in all of its dining outlets ranging from true gourmet to casual.

Eiffel Tower Restaurant	Gourmet French
La Rotisserie	Gourmet French
Brasserie	Parisian-style café
La Provence	Provence region
Le Café	Coffee shop
La Boulangerie	Café in a bakery
Le Pool Café	Poolside café

Rio Suite Hotel

702-252 7777. Many of the Rio's restaurants are consistently highly rated by the Zagat survey.

Napa*	Gourmet French
Búzios*	Seafood
Fiore Rotisserie & Grille*	Fusion
The Wine Cellar Tasting Room	Wine-tasting
Fortunes	Oriental/Western
Mask	Oriental
Mama Maria's Cucina	Italian
Bamboleo	Mexican
Antonio's	Italian
VooDoo Café*	Cajun/creole
All-American Bar	American
Beach Café	Casual mixture
Toscano's Deli	New York deli

Stratosphere

702-380 7777. The tallest free-standing tower in America not only houses two of the biggest rides in Las Vegas, but also the amazing revolving restaurant, the award-winning Top of the World. Then there is the 'fun 50s' Roxy's Diner in which servers are dressed in rock 'n' roll outfits, plus a selection of other restaurants that serve good meals at good prices.

Top of the World	Revolving restaurant
Roxy's Diner	1950s America
Sister's Café and Grille	24-hour bistro
Tower of Pasta	Italian
Big Sky Steakhouse	Steaks and barbecues

Ferraro's Italian Restaurant	Italian

Treasure Island

702-894 7111. The resort tribute to the world of pirates of the Caribbean is home to some great restaurants decked out in the pirate theme.

Buccaneer Bay Club*	American
The Plank	Steak and seafood
Madame Ching's	Chinese
Francesco's	Italian
The Black Spot Grille	Gourmet American
The Delicatessen	Deli
The Lookout Café	24-hour bistro
Sweet Revenge	Ice creams and snacks
Starbucks Coffee	Coffee bar

Tropicana

702-739 2222. There is a distinctly tropical theme to many of the restaurants at this resort hotel – with delicious food to match. After watching the high-roller baccarat players in action you won't go far wrong taking the time out to dine at any of these eateries.

Bella Roma's	Italian
Papagayo's	Italian
Calypso's	24-hour bistro
El Gaucho	Steaks and seafood
The Player's Deli	New York deli
Mizuno's Teppan Dining	Japanese

The Venetian

702-414 4100. Aiming at the more sophisticated traveller and diner, it has a host of celebrity-chef restaurants.

Canaletto	Italian
Delmonico Steakhouse*	Steakhouse
Grand Lux Café	American
Lutece	Gourmet French
Pinot Brasserie*	Gourmet French
Postrio*	Italian
Royal Star	Californian Chinese
Star Canyon	Texan

Valentino	Italian
Zeffirino	Italian

Buffets

These all-you-can-eat-for-little-bucks feasts are what Las Vegas used to be most famous for in the culinary stakes and they are still going strong. The mega-feasts date back to the 1940s when the owner of the El Rancho devised a plan to offer a Midnight Chuck Wagon Buffet – 'all you can eat for a dollar' – and found the crowds rolling in. Other hotels quickly followed suit, introducing breakfast, lunch and dinner spreads and the buffet boom was born.

Now they are known as the gambler's revenge – a way to fill up on food for as little as $3 for breakfast to $15 for dinner – though some of the more upmarket, speciality buffets run to $30 a head. You'll find buffets at just about every hotel on the Strip and Downtown but the choice and turnover varies considerably. Circus Circus is famous for its massive buffet and once fed more than 17,600 people in one day, but the food is not worth the wait.

Buffets on (or near) the Strip

Carnival World Buffet: At the **Rio Hotel** on Flamingo Road. Both the biggest and best, the food is laid out in separate kiosks that have different cuisines from around the globe such as American, Chinese, Japanese and Mexican. It's so impressive you'll want to go back again and again, but the long queues may put you off as this is a real favourite with locals. The Rio also does a Village Seafood Buffet, which is much more expensive than the norm (around $18) but offers an incredible selection of all the different types of seafood in the world in the new Masquerade Village, an indoor New Orleans-style attraction.

★ ★ ★ ★ **INSIDE TRACK** ★ ★ ★
★   ★
★   ★
★ If staying at the Rio or playing in ★
★ the casino, don't forget to use ★
★ the VIP queue to get a head start ★
★ on the crowds! ★
★ ★ ★ ★ ★ ★ ★ ★ ★ ★ ★ ★ ★ ★ ★ ★ ★

The Stratosphere: At the top end of the Strip. This has a wide selection of good quality food at very good prices and the **Frontier** in the middle of the Strip is also well worth queueing for. The **San Remo** on Tropicana Avenue, just east of the Strip, has a small but good buffet in an intimate

Getting the most out of buffets

Generally, avoid breakfast buffets as you won't be able to walk for the rest of the day and the choice is not as good as at other times.

A lot of buffets change from breakfast to lunch at around 11am. Arrive at 10.45am to pay the breakfast rate and get the lunch spread!

Never, ever attempt more than one buffet a day or you will explode!

Try to avoid peak lunch and dinner times or you'll find yourself standing in a queue for an hour and a half. At weekends, even going off-peak times, the queues can take 45 minutes.

If the queues are long, take a good book or magazine to read!

Always check out the local magazines for two-for-one coupons.

atmosphere. Generally the queues are short as this is slightly off the beaten track, and the prices are excellent.

Other places on the Strip that are worth going to but are a little more expensive are at the **Mirage, Caesars Palace** and **Bally's**. The **Excalibur** is one of the biggest and has costumed staff with Robin Hood-style trumpets to add to the atmosphere. The **MGM Grand** is also good but the queues are incredibly long.

The Brown Derby: A grand champagne brunch at the MGM Grand from 9am to 2pm on Sunday. Adults $30, children $12.

The Buffet of Champions: A champagne brunch at the Las Vegas Hilton from 8am to 2.30pm on Saturday and Sunday. $12.

Imperial Buffet: A champagne brunch in the Imperial Palace on Saturday and Sunday from 8am to 3pm. $7.

The Luxor Steak House: Open from 10am to 3.30pm for a champagne brunch on Sunday. $25.

The Mirage: Champagne brunch from 8am to 9.30pm. $14.

Monte Carlo: Champagne brunch from 7am to 3pm. Adults $9 and under 10s $6.

Palatium Buffet: Caesars Palace do a champagne brunch from 10.30am to 3.30pm on Sundays. Adults $16, under 12s $8.

The Steak House: At Circus Circus, a great champagne brunch on Sundays from 10am to 2pm. $18 adults, $10 under 12s.

Sterling Brunch: At Bally's Hotel on the Strip, this is truly expensive ($50) but also truly worth it if you want to splash out on a great dining experience. From 9.30am to 2pm.

Treasure Island: Champagne brunch from 7.30am to 3.30pm. $9.

Tropicana: Champagne brunch in the El Gaucho restaurant from 10.30am to 2pm. Adults $26 and under 10s $16. The hotel's **Island Buffet** also has a cheaper champagne brunch from 10.30am to 2.30pm on Saturday and Sunday. $10.

Downtown buffets

Generally these do not have a good reputation, but the **Garden Court Buffet** at Main Street Station on Main Street was reopened in 1996 and since then has been serving a great choice of food in pretty surroundings. You can also try the **Paradise Buffet** at the **Fremont**, which has a great seafood buffet in the evening and an excellent breakfast choice.

Bourbon Street Hotel: Creole Bloody Mary brunch both Saturday and Sunday from 10.30am to 2pm for $6.

Fitzgeralds' Hotel: Champagne brunch on Saturday and Sunday from 8am to 4pm. $8.

Main Street Station: Champagne brunch from 7am to 3pm. $8.

The Golden Nugget: Champagne brunch is open from 8am to 10pm. $12.

Paradise Buffet: At the Fremont hotel, a champagne brunch from 7am to 3pm. $8.

★ ★ ★ ★ **INSIDE TRACK** ★ ★ ★
★　　　　　　　　　　　　★
★　　　　　　　　　　　　★
★　For Sunday champagne (and　★
★　other) brunches, expect to find　★
★　long queues at most places　★
★　because Las Vegas is so crowded　★
★　at the weekends – and always,　★
★　always avoid the lunchtime peak.　★
★ ★ ★ ★ ★ ★ ★ ★ ★ ★ ★ ★ ★ ★ ★

Greater Las Vegas

If you really want to get the best out of a Las Vegas buffet then you will need to travel a little farther afield than the Strip or Downtown. The **Festival Buffet** at the **Fiesta** on Rancho Drive at Lake Mead Boulevard (north-west Las Vegas) was modelled on the Rio Carnival Buffet and some locals reckon it now does a better job of things than the Rio! The food is more interesting and the quality and selection on offer is excellent.

In the opposite direction, the **Feast** at Boulder Station on the Boulder

Bars

Most restaurants close by 11pm, but the bars usually stay open later – some 24 hours. Many of the best are attached to restaurants and tend to be near to the Strip.

Drai's

Barbary Coast at Flamingo, 702-737 7111. A smart/casual joint with the most expensive cocktails in town. Don't be put off by its location in the basement of the Barbary Coast Hotel, this is a plush bar with plenty of atmosphere, which also has a quiet jazz combo playing in the corner. Open from 5.30 to 11pm.

Drink & Eat Too

200 East Harmon at Koval, 702-796 5519. If you can make it through the madding crowds, the VIP room above the cigar room is the place to go. Unheard-of drink combinations are served in baby bottles, test tubes and small plastic buckets, but you'll have to pay to get in (between $5 and $10 depending on the day of the week). Open 8pm to 5am Tuesday to Saturday.

Frogeez on 4th

Bank of America Building, 300 South Fourth Street, 702-380 1122. Tends to get packed with lawyers who work nearby, but it's one of the better bars downtown and the eating area is open till about midnight. Gets absolutely packed on a Friday night. Open 24 hours Monday to Saturday and until 3am on Sundays.

Gordon Biersch

3987 Paradise Road at Flamingo, 702-312 5247. Filled with beautiful people, this is one of the city's hottest pick-up parlours. Great brews, good food and live swing music make it a fun place to go. Open 11.30am to midnight daily and till 2am Tuesday to Saturday.

Hamilton's

New York-New York, second floor, 702-740 6400. Owned by the king of the tans, George Hamilton, this swanky martini and cigar bar attracts the smart wannabe crowd, all dressed up in tux and cocktail dresses. Modern-day 'Rat Packer' George is known to turn up from time to time and puff on a cigar. From the patio you can see the stage of the Empire Bar downstairs, where jazz and swing bands play every night. For something a little different, try martinis made from tangerine vodka. Open 4pm to 2am.

Holy Cow Casino & Brewery

2423 The Strip at Sahara, 702-732 2697. Las Vegas' oldest microbrewery is well placed to be a good stop-off point as you stroll along the Strip.

Monte Carlo Pub & Brewery

Monte Carlo Resort, 702-730 7423. You can get meals, music and brews with live nightly entertainment from 11am to 2am

5

Top of the World Lounge

Stratosphere, 702-380 7777. A casino lounge without live music on the 104th floor. Entrance to the Tower is $6, though you can avoid that by booking a table for dinner at the revolving restaurant.

Viva Las Vegas Lounge

Hard Rock, 4455 Paradise at Harmon, 702-693 5000. There's no live music, but people still flock to this joint. It's a place to people-watch even if the drinks are a little pricey. Open 11am to 11.30pm daily.

VooDoo Lounge

Rio Suite Hotel, 3700 West Flamingo, 702-252 7777. A great place to people-watch, though the drinks are very expensive. Still, 51 floors up, the view is spectacular. Open 11am to 2am daily.

Highway provides an excellent stop on your way to or from Hoover Dam. Here you'll find a good choice of quality foods ranging from tacos to pizzas and rotisserie chicken.

The Broiler: At Boulder Station on the Boulder Highway, a champagne brunch on Sundays from 10am to 3pm for under $15.

Garduno's: At the Fiesta on North Rancho Drive at Lake Mead Boulevard, you'll find a margarita Sunday brunch from 10am to 3pm. $10.

San Remo: Champagne brunch runs from 7am to 2pm Saturday and Sunday. $7.

Wine Cellar

The Wine Cellar Tasting Room

Rio Suite Hotel, 3700 West Flamingo, 702-252 7777. The world's largest and most extensive collection of fine wines includes more than 600 different wines once only enjoyed by kings, presidents and the cultural élite. Open Monday to Thursday 11am to midnight, Friday to Sunday 10am to 1.30am.

6 FAMILY FUN

From local rides and theme parks to museums and the great outdoors

There is so much more to Las Vegas than bright lights and chips. Many of the resort hotels have thrill rides from the heart-stopping, toe-tingling Sky Screamer at MGM to the Manhattan Express roller coaster at New York-New York, with its 'heartline' twist that simulates the sensation felt by pilots during a high-speed barrel-roll. Then there is the exciting Race for Atlantis at the Forum Shops and the terrifying Big Shot at the Stratosphere.

Kids will have plenty of fun at the Grand Slam Canyon Adventuredome, Fun House Express and Xtreme Zone, all at Circus Circus, or in Virtualand at Luxor, among many other bright spots. And the whole family can take their pick from a line-up of interesting museums including the not-to-be-missed former home of rhinestone king, Liberace.

Then there is the great outdoors and all the amazing ways you can experience it, from white water rafting to rock climbing, horse riding to following the cowboy trail. At certain times of the year it is possible to go skiing in the morning at Lee Canyon on Mount Charleston and head off to Lake Mead for a spot of waterskiing in the afternoon.

Everything you could possibly want to do is available just on the doorstep of Las Vegas and in stunning environments. Nearby is Red Rock Canyon, where ponderosa pines and Joshua trees grow out of towering cliffs of Aztec sandstone, the Valley of Fire, a Martian landscape of vivid red, pastel and white sandstone, and Mount Charleston, which looms 12,000 feet above sea level.

The biggest jewel in Las Vegas' crown of outdoor splendours, though, is the Grand Canyon. A whole raft of companies organise plane and helicopter flights to – and even down to the bottom of – the ten-mile-wide and one-mile-deep natural wonder. Many of those companies also offer trips a little further north to the stunning Bryce Canyon and Zion National Park, famous for its cascading waterfalls.

It has to be said, arrive in Las Vegas, and a world of beauty and fun could be your oyster.

Fun at resort hotels

Grand Slam Canyon Adventuredome   Kids' choice

Circus Circus on the Strip, 702-734 0410. The desert may get scorching hot outside, but here in this five-acre, fully enclosed **elevated theme park** – the largest space-frame dome in America – the temperature stays a comfortable 22°C/72°F year round. What's more, the dome is specifically designed to block dangerous ultra-violet rays while allowing natural light to get in. Grand Slam Canyon is designed to look like a desert canyon with a large rock canyon that gives way to caverns, pinnacles and steep cliffs, while a stream flows gently through the lush landscape. But this canyon is home to **prehistoric creatures** – well, life-sized replicas of them at least – who make themselves known among two **140-foot peaks**, a **fossil wall**, **archeological dig** and a **replica of a Pueblo Indian cliff dwelling**. The ride for thrills is the **Canyon Blaster**, the only indoor, double-loop, double-corkscrew roller coaster in America, which sends people on rockets through canyon walls at 55mph. A more relaxing ride is the **Rim Runner** which takes you on a scenic journey through botanical

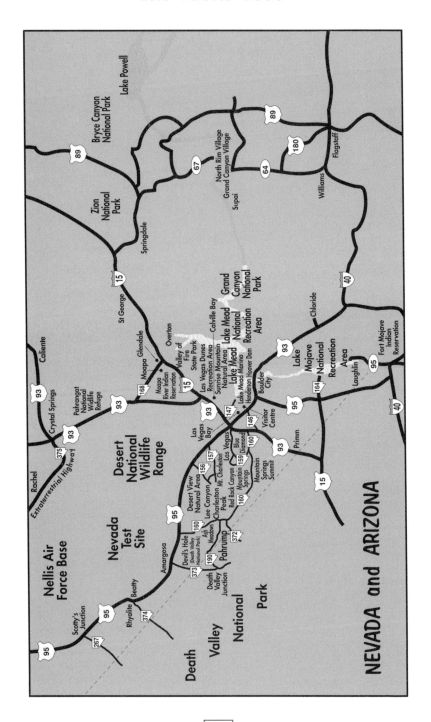

NEVADA and ARIZONA

★ ★ ★ ★ ★ ★ ★
★ **INSIDE TRACK** ★
★ ★
★ The Buccaneer Bay Battle gets ★
★ packed very quickly so arrive ★
★ early to get a good view. ★
★ ★ ★ ★ ★ ★ ★ ★ ★ ★ ★ ★ ★ ★ ★ ★ ★

landscaping before plunging over a heartstopping 60-foot waterfall. At **Hot Shots Laser**, sharpshooters take part in a hi-tech war. There are also plenty of younger children's rides from planes and trains to bumper-mobiles, plus strolling entertainers who juggle, mime and do magic tricks. Open daily from 11am. Unlimited Rides Pass cost $11.95 for people 33–48 inches tall, and $15.95 for those above four feet. Children under 33 inches ride free when with an adult.

Fun House Express

Grand Slam Canyon at Circus Circus. Here all the visual special effects of the **IMAX 3-D** cinema are used to bring to life a fun film about Jimmy, a retired clown, who operates a cheesy old fun-house ride. As the car creaks and rolls through the ride it breaks down and Jimmy is fired. The adventure begins when Jimmy seeks his revenge, dropping unsuspecting passengers through a trap door into a wild underground ride of his own creation – **Clown Chaos**. Open daily. Admission $5. You must be over 42 inches tall.

Xtreme Zone   Action choice

Grand Slam Canyon at Circus Circus. A combination of **rock climbing** and aerial **bungee jumping** creates an

interactive experience with multiple difficulty levels. The Zone's rock-climbing attraction combines traditional harnesses and handholds with cutting-edge belay technology to make the whole climbing experience as safe as possible. The aerial trampoline combines a standard trampoline with a hydraulic system and bungee cords so you can climb up to 20 feet and then flip and spin yourself back and forth. You must weigh 40 to 265 pounds to climb the wall and between 30 and 220 pounds to experience the bungee. Admission $5.

Buccaneer Bay Sea Battle

Treasure Island on the Strip. The amazing **sea battle** between an English frigate and a pirate ship in the nineteenth-century Caribbean is the action-packed free show at the Treasure Island Hotel. Spectacular **special effects** and **stunts** have the frigate sinking in shows at 4pm, 5.30pm, 7pm, 8.30pm and 10pm every day, with an extra show at 11.30pm on Friday and Saturday.

Manhattan Express   Thrill choice

New York-New York on the Strip, 1-800 NYFORME. Based on the kind of **roller coaster** that made Coney Island in the real New York so famous, this ride twists, loops and dives around the perimeter and even through the centre of the New York-New York hotel. It has the world's first **'heartline' twist and dive** that simulates the sensation felt by a pilot during a barrel-roll in an airplane when the centre of rotation actually

6

Top Five thrill rides

The Big Shot at the Stratosphere

Sky Screamer at MGM Grand

Race for Atlantis at the Forum Shops at Caesar's

Manhattan Express at New York-New York

Turbo Drop and Desperado at Buffalo Bill's in Primm

Good for Kids

Grand Slam Adventuredrom, Fun House Express,
Buccaneer Bay Sea Battle, MGM Grand Adventure,
Merlin's Monster Battle, Lied Discovery Children's Museum, Art Encounter,
Guinness World of Records, Las Vegas Natural History Museum,
Magic and Movie Hall of Shame O'Sheas, Wet 'n' Wild,
Ethel M Chocolate Factory, Ocean Spray Cranberry World West,
Ron Lee's World of Clowns, Virtualand at Luxor,
Famous Brands International Marshmallow Factory.

becomes the same as your centre of gravity! Open 10am to 11pm daily. Admission $5.

Masquerade Village   Free
Rio Suite Hotel, 3700 West Flamingo, 702-252 7777. A $25-million Disneyesque spectacle in which dozens of Mardi Gras floats containing exotically-costumed dancers literally 'float' about 20 feet above your head, all accompanied to music. The free display happens every two hours and for a small fee you can even take part.

MGM Grand Adventures
Thrill choice
MGM Grand on the Strip, 702-891 7979. This outdoor entertainment complex includes thrilling rides, shows, shops and cafés with themed streets and city façades. The **Sky Screamer** lifts up to three flyers 220 feet off the ground before the flyers pull their own ripcords to set in motion a free-fall drop at speeds of up to 70mph. The **Lightning Bolt** is an adventurous roller coaster that twists and turns over Grand Canyon Rapids, **Over the Edge** is a log-flume ride with a 42-foot drop and at **Grand Canyon Rapids** you take a free-floating raft down the rapids past an old Western gun fight and tunnel explosion. Check the times for the **live entertainment shows** at the indoor theatres, which includes **Duelling Pirates** in hand-to-hand combat,

exploding towers and breakaway masts at the Pirate's Cove Theater; **New Orleans street entertainment** at the Magic Screen Theater and an **exotic bird show** at the Gold Rush Theater. At Canterbury Square you will find lockers, lost and found and stroller and wheelchair rentals. Opening hours and days are seasonal. General admission is $12 over 12s and $10 a child, which includes $2 entrance and a one-day unlimited rides and shows wristband. The Sky Screamer costs $12.50.

★★★★ ★★★
★ To get the best out of the MGM ★ Grand Adventures theme park, ★ go during the week to avoid long ★ queues. ★
★★★★★★★★★★★★★★★★★★

Race for Atlantis   Thrill Choice
The Forum Shops at Caesars on the Strip, 702-733 9000. The world's first giant-screen **IMAX 3-D motion simulator ride** is a teeth-rattling, hair-raising, computer-animated chariot race through the legendary kingdom. Passengers are 'chosen by gods' to race against a fierce field of competitors – including Neptune, the reigning monarch, and Ghastlius, champion of evil – in a fight to the finish that will determine the ruler of Atlantis for the next millennium.

Launched into action by a **giant catapult**, riders have to dodge evil villains, fantastic obstacles and crashing competitors as **3-D computer-animated visuals** take you careening through beautiful vistas and plunging deep into the sea. Open from 10am to 11pm Sunday to Thursday, 10am to midnight Friday and Saturday. Admission: adults $9.50, students $8 and under 12s $6.75.

Star Trek: The Experience™

Las Vegas Hilton, 3000 Paradise Road, 702-732 5111. Prepare to beam up in the $70-million *Star Trek* ride in which your mission is to boldly go through space and time. You will be transported aboard the USS *Enterprise* and venture on the famous bridge before travelling on a TurboLift and speeding along the Grand Corridor. The attraction also includes a complete re-creation of the promenade in **Star Trek: Deep Space Nine®**, where you can eat at **Quark's Bar and Restaurant**, check out the largest collection of *Star Trek* merchandise under one roof, and even meet Ferengi, Klingons and other interplanetary visitors. Open from 11am to 11pm daily. Admission $9.95.

Stratosphere Tower

Thrill choice

Stratosphere Hotel on the Strip, 702-380 7777. The tallest free-standing observation tower in America has an indoor and outdoor **Observation Deck** where each of the landmarks seen from each point of the circular deck is explained. The best time of day to see the Strip is just before sunset when you can make out all the landmarks before the town goes dark and everything lights up. For many visitors, this is thrilling enough, but for die-hard ride fans, the Stratosphere has two – the Big Shot and the High Roller. The **Big Shot** thrusts 16 passengers 160 feet into the air along the 228-foot spire at speeds of around 45mph, producing up to four Gs with negative Gs on the way back down. What is so scary about the ride is not just the speed and force of it all, but the fact that you are so high up in the air in the first place!

★ ★ ★ ★ **INSIDE TRACK** ★ ★ ★
★ ★
★ ★
★ If it's serious thrills you're after, ★
★ then opt to do the Big Shot ★
★ twice on your all-inclusive ★
★ Stratosphere Tower ticket! ★
★ ★ ★ ★ ★ ★ ★ ★ ★ ★ ★ ★ ★ ★ ★ ★ ★

In comparison, the **High Roller**, one of the highest in the world, is a fairly tame experience. The rides are open from 10am to midnight Sunday to Thursday and from 10am to 1am Friday, Saturday and holidays. Tower admission plus the High Roller is $9. Tower admission plus the Big Shot is $10. Tower admission plus both rides is $14. Minimum height requirement for both rides is four feet.

VirtuaLand

Luxor Hotel on the Strip, 702-262 4000. Home of Sega's state-of-the-art **hi-tech games** including Virtua-Formula, a 14-foot-by-50-foot interactive racing game with 3-D polygon graphic technology. A **big screen**, live **monitors** and individual **motion-based race cars** are used to pit eight racers against each other. Another great game is the **R360**, which is a **dog-fight simulator** that has 360-degree manoeuvring and a gyro-moving spherical cockpit system. Open daily from 9am to 11pm. Admission $6. The Luxor also houses the **King Tut Museum**, with reproductions of artefacts found at the original site. Open daily from 9am to 11pm. Admission $3.

Top Five action sports

Rock/bungee climbing with Xtreme Zone at Circus Circus

Bungee jumping with AJ Hackett

Learning to fly at Flyaway Indoor Skydiving

Skydiving with an instructor at Boulder city near the Hoover Dam

Horse riding on an old cowboy trail

Merlin's Monster Battle

Excalibur Hotel on the Strip, 702-597 7777. A robotic Merlin the Magician battles it out with a giant, scaly, fire-breathing dragon for domination of the mystical moat outside the Excalibur every hour from 6pm until 1am, depending on weather conditions, seven days a week. Admission free.

★★★ **INSIDE TRACK** ★★★
★ ★
★ ★
★ Merlin's battle with the dragon at ★
★ the Excalibur may be free, but ★
★ don't feel you have to go out of ★
★ your way to see it! ★
★★★★★★★★★★★★★★★★★★★

Secret Garden

Mirage Hotel on the Strip, 702-791 7111. Here is your chance to get a closer look at the **rare breeds of animals** which Siegfried and Roy use in their magical illusion show. The $15-million, 2.5-acre natural habitat was specially built to house their royal white tigers, Bengal tigers, panthers, snow leopards and Asian elephants. Next door and included in the admission price is the **Dolphin Habitat**, which contains several dolphins in a habitat that copies their natural environment. Open daily from 11am to 5.30pm. Entrance $10.

Imperial Palace Auto Collection

Imperial Palace Hotel on the Strip, 702-731 3311. There are more than 600 cars in the collection but only 200 are ever on show at one time. Some of the **vintage, classic and special-interest cars** include the **Chaser**, the world's fastest petrol-powered police car, a 1986 Ford Mustang, which was specially built for the Nevada Highway Patrol, President Woodrow Wilson's 1917 Pierce Arrow car and a 1961 Lincoln Continental that was once owned by Jacqueline Kennedy Onassis. Open daily from 9.30am to 11pm. Admission: adults $6.95, children $3.

Museums, galleries, parks and factories

Liberace Museum

Liberace Plaza, 1775 East Tropicana Avenue, 702-798 5595. The man known as Mr Showmanship lives on in one of the most popular attractions in Nevada, that includes a collection of three buildings near where the artist once lived. One building houses 18 rare and antique **pianos** including Liberace's favourite Baldwin grand piano, and others owned by Chopin and George Gershwin, plus Liberace's **cars**. Another building is devoted to his famous **stage wardrobe** of multi-sequinned, bejewelled and rhinestone-studded costumes and famous rings that used to dazzle audiences around the world. The third contains an extensive collection of **Liberace's memorabilia** including hundreds of rare Moser crystal from Czechoslovakia, a monogrammed set of dinner plates that once belonged to President John F Kennedy, and Liberace's violin, made by the famous violin maker George Winterling. There are also re-creations of Liberace's office and bedroom at the Cloisters, his Palm Springs hacienda, complete with an ornately inlaid Louis XV desk originally owned by Czar Nicholas II of Russia. Open Monday to Saturday 10am to 5pm and from 1pm to 5pm on Sunday. Admission: adults $6.50, 6–12s $2, though children must be accompanied by an adult. All the proceeds go to the Liberace Foundation for the Performing and Creative Arts, which regularly donates thousands of dollars to schools, universities and other organisations for music, dance, drama, film and visual arts.

Lied Discovery Children's Museum

833 Las Vegas Boulevard North, 702-382 5437. Here children can touch, see, explore and experience more than 100 hands-on exhibits in one of America's largest – and most exciting – children's museums. Children crawl and slide through the **Toddler Towers**, become a star on the **Performing Arts stage**, pilot the **Space Shuttle** or **Gyrochair**, create colour **computer prints** and toe-tap a tune on the **Musical Pathway**. They can also stand in a giant bubble, play at being a disc jockey at the KKID radio station or use their bodies to generate electricity. Open Tuesday to Saturday 10am to 5pm, Wednesday 10am to 7pm and Sunday noon to 5pm. Closed Monday except most school holidays. Adults $5, over 12s, $4, 3–11s $3 and toddlers free. Children under the age of 11 must be accompanied by an adult.

Art Encounter

3979 Spring Mountain Road, 702-227 0220. Nevada's largest **fine art gallery** houses paintings, sculpture, jewellery, pottery and glass by international, national and local artists. Open Tuesday to Friday from 10am to 6pm and Monday and Saturday from noon to 5pm.

Desert Demonstration Gardens

3701 West Alta Drive, 702-258 3205. Offers free literature, classes and a self-guided tour to people interested in creating a **'water smart' garden** in the middle of a desert. Open Monday to Friday from 8am to 5pm and until 4.30pm at weekends.

Guinness World of Records

2780 Las Vegas Boulevard South, 702-792 3766. Affiliated to the book, record-breakers are brought to three-dimensional life with the help of **life-sized replicas, colour videos** and **computerised databanks**. Included are the tallest man, the fattest man and fastest-talking man, plus the musical records of Michael Jackson and videos of world records being set. Open daily. Admission: adults $4.95, students $3.95 and 4–12s $2.95.

Las Vegas Art Museum   Free

3333 Washington Avenue, 702-647 4300. **Fine art exhibits** in three galleries that are changed on a monthly basis. It also runs **art classes** for adults and children and art competitions. Open from Monday to Saturday 10am to 3pm and from noon to 3pm on Sunday.

Las Vegas Natural History Museum

900 Las Vegas Boulevard North, 702-384 3466. Wildlife existed in the Las Vegas valley long before man arrived and created casinos! Here you can take a walk on the wild side and discover the scenic and wild natural beauty of southern Nevada. It includes exhibits representing the many different habitats in the Las Vegas area with a diverse variety of **plants** and **wildlife**. The historical side is represented by **animated dinosaurs**, while there is an **international wildlife room**, small live

sharks in the **aquarium** and a **hands-on exploration room** for children. There is also an extensive wildlife **art gallery** and award-winning wood **sculptures**. Open from 9am to 4pm daily. Entrance: adults $5, students $4 and 4–12s $2.50

Magic and Movie Hall of Fame O'Sheas

3555 Las Vegas Boulevard South, 702-792 0788. A 20,000-square-foot attraction with a museum of magic, ventriloquism and movie memorabilia. The **Magic Museum** has a collection of equipment used by past master magicians including Houdini artifacts. The **Movie Museum** has costumes from *Cleopatra* and *Gone with the Wind* and a Frankenstein monster that comes to life. The ***That's Magic* illusion show** costs $21.95 for adults and $7.95 for children and includes free entry to the exhibits, a magic gift and one drink. Shows at 5.30pm, 7.30pm and 9.30pm Monday to Saturday.

Moonstruck Gallery

6322 West Sahara Avenue, 702-364 0531. Voted the best gallery in Las Vegas, here you will find limited-edition prints, music, books, pottery, jewellery, handcrafted gifts and musical instruments. Open from 10am to 6pm Tuesday to Saturday.

Nevada State Museum and Historical Society

700 Twin Lakes Drive, 702-486 5205. The history of southern Nevada from mammoths to gambling is presented in three galleries – Biology, Earth Science and History/Anthropology. There is also a display explaining how neon has been used in the city. Open from 8.30am to 4.30pm daily. Admission: adults $2, under 18s free.

Nevada Zoological-Botanical Park

1755 North Rancho Drive, 702-648 5955. This is a small zoo committed to **conservation, education** and **recreation**. It has more than 50 species of reptiles and small animals of the great South-western desert, plus other animals including an African lion, Bengal tiger, Barbary apes, monkeys, wallabies, flamingos, king vultures and North America's only tigrina, an endangered tropical cat. Open from 9am to 5pm daily. Admission: over 12s $5, 2–12s $3 and under 2s free.

Old Las Vegas Mormon Fort

State Historic Park, 908 Las Vegas Boulevard North, 702-486 3511. This is the oldest surviving non-Indian structure in Las Vegas and dates back to 14 June 1855 when the Mormon missionaries arrived in New Mexico Territory. Their aim was to convert the Indians and provide a safe way-station between Mormon communities in Great Salt Lake City to the north and San Bernardino to the east. The 150-square-foot adobe-walled fort was still being built when the fort was largely abandoned in 1858 and subsequently was used by lead miners before becoming a ranch. It was sold to the San Pedro, Los Angeles and Salt Lake Railroad in 1902, which created a railroad watering stop and townsite. It was three years later, on 15 May 1905, that the townsite lots were auctioned off and this is now considered to be the birthday of the modern city of Las Vegas. Since then it has been used as a restaurant and as a lodge before being bought by the city of Las Vegas and becoming registered as a Historic Place. The Nevada Division of Parks has launched a project to rebuild the entire site, plus a visitors' centre and vegetable garden where the crops will be identical to those planted by the Mormon pioneers. Open from 8.30am to 3.30pm every day. Entrance fees to be decided.

Planetarium and Observatory

Community College of Southern Nevada, 3200 East Cheyenne Avenue, 702-651 5059. Southern Nevada's only public planetarium and observatory has **multimedia shows** on astronomy plus **hemispheric motion pictures**. Public observing sessions are held after the last showings. Showing at 6pm and 7.30pm on Friday and 3.30pm and 7.30pm on Saturday. Store is open from 5pm to 8pm on Friday and from 3pm to 8pm on Saturday.

Action

Wet 'n' Wild   Action choice

2600 Las Vegas Boulevard South, 702-737 7873. Here you will find 15 acres of rides, slides, chutes, floats and flumes to beat the summer heat. Wet 'n' Wild favourites include the **Lazy River®**, **Der Stuka®** and **Kids' Park**, while you can battle the monster surf of the **Wave Pool** or tackle the ultimate terror of the **Banzai Banzai®**. Then there is the whirlpool wonder of **Willy Willy®** and **Bubble Up** for children. Facilities include lockers, changing areas, showers, shops with swimwear and snack bars, though you are allowed to bring your own **picnics**. Open from April to September, times vary according to the season, but from the end of June to early August, it is open from 10am to 11pm every day. Parking is free. Entrance costs $21.95 for 10 and over, $15.95 for 3–9s. Under 3s free.

AJ Hackett Bungee
Action choice

810 Circus Circus Drive, 702-385 4321. If it's sheer exhilaration you want to experience, jump off the 180-foot tower and then cool off in the pool! Hours are seasonal, so phone in advance. Various packages are available with T-shirts and videos. Prices start at $49 for the jump only.

★ ★ ★ ★ **INSIDE TRACK** ★ ★ ★
★   ★
★   Although you are allowed to   ★
★   bring your own picnics to   ★
★   Wet 'n' Wild, do make sure   ★
★   that they are alcohol free!   ★
★ ★ ★ ★ ★ ★ ★ ★ ★ ★ ★ ★ ★ ★ ★ ★ ★

Flyaway Indoor Skydiving
Action choice

200 Convention Center Drive, 702-731 4768. Learn how to fly at America's only indoor skydiving simulator, where the **vertical wind tunnel** allows you to beat gravity and fly! First-time flyers are given a 25-minute class in safety and body control techniques. Experienced skydivers can also get valuable 'air' time to improve their skills without having to pack a rig and wait for the right weather. There are also **video coaching programmes** available where your air tunnel flight is recorded so you can improve your style. Prices depend on the package you go for. Open from 10am daily. Classes every 30 minutes on a first-come, first-served basis. Dress in comfy clothes with socks and trainers. A single flight is $35 including class, equipment and 15-minute flight shared by five flyers. Double flights are $55. Videos of flight cost $15.

Las Vegas Skydiving Center

Just behind the Goldstrike Hotel at Jean Airport, 702-877 1010 (southwest of Las Vegas). Take a tandem skydive after a 20-minute lesson for $159 ($179 including transport from your hotel). Open daily from 8am till dusk, jumps are by appointment only.

Skydive Las Vegas

Boulder City Airport, Boulder City, 702-293 1860 (near Hoover Dam). You freefall for 45 seconds before enjoying a seven-minute parachute ride in a tandem jump. By appointment only.

6

Las Vegas Mini Grand Prix

1401 North Rainbow Boulevard,
702-259 7000. Take exit 82a off US
95 for the ride of a lifetime on adult
Gran Prix, Nascars, go-karts and
kiddie karts. There is also a games
arcade and snack bar. Open daily
according to the season.

Rocks and Ropes

3065 East Patrick Lane, Suite 4, 702-
434 3388. The **indoor climbing
facility** has more than 7,000 square
feet of sculpted and textured walls for
climbing, 30-foot ceilings, top rope
and lead climbing and a mega-cave
with a leadable 40-foot roof so
people can learn everything they
need to know to go rock climbing for
real! A five-visit pass costs $45.

Ultrazone: The Ultimate Laser
Adventure   Action choice

2555 South Maryland Parkway, 702-
734 1577. This is the place where
'virtual' stops and reality begins as
three-man teams play a laser
adventure in thick fog. Sharp reflexes
and hi-tech lasers are your only
defence!

Turbo Drop and Desperado
Thrill choice

Buffalo Bill's Hotel, Primm, 1-800 367
7383. At the border with California,
35 miles south of Las Vegas on
Interstate 15. The hotel is now home
to two of the most thrilling rides in the
Las Vegas Valley. **Desperado**, the
world's tallest and fastest roller
coaster has a top speed of around
90mph and creates a G-force of
nearly 4. It starts inside the casino
and then loops its way outside the
resort hotel. It is also home to the
Turbo Drop, which creates a similar
sensation as flying straight towards
the ground in a jet fighter. Riders are
nestled in padded saddles and
shoulder harnesses, lifted 200 feet in
the air and plunged to earth at
45mph, creating postive G-forces
close to 4.5. Other rides include
Adventure Canyon Log Flume and

Ghost Town Motion Theaters. Open
Sunday to Thursday 10am to 9pm
and until midnight on Friday and
Saturday. Desperado and Turbo Drop
cost $5 each, the log flume $4 and
the motion theatres $3.

Clark County Heritage
Museum

1830 South Boulder Highway,
Henderson, 702-455 7955. Covers a
timespan of 12,000 years of southern
Nevada history and includes **Heritage
Street**, a living history area, and
Nevada ghost town. There are old
railroad cars, a fully restored 1920s
bungalow built by a pioneer Las
Vegas merchant, a replica of a
nineteenth-century frontier print shop,
plus ranching displays and a nature
walk. Open 9am to 4.30pm.
Admission: adults and children
$1.50, under 3s free.

Ethel M Chocolate Factory
Free

2 Cactus Garden Drive, Henderson,
702-433 2500. Chocoholics will be
in heaven at this ultra-modern
chocolate sweet factory on the way
to Hoover Dam. Ethel Mars was the
mother of Forrest Mars, creator of the
Mars bar, M&Ms and Milky Way
among others. Forrest Mars is now
one of the world's richest men and
visitors can see his famous sweets
being made. Outside the factory is
also a beautiful cactus garden
featuring more than 300 cacti and
desert plants. Self-guided tours are
offered daily from 9am to 5.30pm.

Famous Brands International
Marshmallow Factory   Free

1180 Marshmallow Lane, Henderson,
702-564 5400. Another paradise for
those with a sweet tooth, here you get
free self-guided tour with a bag of
marshmallows. Open daily from 9am
to 4.30pm

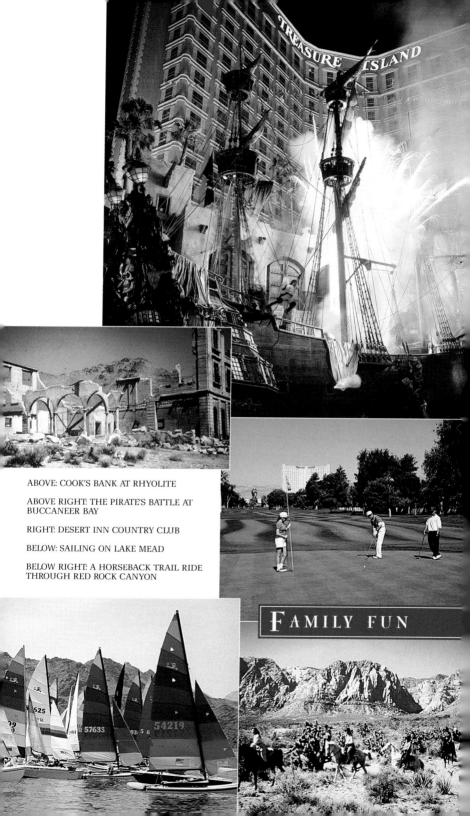

ABOVE: COOK'S BANK AT RHYOLITE

ABOVE RIGHT: THE PIRATE'S BATTLE AT BUCCANEER BAY

RIGHT: DESERT INN COUNTRY CLUB

BELOW: SAILING ON LAKE MEAD

BELOW RIGHT: A HORSEBACK TRAIL RIDE THROUGH RED ROCK CANYON

FAMILY FUN

HELICOPTER IN GRAND CANYON

THE HOOVER DAM

FAMILY FUN

THE ROLLERCOASTER AT NEW YORK-NEW YORK

NATIONAL RODEO FINALS

DESERT PRINCESS CRUISES
PADDLEBOAT ON LAKE MEA

Ocean Spray Cranberry World West — Free

1301 American Pacific Drive, Henderson, 702-566 7160. A Las Vegas-style dancing showgirl called the Cran-Cran Girl greets visitors to Ocean Spray's family attraction. Using a blend of interactive displays, artefacts and audio visuals, you are shown the cranberry's journey from the wetland bogs of north-west America to this drinks plant. There is also a **100-seat cinema** with movable seats, a **demonstration kitchen** and a **gift shop**. Open 9am to 5pm.

Ron Lee's World of Clowns — Free

330 Carousel Parkway, Henderson, 702-434 1700. Here you can see how clown and animation characters are made in an impressive 35-minute **self-guided tour**. A Warner Bros production facility, you will see famous **cartoon characters** including Popeye, Betty Boop, ET and Rocky. Includes a **museum of clown memorabilia, Jitters Café** and **gift shop** and a beautiful, jewel-encrusted **musical carousel**, which you can ride for $1. Open daily.

Spooky sights

ET Highway — Free

About 140 miles north of Las Vegas. A 98-mile stretch of road on Route 375, a few miles north of the notorious Area 51 and the super-secret Groom Lake Air Force Base. This is where the American Air Force is believed to have tested the Stealth and U-2 aircraft and where numerous American TV shows have claimed aliens from outer space have undergone examinations at the top-secret Department of Defense site. UFO buffs often gather on ridges above Area 51 and use high-powered telescopes and binoculars to spy on the secret location. Their favourite meeting points are at the bars in nearby Rachel, where they exchange tales about extra-terrestrials. Now the road has been officially dubbed the ET Highway by the Nevada Commission on Tourism, which has even created a new programme called the ET Experience. You can call a toll-free number (1-800 237 0774) to get an information kit on the highway and nearby attractions. The kit also contains a mileage chart and suggested (earthbound) travel itinerary. If you travel the route and can prove it with receipts from businesses along the highway you can become an official member of the ET Experience Association. Members can get a T-shirt, glow-in-the-dark licence plate frame, bumper sticker and collar pin. Call the Commission on 1-800 NEVADA 8 for more information.

Pioneer Saloon — Free

Goodsprings, south of Las Vegas, 702-874 9362. Founded in the old mining town, it has much historical memorabilia and is worth dropping into to soak up some old-Americana atmosphere. Sitting on top of the US Army Cannon Stove, once used to warm people up on cold winter nights, is a piece of melted aluminium from the airplane in which film star Carole Lombard and her mother died. The plane crashed into Double Deal mountain in January 1942 and her husband Clark Gable sat in the bar for days after, hoping for a miracle. Open daily from 10am.

Bonnie and Clyde's 'Death Car' — Free

Whiskey Pete's Hotel, Pimm (off Interstate 15), 702-679 6624. The original car driven by Bonnie Parker and Clyde Barrow in their final shoot-out with the FBI on 23 May 1934 is on display at the hotel. The infamous duo who held up gas stations, restaurants and small banks in Texas, New Mexico, Oklahoma and Missouri were shopped by a friend. At a cost of $75,000, Clyde's bullet-

6

ridden and bloodstained shirt is now on display too! Worth visiting if you're going to Buffalo Bill's Turbo Drop and Desperado.

Places to see

Hoover Dam

The amazing construction – it's 726 feet high and 1,244 feet long and is filled with enough concrete to build a two-lane highway from San Francisco to New York – literally changed the face of America's West. It blocks the Colorado River at the Black Canyon, which spans Nevada and Arizona, and put an end to the centuries of droughts and floods caused by the mighty Colorado. Work began on the dam in 1931 and the $165-million project was completed by 1935. Its offspring, Lake Mead, now produces drinking and irrigation water for the entire Las Vegas Valley, while the electric power plant creates enough energy to sell to Nevada, Arizona and California.

You can get a feel for its scale by taking a tour from the Visitors' Center (702-293 8321), which is open every day of the year except for Christmas Day. The three-level, 110-foot-diameter circular building stands 700 feet above the base of the dam and includes a rooftop viewing point where you can get stunning views of the dam, Lake Mead and the waters of the Colorado River re-entering the Black Canyon after going through the dam's giant turbines. The gallery houses an environmental exhibit, technology exhibit and the story of the settlement of the lower Colorado River area. The rotating theatre is divided up into three segments and you move between the three areas to see three different films about the making and history of the dam. Tours leave the Visitors' Center lifts every few minutes between 8.30am and 6.30pm every day of the week. Hour-long hard-hat tours begin at 9.15am and go on throughout the day until

4.45pm, giving a detailed look at the gigantic, concrete structure. Included in the tour is the turbine gallery, generator shaft gallery, cable gallery, sump room and other behind-the-scenes locations. Admission to the Visitors' Center, including tour, is $5 for adults, $2.50 for 10–16s and free for under 10s. Parking costs $2.

★ ★ ★ ★ **INSIDE TRACK** ★ ★ ★
★   ★
★   If you're touring in an RV   ★
★   (recreational vehicle, ie a
★ motorised caravan) you will have ★
★ to park on the Arizona side of   ★
★   the dam as they have been   ★
★   banned from the new parking   ★
★   garage at Hoover Dam for   ★
★   security reasons.   ★
★ ★ ★ ★ ★ ★ ★ ★ ★ ★ ★ ★ ★ ★ ★ ★ ★

Other things to do in the area include a river raft trip (see Things to do, page 112) and visiting **Boulder City/ Hoover Dam Museum** (444 Hotel Plaza, Boulder City, 702-294 1988). Here you'll see a **free movie** about the building of the dam plus **historical memorabilia** from the workers. Open 10am to 4pm for a donation. Daredevils can try a tandem jump with Skydive Las Vegas (see page 101).

Lake Mead

The dazzling-blue Lake Mead, created by the construction of Hoover Dam, is about 25 miles east of Las Vegas. It is 110 miles long and has 550 miles of freshwater shoreline. Here you can try out anything from boating to swimming, scuba-diving, waterskiing, camping and fishing, while six **marinas** provide docking space for boats, plus restaurants and other services. Every December, a **Parade of Lights** is held at Lake Mead Marina, with a flotilla of powerboats, houseboats and sailboats covered in lights. A newer, annual event is the **hydroplane race** held in September.

The Visitors' Center (702-293 4041) is four miles north-east of

Boulder City and contains a **botanical garden** and exhibits on **natural history**. Here you will find details of a **self-guided tour,** with tape-recording, of the lake's Northshore and Lakeshore roads, plus information about facilities and services in the area. It is open from 8.30am to 4.30pm every day. Admission free.

Dotted around the lake are **Callville Bay Marina, Lake Mead and Cottonwood Cove Marina** and **Lake Mohave**, all full-service marinas offering houseboat and daily deck cruiser rentals, restaurants and gift shops. At night Callville Bay offers barbecues on the patio overlooking Lake Mead.

For jetskiing and cruising the lake in the summer see Things to do, page 112. During the cooler winter and early spring months, you can take a

hike in the **Lake Mead National Recreation Area** on Saturday mornings to learn about the history of the people of the area, from the mining era on. Each hike is limited to 25 people and you can make reservations by phoning 702-293 8990.

Useful numbers: Lake Mead Marina 702-293 3484; Lake Mead National Park Service 702-293 8907; Alan Bible Visitor Center 702-293 8906; Callville Bay 702-565 4813.

If you don't mind travelling a little further afield, head off south to Lake Mohave and Cottonwood Cove Resort and Marina at 1000 Cotton-wood Cove Road, Cottonwood, 702-297 1464. It's a full-service marina offering luxury houseboats, small boats and personal watercraft rentals about 1½ hours south of Las Vegas.

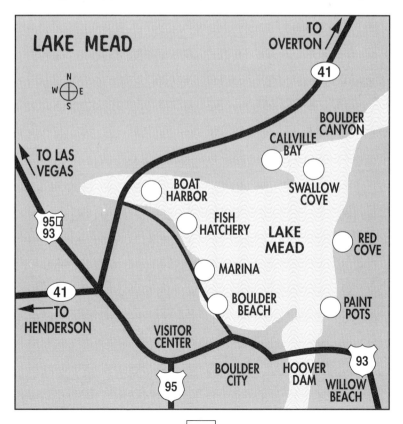

Red Rock Canyon

Once the home of ancient Native American Indian tribes, this magnificent canyon was formed by a thrust fault – a fracture in the earth's crust where one plate is pushed horizontally over another – 65 million years ago. It is home to feral horses and burros, as well as various species of native wildlife including desert bighorn sheep and coyotes, which you can see on the 13-mile **Loop Drive**. Best places to stop are at the **Calico Vista** points which offer great views of the crossed-bedded Aztec sandstone. For easy access to the sandstone, stop at the **Sandstone Quarry** parking lot where you can see large blocks of stone and other historic evidence of quarry activity at the turn of the century. You can have a picnic at **Red Spring** and **Willow Spring**, while there are also great views of wooded canyons and desert washes at **Icebox Canyon, Pine Creek Canyon** and **Red Rock Wash**. The Bureau of Land Management (PO Box 26569, 702-872 7098) runs the area and there is a free visitors' centre for touring information.

Entrance to the scenic loop, a 13-mile one-way-only drive through the canyon, costs $5 for motorists and $2 for motorcyclists, though hikers and bicyclists can still use the area free of charge.

★ ★ ★ ★ **INSIDE TRACK** ★ ★ ★
★   ★
★   It is worth stopping at the   ★
★ visitors' centre before going into ★
★   the park 'loop' to acquaint   ★
★   yourself with the latest park   ★
★ regulations including where you ★
★   can drive and park.   ★
★ ★ ★ ★ ★ ★ ★ ★ ★ ★ ★ ★ ★ ★ ★ ★ ★

If you want to do a bit of hiking or rock climbing in Red Rock or Mount Charleston, see pages 111 and 113 under Things to do.

Bonnie Springs Old Nevada

West on Charleston Boulevard, just past Red Rock Canyon, 702-875 4191. Originally built in 1843 as a stopover for the wagon trains going to California down the Old Spanish Trail, it has been used as a tourist attraction since 1952. Old Nevada Village attractions include **gunfights** in the street, **hangings**, an 1880 **melodrama**, miniature **train, US Post Office, blacksmith display** and **Boot Hill Cemetery**. You can also go **riding** from here, while there is a **petting zoo, duck pond** and **aviary** and breakfast, lunch, dinner and cocktails are also available. Admission to the zoo is free. It costs $6.50 for over 12s and $5 for over fives to enter Old Nevada.

Within the recreation area is **Spring Mountain State Park** beneath the cliffs of the Wilson Range, a picturesque ranch that was once owned by Howard Hughes.

Pahrump Valley Vineyards
Free

3810 Winery Road, Pahrump, 702-727 6900. Just north of Red Rock is Nevada's only vineyard and it regularly produces award-winning Chardonnay, Cabernet, Burgundy and sherry. Tours are available from 10am to 4.40pm, lunch from noon to 3.30pm and dinner from 5pm to 9pm (until 8pm on Sunday). Dinner costs between $13 and $20.

Mount Charleston

Part of the Spring Mountain Range and set in beautiful Toiyabe National Forest, Mount Charleston looms nearly 12,000 feet above sea level just 45 miles north-west of Las Vegas on Highways 95 and 157. One of the most beautiful areas in the Las Vegas Valley, Lee Canyon Road, the Kyle Canyon section of Charleston Park Road and Deer Creek Road have all been designated Scenic Byways because of their extra-ordinary scenery and panoramic views. The whole area is about

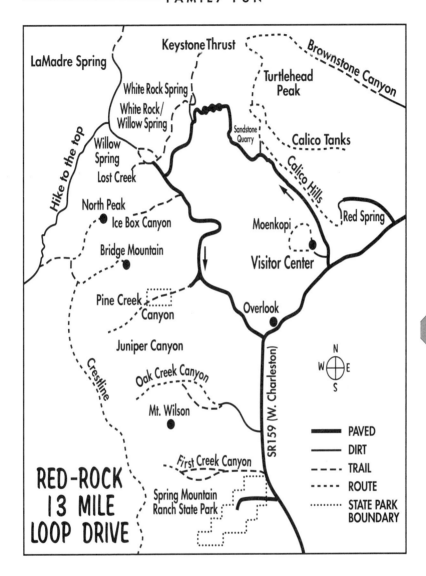

LaMadre Spring

Keystone Thrust

Brownstone Canyon

White Rock Spring

Turtlehead Peak

White Rock/
Willow Spring

Sandstone
Quarry

Calico Tanks

Willow
Spring

Calico Hills

Lost Creek

North Peak

Ice Box Canyon

Moenkopi

Red Spring

Bridge Mountain

Visitor Center

Pine Creek
Canyon

Overlook

Juniper Canyon

Oak Creek Canyon

Crestline

Mt. Wilson

SR159 (W. Charleston)

N
W ✦ E
S

First Creek Canyon

RED-ROCK
13 MILE
LOOP DRIVE

Spring Mountain
Ranch State Park

▬▬▬	PAVED
——	DIRT
– – –	TRAIL
· · · ·	ROUTE
········	STATE PARK BOUNDARY

6

17°C/30°F cooler than Las Vegas, making it a perfect escape from the city heat for a day. Camping is allowed from May to September and fees are $8 per site per day for a single family. Some sites can be reserved in advance by phoning 1-800 280 CAMP. For further information, call 702-873 8800. You can also go horse riding and in the winter you can ski at Lee Canyon (see Things to do, page 113).For the Native American Indians, Charleston Peak was the birthplace of the Paiute people and is sacred land. To respect this, the scale and extent of the road system will stay fairly limited.

Valley of Fire State Park

PO Box 515, Overton, NV, 702-397 2088. This is 50 miles north-east of Las Vegas on Highways 15 and 169. It gets its name from the red sandstone formations that were formed from great, shifting sand dunes during the age of the dinosaurs 150 million years ago. Complex geological movements followed by extensive erosion have created the spectacular wind carvings around and through the beautifully coloured rock formations. This whole area was extensively used by the Basket-maker people and later by the Anasazi Pueblo farmers from the nearby Moapa Valley. It was probably visited for hunting, food gathering and religious ceremonies, though the lack of water limited their stays. Wonderful reminders of the time these ancient tribes spent at Valley of Fire are the extraordinarily detailed Indian petroglyphs that tell the stories of their lives. The combination of fantastic scenery and fascinating history make it well worth a day's visit.

Grand Canyon

If you're planning to tour around the West, then you're bound to want to see the Grand Canyon close up and for real. But it is also possible to take plane and helicopter rides to this, the most spectacular canyon on earth – even landing on the canyon floor and having a spot of lunch on the banks of the Colorado. Full details of its size and activities are given in Chapter 11 and details of air and bus tours follow in this chapter.

Zion National Park

North of Las Vegas and the Grand Canyon in southern Utah is the majestic Zion National Park with its beautiful waterfalls cascading down red rocks and hanging gardens. Once a home to the ancient Anasazi, its history and majesty are presented in an adventure film on a giant screen at the Zion Canyon Cinemax Theatre (435-772 2400).

Bryce Canyon

Nearby, and also in Utah, is the equally beautiful Bryce Canyon, once home to both Native Americans and cowboys of the old West. Both Zion and Bryce offer hiking, biking, horse riding, rock climbing and bird watching.

Death Valley

The hottest place on earth with average summer temperatures of 45°C/131°F, here you will see miles and miles of sand that has been hardened into a sea-like landscape by the melting sun, extinct volcanos and wind-carved rock formations. A full description of the Valley and how to drive through it is given in the Grand Tour chapter, starting on page 225, but it is now possible to visit Death Valley on day trips from Las Vegas.

Many companies offer tours to the Valley and to break up the monotonous terrain on the way, you'll be taken through the beautiful Titus Canyon, ghost towns and be shown Native American petroglyphs. Once there you'll see all the Valley highlights including Furnace Creek, Zabriski Point, Bad Water and Scotty's Castle.

★ ★ ★ ★ **INSIDE TRACK** ★ ★ ★
★   ★
★   ★
★   At around $179, Death Valley ★
★ tours are not cheap so you may ★
★   prefer to see it as part of a   ★
★   touring trip of the West.   ★
★ However, Rocky Trails do offer a ★
★   great hiking experience if you   ★
★   want to see it close up!   ★
★ ★ ★ ★ ★ ★ ★ ★ ★ ★ ★ ★ ★ ★ ★ ★

Ghost Towns

The old gold and and silver mining towns are the stuff of many a Western movie, and it is possible to visit some of these abandoned sites.

Goldfield Ghost Town (on Interstate 95 north of Scotty's Castle) was once Nevada's largest city after gold was dicovered in 1902. Known for its opulence, it was called the Queen of Camps and had 20,000 residents at its peak, with mines producing $10,000 a day in 1907. A flood in 1913 and a fire in 1923 destroyed much of the town, but still standing are the Courthouse and Santa Fe Saloon among other buildings. For details contact the Goldfield Chamber of Commerce (702-485 6365).

In 1904 gold was discovered in the Amargosa Valley and the town of Rhyolite (just outside Beatty on Interstate 95, then 374) was born. At its peak it housed 10,000 people and had more than 50 saloons, 18 grocery stores and half a dozen barbers. But it became a ghost town in 1911 after losing its financial backing. You can still see the Cook Bank Building, school and jail, plus a house built in 1905 entirely of bottles.

Things to do

There's plenty to do outside Las Vegas and as the interest in the great outdoors increases, so do the options. These days you can easily do anything from white water rafting to horse riding, jeep tours, hiking and skiing. Full details of all the companies offering different types of activities are listed in the A–Z of tour companies that follows.

Air tours

You can fly to all the major sights mentioned in this chapter either in a small plane or by helicopter. Flight packages are offered by many of the tour companies listed, though **Eagle Scenic** is the largest and some just specialise in helicopter flights. These tours may a bit pricey – anything up to $399 – but they are a marvellous opportunity to see amazing scenery in a very short space of time.

Generally, a small flight will include the Las Vegas Strip, Western Grand Canyon, Hoover Dam and Lake Mead and will cost around $99. The next step up will be all the above plus a complete aerial tour of the Grand Canyon for around $149. After that you will get extras such as a champagne lunch on the Grand Canyon rim or in the case of helicopter flights, on the Canyon floor next to the Colorado. Combinations also include lunch with Native Americans, river rafting and hiking. In some cases you can even stay overnight at the Grand Canyon, Bryce Canyon or Monument Valley, though these are obviously even more expensive.

Bus tours

The prices are cheaper, but the days are longer as you get to see all the sights covered by the air tours – only on the ground, of course!

Hiking

You can hike just about anywhere with **Rocky Trails**, one of the largest dedicated hiking organisations, which specialises in providing geological tours of everywhere from Red Rock to Valley of Fire, Mount Charleston and even Death Valley. Tours cost $139 to $179 including lunch. Or hike down the Grand Canyon – despite the helicopter tours, still the best way of seeing one of the most beautiful places on earth. **The Grand Canyon Tour Company** do half-day ($50) and full-day ($95) hikes with guides who tell you all about the geology and human and natural history of the Grand Canyon. The tour prices include drinking water, high energy drink mixers and snacks.

Horse riding

Available at Red Rock, Bonnie Springs Old Nevada, Mount Charleston and Valley of Fire. You can go on horseback rides, custom and group trail rides and pack trips in southern Nevada, Utah and Northern Arizona with **Cowboy Trail Rides Inc.** Trips are tailor-made and can last as little as an hour or up to seven days.

6

City slickers can get a taste of the local desert landscape on gentle cowboy-trained trail horses in one- and two-hour trail rides and all-day cattle drives with **Saddle Up** in Primm. **A1 Western** do Rossil Ridge, Canyon Rim and Sunset Rides in Red Rock Canyon.

The **Mount Charleston Riding Stables** (702 872 7009) offer a three-hour ride to the Fletcher Canyon filled with beautiful aspen trees and huge evergreens. Overnight wilderness rides are also available. Three-hour rides are $60 and have to be reserved in advance. Short 25-minute rides cost $8 for adults, $6 for 3–6s. Under 3s go free.

Cruising, boating, fishing and jetskiing

All are available on Lake Mead and the largest provider of cruises and jetskiing is **Lake Mead Cruises**. They run breakfast, midday, dinner and dinner-dance (Friday and Saturday only) cruises on the glassy waters of Lake Mead on board the Desert Princess, an authentic 300-passenger paddlewheeler, which is climate-controlled inside. Breakfast cruises cost $21 (under 12s $10), midday cost $16 (under 12s $6), early dinner cruises cost $29 (under 12s $15) and dinner-dance cruises $43. Under 2s go free. All prices include tax. You can either board at Hoover Dam or at Lake Mead Marina.

The same company also run a two-hour Lake Mead Jetski Tours package, which includes a half-hour orientation class and 90 minutes on the water. Each tour is accompanied by a guide who will narrate the trip via a hands-free, waterproof, two-way radio on each personal jetski. A box lunch is served at the end of the trip, which costs $164.

Further north at Overton Beach Marina you can hire everything from personal watercraft to patio and fishing boats with **Overton Beach Watercraft** (1-800 553 5452).

Overnight packages are even available. There are Personal Watercraft that can seat two or three people and have storage compartments with a built-in cooler for your packed lunch. Patio Boats for up to ten people are perfect for fishing or cruising and come with a motor, radio/cassette, cooler, cushioned bench seating and an awning. Fishing boats hold four people and come with a Fish Finder and Pole Holder to increase your odds of catching the Big One! Costs in each case are $45 an hour, $125 for half a day and $175 for a full day.

Off-road adventures

ATV Action Tours were the first ones in and have the sole licensing permits for many desert regions, mountains and other points of interest in south west Nevada. They combine the off-road experience in Land Rovers, Jeep Cherokees and Wranglers with short hiking excursions, climbing large rock formations and searching for petroglyphs. Definitely the most fun way to get back to nature without breaking into a sweat! Tours cost between $65 and $179.

Since ATV set the ball rolling, many other tour companies are now offering Hummer Tours – the term used to describe off-road adventures in 4x4 Hummers. Those companies include **Grand Canyon Tour Company, A1 Western Tours** and **Rebel Adventure Tours**. The Hummer tours are also often combined with other activities such as jetskiing and rafting.

Rafting

There are two basic types easily available from Las Vegas. You can take a gentle ride in a motorised raft down an 11-mile stretch of the Colorado starting at the base of the mighty Hoover Dam and stopping for lunch (and a cooling swim). Along the way you will see hot water springs bubbling out of cliffs, flora and fauna and the amazing desert bighorn sheep, who think nothing of living on the perilous slopes of the Grand Canyon. These rides usually last around seven hours and cost about $80. **Black Canyon River Raft Tours** are the specialists in these rides, though plenty of other tour companies offer similar tours.

The other kind of rafting is a lot more expensive, but also more authentic, too. You can take one or two-day trips on rapids with strengths of between 4 and 7 (on a scale of 1 to 10) with Native Americans from the Grand Canyon area. The **Grand Canyon Tour Company** offer trips from Lees Ferry in Arizona (about 2½ hours' drive from the South Rim of the Grand Canyon) that can also be combined with a hike down the Grand Canyon. Otherwise most of their trips start at three days and go up to two weeks between April and October and cost around $225 per day.

With **A1 Western Tours** you can do a two-day trip with a Native American river guide. You'll see the rugged mountains, mesas and deep gorges of the West Rim, travelling into the depths of the Canyon, rafting on rapids rated 4 to 7. Your overnight accommodation is either at Haulapai Lodge or camping on the canyon floor. These tours cost $612–$659.

Rock climbing

That is, the real-life outdoors stuff, is available at Red Rock or Mount Charleston with **Sky's the Limit**. Courses in rock and alpine craft are available daily for small groups and cost anywhere from $110 to $200 per day for rock craft and $160 to $250 for alpine craft depending on the size of the group. Levels are anywhere from basic to intermediate and advanced and can last up to a week for the dedicated! For instance, the week-long Basic Alpine Craft course covers balance and technique in face and crack climbing, rope management, climbing signals,

belays, anchors, rappelling, multi-pitch climbing, use of ice axe in climbing and self arrest, route finding, evaluation of hazards and ethics. It costs $900, though, so it's only for the dedicated, but as with all courses, there is a 10 per cent discount for advanced booking and payment.

Skiing

Just 35 minutes outside of Las Vegas in Mount Charleston's Lee Canyon you can ski or snowboard from Thanksgiving to Easter. Beginner packages for skiing cost $40 for ski rental equipment, lift ticket and a one-hour group lesson, for snowboarding it costs $59 for the rental equipment, lift ticket and a one-hour group lesson. Lift prices for those with experience are $28 for adults and $21 for under 12s.

In summer (mid-June to October) ski-lift chair rides to the top of the ski runs are only $4 for adults and $2 for under 12s.

A–Z of tour companies

As you can see, the outdoor options are numerous and to make life a little simpler I have tried to list most of the major tour companies in this simple A–Z format. In many cases the companies have their own websites through which it is possible to book excursions and trips in advance. This is probably most useful for those planning to do something quite specialist, such as rock climbing, or trying to go off the beaten track as times and dates may be specific.

Adventure Photo Tours
(702-889 8687, www.adventurephototours.com) Private or semi-private photo safaris with professional and well-informed guides to Red Rock, Valley of Fire, Lake Mead and ghost towns in seven-seater Ford Expeditions, with pick-up from your hotel.

Cowboys ...

You can't get away from them in Nevada – even the casinos are packed with stetsons bobbing around among the slot machines. One of the most exciting festivals the city has to offer is the annual National Finals Rodeo held in the second week of December. Great contests include saddle bronc riding, bareback riding, bull riding, calf roping, steer wrestling, team roping, steer roping and barrel racing.

You can get a taste for real-life ranch action at any of the many ranches dotted throughout Nevada, Arizona and California that allow non-cowboys on board for a bit of fun (see page 224 for a full description of the different types and how to get in).

If time doesn't permit, there are other ways to get the idea. **Wagons West** run bus tours and horse-riding trips to cowboy country and highlights include the evening cowboy cook-out dinner in the heart of the Nevada desert. They can even arrange a real cowboy rodeo or Western show, depending on the numbers involved. Offering similar deals are **Pioneer Territory Wagon Tours** and **Cactus Jack's Wild West Tour Company.**

Expect to pay around $40 for a day wagon ride including dinner or $75 for overnight stays at the cow camp in Ash Meadows National Wildlife Meadows Refuge with Pioneer.

Valen Transportation do a Wild West and Bryce Canyon tour intended to recapture the Wild West Experience with exciting stories of history, geology and Indian culture. The tour takes you on pioneer trails, to Old West towns, into Indian country and to the Frontier Movie Town, the old Hollywood Western film centre, in Kanab. There you have a traditional cowboy Dutch-oven lunch. These tours cost $129. Also see Horse riding (page 111) for other cowboy trails.

About 20 miles east of Laughlin is Oatman in Arizona. Once a thriving mining town during the gold rush, wild burros now wander the streets of this popular TV and Western movie backdrop. At weekends you can take a trip back to the Old West with free cowboy gunfights and showdowns on Main Street. For details phone the Chamber of Commerce on 520-768 3990. Finally, see Bonnie Springs Old Nevada (page 108) for a taste of the Wild West.

A1 Western Tours
(702-644 7191,
www.a1westerntours.com)
Bus, air and helicopter tours, plus rafting, Lake Mead cruises, riding and ghost towns.
ATV Action Tours
(702-566 7400,
www.atvactiontours.com)
Get to the other side of Las Vegas in a Jeep Cherokee or Wrangler off-roader combined with short hiking trips. Also offer custom tours – including overnight stays at a Dude Ranch, in a mountain cabin or even camping under the stars.
Black Canyon River Raft Tours
(702-293 3776, www.rafts.com)

Cactus Jack's Wild West Tour Company
(702-731 9400)
Cadillac Reservations and Tours
(1-800 556 3566,
www.lvhelicopters.com)
Do a selection of helicopter flights to the Grand Canyon, but do not land in the canyon.
Cowboy Trail Rides
(702-387 2457)
Creative Adventures
(702-361 5565)
Specialists in the Spirits and Ghosts Tour in which you travel the wild country along the Colorado to Native American country before touring Searchlight, once a bustling mining

... and Indians

Three tribes have dominated Nevada's Indian history – the **Northern Paiute, Southern Paiute** and the **Shoshone**. Between them they have etched their stories in the rock petroglyphs of the Valley of Fire and other sacred places including Mount Charleston, while the modern-day Indians still remain an important force in Nevada, with major Indian reservations at **Moapa** and **Fort Mojave Reservation** in the southern-most tip of the state. The Indians still live by their ancient codes and even though they now run their own casinos and restaurants, maintain their heritage through traditional **Pow Wows**. Originally, the Pow Wow was designed to bring various tribes together in a friendly way. It was a festive gathering where they exchanged gifts, heard the latest news and sold foods and crafts. **Rodeos** were an attraction, but the highlight was always the **tribal dance competition** in which they would dress in tribal regalia for the dances.

Pow Wows still take place today and are a wonderful way to experience the Indian culture. Of course, you cannot guarantee a Pow Wow will be organised for your trip, but you can still get a taste of the Indian way of life by visiting the **Moapa River Indian Reservation**, just east of the Valley of Fire off Interstate 15. The store at the entrance is famous for its duty-free tobacco, alcohol and fireworks. But be warned, fireworks are not allowed outside the reservation and police do stop and search cars periodically.

Another great place to go is the **Lost City Museum of Archaeology** (721 South Moapa Valley Boulevard, Overton, 702-397 2193, just north of Red Rock Canyon). Here you will find artefacts from the Anasazi culture that lived in the Moapa Valley from the first to the twelfth centuries. Displays include a reconstruction of the Basket-maker pithouse and pueblo dwellings. The museum is located 66 miles north-east of Las Vegas on Highway 15 and Highway 169 near Overton. Open from 8.30am to 4.30pm daily.

Bruno's Indian Museum (1306 Nevada Highway, Boulder City, 702-293 4865) promotes and gives information about the Native American artists of the South-west, of which 2,000 are represented by the museum. Open 9am to 5pm.

Most of the major tour companies offer Grand Canyon flights or helicopter tours to the West Rim combined with a barbecue lunch with the Hualapai Indians during which you'll have the chance to hear their legends and learn about their culture. The trips have been so successful that the Hualapai have even built a tiny village overlooking the Grand Canyon where you can shop for souvenirs or check out the small museum.

Another way to get the 'Indian' experience is to go on a one- or two-day rafting trips with a Native American river guide on the Colorado River. **Grand Canyon Tour Company** offer rafting from Diamond Creek to Pierce Ferry.

town at the turn of the century.
Desert Action Tours
(702-796 9355)
Drive Yourself Tours®
(702-565 8761,
www.207.217.222.162.drive-yourselftours)
Pop a tape in the cassette machine

and take yourself off to Red Rock, Valley of Fire, Mount Charleston, Hoover Dam and Lake Mead and even the Grand Canyon, listening to information about points of interest along the way. The tapes come with maps for ease of use.

6

Eagle Scenic
(702-638 3300,
www.scenic.com)
Since Eagle Airlines bought out
Scenic, this is now the largest air tour
company in Las Vegas. It offers every
single destination you could think of –
and every different combination. In
addition to the Grand Canyon, Zion
Canyon, Bryce Canyon, Monument
Valley and Lake Powell, you can also
do overnight stops and get the Native
American experience. Plus, of course,
the ubiquitous night flight over the
Strip.

Gourmet Tour
(702-221 0376)
Offer two tours – to Hoover
Dam/Lake Mead and the Valley of
Fire – combined with a gourmet lunch
provided by one of the top restaurants
in town.

Grand Canyon Discount Flights
(702-433 7770,
www.gcflight.com)
Specialise in Grand Canyon flights
and helicopter tours and also
combine them with champagne
lunches, river rafting and trips to
Bonnie Springs Ranch.

★★★★ INSIDE TRACK ★★★
★   ★
★   ★
★ Watch out! Some tour companies ★
★   offer two-for-one or other big ★
★   discounts, but do not include   ★
★ taxes and other extras, which can ★
★ bump up the price considerably. ★
★★★★★★★★★★★★★★★★★★★★★

Grand Canyon Tour Company
(702-655 6060,
www.grandcanyontourcompany.com)
Another of the very big tour
companies, they offer all the Grand
Canyon flights and helicopter rides to
the bottom of the Canyon, bus trips,
overnight stays, trips to Bryce and
Zion Canyon, plus combinations with
rafting, hiking, Hummers, and even a
trip on the Grand Canyon Railway.

Gray Line Sightseeing Tours
(702-384 1234,
www.pcap.com/grayline.htm)
The big bus trip specialist, they cover
everywhere from Hoover Dam and
Grand Canyon to Bryce Canyon and
Death Valley. If you book and pay for
your tour in advance, you'll get a free
round trip transfer from the airport to
your hotel or a free Laughlin Day
Tour.

Guaranteed Tours
(702-369 1000,
www.guaranteedtours.com)
Largely bus tours, but also offers air
tours, river rafting and a good
selection of destinations.

HLA Tourist Services
(702-243 2786,
www.hlatours.com)

Kidz Adventure Tours
(702-564 6631)

Lake Mead Cruises
(702-293 6180,
www.lakemeadcruises.com)
For both cruises and jetskiing at Lake
Mead.

Las Vegas Airlines
(702-735 8007,
www.lasvegasair.com/customer)
Specialise in air tours to the Grand
Canyon area.

**Las Vegas Concierge Sightseeing
Tours**
(1-800 789 4444)
They can arrange for you to see the
Hoover Dam, go on a Lake Mead
Cruise, have a barbecue in Native
American country, go rafting or off-
road or take Grand Canyon air tours.

Las Vegas Host
(702-798 5246,
www.lasvegas.host)
One of the largest agencies for
booking tours and attractions at good
rates. Covers bus, air and helicopter
tours and combinations with Pahrump
Valley Vineyard, Harley Davidson
Café, Grand Canyon champagne
picnics, Native Americans and
overnighters. Also offer a $2 discount
off entrance to Wet 'n' Wild.

Las Vegas Tour Desk
(702-310 1320.
www.lasvegastourdesk.com)
Specialises in air tours to the Grand
Canyon.
Las Vegas Tours
(702-895 8996,
www.lasvegastours.com)
Champagne picnics at the bottom of
the Grand Canyon.

Maverick Helicopter Tours
(702-261 0007,
www.maverickhelicopter.com)
Custom charters and tours to Grand
Canyon, Bryce, Zion, Monument
Valley and Death Valley. Also offer
personalised videos to take home.
Pioneer Territory Wagon Tours
(702-727 8332)
For the real Wild West experience!
Rebel Adventure Tours
(702-380 6969,
www.rebeladventuretours.com)
Off-road Hummer tours to Lake Mead
and Hoover Dam and Grand Canyon
also combined with jetskiing, lunch
with Native Americans and white
water rafting.
Rocky Trails
(702-869 9991,
www.rockytrails.com)
Run by a geologist, they specialise in
hiking tours that give you a real
insight into the wonders of Red Rock,
Valley of Fire, Mount Charleston and
Death Valley.
Sky's The Limit
(702-363 4533,
www.skysthelimit.com)
Hiking and rock climbing.

Sundance Helicopter Tours
(702-736 0606,
www.helicopter.com)
Mostly helicopter trips to the Grand
Canyon – landing on the canyon floor
– but also do combinations with
rafting, the Harley Davidson Café
and Pahrump Valley Vineyard.
Valen Transportation and Tours
(714-956 2252,
www.valenbus.com)
Coach trips to the Grand Canyon,
Zion and Bryce Canyons, Death
Valley and the Wild West Tour.
Wagons West
(702-494 8235)
Wild West Tour Co
(702-731 2425)

Sports

Las Vegas is most famous for staging
big-name fights between boxers, but
its climate – especially in the spring,
autumn and winter months – make it
perfect for golf and there has been a
huge increase in the number of courses
available over the last decade.

Golf

The irony is that the time when most
Brits will be in Las Vegas – the
summer months – is actually low
season, so you should get some pretty
good deals at golf courses. The peak
season is October to May, as the
Americans consider the summer
months far too hot to play! However,
golf is still available early in the
morning or later in the afternoon in
the summer. Many hotels are affiliated
to different golf courses, which offer
resort guests reduced-price tee fees.
All the same, fees for those courses
and others in central Las Vegas will
be two to three times more expensive
than those a drive away out of the
city, so I have given details of golf
courses in Boulder City, North Las
Vegas, Henderson, Laughlin and
Pahrump.

6

★★★★ **INSIDE TRACK** ★★★
★   ★
★   ★
★ If you want to arrange a round of ★
★ golf, go for an afternoon slot as ★
★ the early mornings tend to get ★
★ very busy. It's also a lot cheaper ★
★ at many places – ask about ★
★ 'twilight' rates, which mean ★
★ any time after 1pm. ★
★★★★★★★★★★★★★★★★★★★

A full listing of golf courses open to tourists follow, but two very useful numbers are:

Stand-By Golf, 702-597 2665 (7am to 9pm) for same-day and next-day play at reduced prices at many golf courses in the Las Vegas area.

Golf Reservations of Nevada, 702-732 3119, for advance tee-time reservations for individuals and groups at major courses in the area.

Golf courses

Codes:
GF green fees
WC with cart (in some cases obligatory and it means a cart to ride as opposed to a pull-cart!)
CR club rentals.
In some cases locals pay less, where this is the case, prices for non-residents have been given.

LAS VEGAS

Angel Park Golf Club: 100 South Rampart Boulevard, 702-254 4653. Two 18-hole resort courses. GF (WC) $110. Twilight rates: $60. 12-hole course: GF $22, WC $32. CR $25. Reduced summer rates.

Badlands Golf Club: 9115 Alta Drive, 702-242 4653. 27-hole resort course. GF (WC) $99 Monday to Thursday, $119 Friday to Sunday. After 1pm $50. After 2pm $29.

Callaway Golf Center/Divine Nine: 6730 Las Vegas Boulevard South, 702-896 4100. GF $30 on synthetic tees, $45 on grass tees. Carts $7 per person. CR $25. Driving range hits on to 12 greens with various hazards.

Desert Inn Golf Club: 3145 Las Vegas Boulevard South, 702-733 4290. GF (WC) $150 for Desert Inn lodgers, $215 non-lodgers. CR $40. Reservations recommended and taken one year in advance for hotel guests.

Desert Pines Golf Club: 3415 East Bonanza Road, 702-388 4400. 18-hole public course. GF (WC) $115 Monday to Thursday, $130 Friday to Sunday.

Desert Rose Golf Course: 5483 Club House Drive, 702-431 4653. 18-hole County course. CF (WC) Non-residents $65 Monday to Thursday, $75 Friday to Sunday. Twilight rates available. CR $15. Tee times seven days in advance.

Las Vegas Golf Club: 4300 West Washington, 702-646 3003. 18-hole city course. GF non-residents $37 to walk, $46 to ride. CR $15. Reservations taken seven days in advance.

Las Vegas National Golf Club: 1911 East Desert Inn Road, 702-382 GOLF. 18-hole public course. GF (WC) $145 Monday to Thursday, $175 Friday to Sunday. Twilight rates. CR $25 and $40. Floodlit driving range. Reservations 90 days in advance.

Las Vegas Paiute Resort: 10325 Nu-Wav Kaiv Boulevard, 20 miles north of city on the Snow Mountain exit near Mount Charleston, 702-658 1400. Two 18-hole public courses on the Las Vegas Paiute Tribe Indian Reservation. GF (WC) $100 Monday to Thursday, $110 Friday to Sunday.

Links Las Vegas: Stephanie between Vegas Valley Drive and Desert Inn Road, 702-388 4400. Phone for green fees.

Los Prados Country Club: 5150 Los Prados Circle, 702-645 5696. 18-hole semi-private course. GF (WC) visitors $40 weekdays, $45 weekends and holidays. After 12 noon $25. CR $20. Reservations three days in advance for visitors.

Painted Desert: 5555 Painted Mirage Drive, 702-645 2568. 18-hole public course. GF (WC) $110 Monday to Thursday, $130 Friday to Sunday.

After 1pm $70 Monday to Thursday, $80 Friday to Sunday. After 2pm $40. CR $40.

Rhodes Ranch Golf Club: 9020 Rhodes Ranch Parkway, 702-740 4114. GF (WC) non-residents $110 Monday to Thursday, $140 Friday to Sunday. After 1.30pm $69 and $79.

Sun City Las Vegas Golf Club (three courses). **Palm Valley:** 9201-B Del Webb Boulevard, 702-363 4373. 18-hole semi-private (preference is given to residents). GF (WC) $95. After 1pm $53. CR $30. **Highland Falls:** 10201 Sun City Boulevard, 702-254 7010. 18-hole course, prices as Palm Valley. **Eagle Crest:** 2203 Thomas Ryan Boulevard, 702-240 1320. 18-hole course. GF (WC) $55. CR $20.

Tournament Players Club at the Canyons: 9851 Canyon Run Drive, 702-256 2000. 18-hole resort course. GF (WC) $130 Monday to Thursday, $150 Friday to Sunday. Summer and summer twilight rates. Reservations for groups taken 30 days in advance.

NORTH LAS VEGAS

Craig Ranch Golf Course: 628 West Craig Road, 702-642 9700. 18-hole public course. GF $15 to walk, $23 to ride. CR $8. Reservations seven days in advance.

North Las Vegas Golf Course: 324 East Brooks, 702-633 1833. 9-hole city course (the ninth hole is on a hill and has a great view of Las Vegas). GF $5 weekdays, $6.50 weekends. Floodlit golf. Carts not allowed. CR $10 with pull-cart. Reservations seven days in advance.

Shadow Creek: phone the Mirage 702-791 7111. 18-hole resort course specifically for the Mirage. Ranked 15th best course in America and it's unlikely you'll go there unless you fancy parting with $1,000 in green fees, though this does include a suite at the Mirage. Bargain!

BOULDER CITY

Boulder City Municipal Golf Course: 1 Clubhouse Drive, Boulder City, 702-293 9236. 18-hole city course. GF $27, WC $36, CR $15. Reservations one week in advance.

HENDERSON/GREEN VALLEY

Black Mountain Golf and Country Club: 500 Greenway Road, Henderson, 702-565 7933. 18-hole semi-private course. GF (WC) $52 weekdays, $57 weekends, CR $13. Tee times up to four days in advance.

Lake Las Vegas Resort Course: 75 MonteLago Boulevard, Henderson, 702-558 0022. 18-hole, daily-fee resort course. Call for green fees.

Legacy Golf Club: 130 Par Excellence Drive, Henderson, 702-897 2187. 18-hole resort course. GF (WC) $115 Monday to Thursday, $125 Friday to Sunday. Tee times two months in advance.

Rio Secco Golf and Country Club: 2851 Grand Hills Drive, Henderson, 702-889 2400. 18-hole resort course owned by the Rio Suite Hotel. GF (WC) for Rio Suite Hotel guests $190, for locals $300. CR.

Wildhorse Golf Club: 2100 Warm Springs Road, 702-434 9000. 18-hole public course. GF (WC) $110 Monday to Thursday, $135 Friday to Sunday. CR.

★ ★ ★ ★ **INSIDE TRACK** ★ ★ ★
★ ★
★ Don't forget your sun protection ★
★ factor 50 and a hat when playing ★
★ in summer. In autumn, take a ★
★ sweater with you for late- ★
★ afternoon games as it can get ★
★ quite chilly when the sun goes ★
★ down. ★
★ ★ ★ ★ ★ ★ ★ ★ ★ ★ ★ ★ ★ ★ ★ ★ ★

LAUGHLIN

Emerald River Country Club: 1155 West Casino Drive, Laughlin, 702-298 0061. 18-hole resort course next to the Colorado including five holes along the river! GF (WC) $65 Monday to Thursday, $75 Friday to Sunday. CR $15.

Mohave Resort Golf Club: 9905 Aha Macav Parkway, Laughlin, 702-535 4653. 18-hole course. GF (WC) $60 Monday to Thursday, $70 Friday to Sunday. CR $25. Reservations one week in advance or 30 days with a credit card.

PAHRUMP

Calvada Valley Golf and Country Club: 1500 Red Butte Drive, Pahrump, 702-727 4653 for the 18-hole Championship Course. GF (WC) $54. CR $15. Phone 702-727 6388 for the 18-hole Executive Course. GF $22. Power carts not allowed. $2.25 for pull-carts. CR $15.

Spectator sports

Las Vegas Speedway Park: 6000 Las Vegas Boulevard North, 702-644 7774. Lying 17 miles north of the Strip, the 1,500-acre Speedway opened in 1996 at a cost of $200 million and seats 107,000. Facilities include a 1.5-mile **superspeedway**, a 2.5-mile **road course**, a half-mile **dirt oval, drag strip, go-kart tracks** and **racing school.** Checkout **Midnight Madness** on Fridays and Saturoadays for drag racing which starts at 10pm as part of the test and tune sessions that begin at 5pm. Phone ahead for schedules of upcoming events and tickets.

If you want to catch some football action, try the **Canadian Football League** on 702-242 4200 for their schedules. For **hockey**, try the **Las Vegas Thunder Hockey** on 702-798 PUCK and for **general sports events, UNLV Sports** on 702-895 3900.

Annual sporting events

March: Big League Weekends – Cashman Field Center, 702-386 7200.

April: Spring Pro-Am Golf Tournament – Sunrise Golf Club, 1-800 332 8776; and **Las Vegas Senior Classic** – Senior PGA Golf Tournament, 702-382 6616.

September: Pro-Am Golf Tournament – Sahara Country Club, 1-800 332 8776.

October: Ice Hockey Season. A schedule is available in August for the **Las Vegas Thunder International Hockey League** at the Thomas and Mack Center, 702-798 7825; and for the **Las Vegas Invitational PGA Golf Tournament** on 702-382 6616.

December: National Finals Rodeo Christmas Gift Show at Cashman Field Center, 702-386 7100.

National Finals Rodeo at the Thomas and Mack Center, 702-895 3900.

Las Vegas Rugby Challenge – 64 American and Canadian teams battle it out at Freedom Park or Sam Boyd Silver Bowl. For a schedule call 702-656 1401. **Las Vegas Bowl Collegiate Football Game** – Big West Conference v Mid-American Conference at Sam Boyd Silver Bowl, 702-731 2115.

★★★ **INSIDE TRACK** ★★★

★ ★
★ Try Nevada Ticket Services on ★
★ 702-597 1588 to book anything ★
★ from basketball to football, ★
★ hockey, baseball, National Finals ★
★ Rodeo, pro bull rides, Superbowl ★
★ and Final Four. ★

★★★★★★★★★★★★★★★★★★

SHOP TILL YOU DROP

On the trail of the best buys in the shopping malls

They're a canny lot in Las Vegas – if they don't get you in the casinos, they've come up with another brilliant way to separate you from your cash – and it's called shopping. It is such big business that Nevada shopping malls took a massive $24.5 billion in 1998, with most of that money being spent in Las Vegas. That is even more money than the casinos took in gambling in the same year. But then the Las Vegas malls do it in such style, with so much fun and by offering such good value that people simply can't resist.

Top of the pile, of course, is the **Forum Shops** at Caesars Palace, one of the biggest and most amazing entertainment and shopping complexes in the world, and now known as the Shopping Wonder of the World. In addition there is the **Showcase Mall**, home to the **World of Coca-Cola**™, the **Fashion Show Mall** and two factory outlet shopping malls where you really can get some great deals. Here is a guide to the shopping experience on offer in Las Vegas.

Hints and tips

Sizes: Clothes sizes are one size smaller in America, so a dress size 10 in the US is a size 12 in the UK. It means you can travel out in a size 12 and come back in a size 10! It is the same for men: a jacket size 42 is the English size 44. But it's the opposite with shoes: an American size 10 is our size 9.

Measurements: The Americans still work in feet and inches, which is great for anyone over the age of 30!

Taxes: In all cases you will have to add local taxes on to the cost of your goods. This can add anything from 7% to 9% on to the price, depending on where you are buying. Nevada sales tax is 7.5%.

UK shopping allowances: Your duty-free allowance is just £145 and given the wealth of shopping opportunities you're likely to exceed this, but don't be tempted to change receipts to show a lesser value as the goods will be confiscated and you'll face a massive fine. In any case, the prices for some goods in America are so cheap that even paying the duty and VAT on top will still work out cheaper than buying the same item in Britain. Duty can range from 3.5% to 19% depending on the item, eg computers are charged at 3.5%, golf clubs at 4%, cameras at 5.4% and mountain bikes at a massive 15.8%. You pay this on goods above £145 and then VAT of 17.5% on top of that.

Duty free: Buy your booze from US liquor stores – they're better value than the airports, but remember your allowance is one litre of spirits and two bottles of wine.

Videos: US video tapes may not be compatible with British machines.

The Forum Shops at Caesars

This is such an amazing place that it should be on your must-visit list for Las Vegas regardless of whether you want to buy anything. It was deliberately built as an entertainment mall and transports people back in time to the great Roman Empire era with architecture, materials and street lighting to match. Even the piazzas and streets are laid out in the traditional format of a Roman town. The entire mall is enclosed, temperature-controlled and covered with a 'sky' that changes throughout the day from a rosy-mauve dawn to high noon, the fading gold of the afternoon, twilight and finally night-time with twinkling stars.

The original $110-million complex, which opened in 1992, proved so successful that it was expanded and a further 35 stores and entertainment outlets opened in 1997. On average 50,000 people visit every day, rising to 70,000 at the weekends and even 80,000 a day during the Christmas period. It amounts to 20 million visitors a year, who spend $1,200 per square foot annually to make it America's most successful mall for retailers – the norm is $350. The outlook is so bright that a second extension to the Forum Shops will be opening by the summer of 2000, adding another 240,000 square feet to the existing 533,000 square feet. The new mall maintains the Roman theme with classic columns, arches, ornate fountains and statues. There will be a 150-foot-high Pantheon at the entrance and an 85-foot-high centrepiece in the main hall called Atlantis.

From the Strip, you enter the Forum through the rotunda under the magnificent **Quadriga** statue of gold-leafed horses and charioteers, and the moving walkway takes you to the five giant heroic arches that are an ancient symbol of great achievement. Once inside you can go down to the lower level of attractions of the **CyberStation** game arcade and the **Cinema Ride** or head on past the ticket, concierge and postal desks. You will then arrive at the **Festival Fountain** where you will see the seven-minute special effects show in which Bacchus, god of merriment and wine, wakes up and decides to throw a party for himself and visitors to the Forum. He enlists the help of Apollo, who provides the music with his lyre, and Plutus, the god of wealth, who brings the fountain to life with cascades of jewel-like effects in the waters while the goddess of love, Venus, also puts in an appearance. Music, sound effects, animatronics and special scenic projections on the dome combine with a computer-controlled waterscape and theatrical lighting for a dazzling show. After thanking his companions and inviting his guests to enjoy the pleasures of the shops, Bacchus then becomes a marble statue again.

Before leaving the area you can tuck into a sandwich at the nearby deli, get a bite to eat at **La Salsa** or enter the world of the **Magic Masters**. Designed as a replica of Houdini's private library, Magic Masters features magical demonstrations, and prospective buyers are taken through a secret door to a secret room to learn how to perform an illusion. Afterwards, drop in at the athletic shoe store **Just for Feet**, where a half-court basketball arena and treadmill machines are provided so you can test out your purchases.

As you head on down towards the **Fountain of the Gods**, you'll pass the **Disney Store** on your right and **Planet Hollywood** on your left. But before you decide to have lunch, just remember that the Forum Shops houses some of the finest restaurants in Las Vegas, including **Bertolini's** Italian restaurant, celebrity chef Wolfgang Puck's two outlets, **Spago** and **Chinois**, and the **Palm Restaurant**.

To the left of the Fountain of Gods is the **Fortuna Terrace**, which houses

THE FORUM SHOPS AT CAESARS

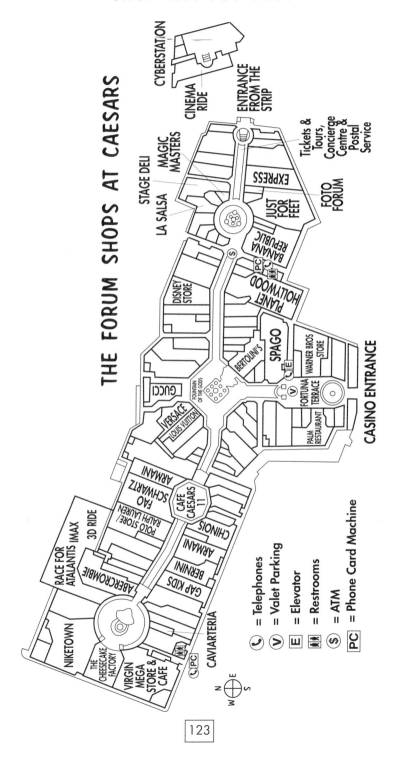

CYBERSTATION

CINEMA RIDE

ENTRANCE FROM THE STRIP

Tickets & Tours, Concierge Centre & Postal Service

MAGIC MASTERS

STAGE DELI

EXPRESS

LA SALSA

JUST FOR FEET

FOTO FORUM

BANANA REPUBLIC

DISNEY STORE

PLANET HOLLYWOOD

PC

SPAGO

BERTOLINI'S

WARNER BROS STORE

GUCCI

FOUNTAIN OF THE GODS

FORTUNA TERRACE

CASINO ENTRANCE

VERSACE

LOUIS VUITTON

PALM RESTAURANT

ARMANI

FAO SCHWARTZ

POLO STORE/ RALPH LAUREN

CAFE CAESARS 11

3D RIDE

CHINOIS

RACE FOR ATALANTIS IMAX

ARMANI

ABERCROMBIE

BERNINI

GAP KIDS

NIKETOWN

THE CHEESECAKE FACTORY

VIRGIN MEGA STORE & CAFE

PC

CAVIARTERIA

📞 = Telephones

Ⓥ = Valet Parking

Ⓔ = Elevator

🚻 = Restrooms

$ = ATM

PC = Phone Card Machine

N W E S

7

many of the restaurants and the **Warner Bros Studio Store**, which has a video wall showcasing new movie trailers, cartoons and take-outs from classic films. Youngsters can also learn how to make their own cartoons. The focal point in this area is the statue of the goddess **Fortuna**, which is surrounded by a Roman colonnade and ceiling-high recessed arches with replicas of classic statues. It also leads out to the casino at **Caesars Palace** and houses the valet parking desk. If you return to the Fountain of the Gods you will once again be surrounded by some of the top designer shops that are in the Forum – **Gucci, Versace, Louis Vuitton** and **Armani**. Head down the promenade to your left and you'll find the **Café Caesars II** restaurant, where you dine al fresco, and continue on to the new **Great Roman Hall**.

Here the **Atlantis** comes to life in a spectacle that has the gods unleashing their wrath on the ancient city. Fire, water, smoke and special effects are used to create a show in which the animatronic characters of Atlas, Gadrius and Alia struggle to rule Atlantis.

★★★★ **INSIDE TRACK** ★★★
★ ★
★ ★
★ Arrive early for the Atlantis shows ★
★ as the crowds build up early and ★
★ you'll want a good view of the ★
★ sunken city. ★
★★★★★★★★★★★★★★★★★★★

Surrounded by a 50,000-gallon saltwater aquarium, the mythical sunken continent rises and falls before your eyes. The **Great Hall** is surrounded by giant projection screens which, together with lasers and other special effects, help create the illusion that you are genuinely part of the action. Shows are held every 90 minutes starting at 10am every day of the year.

Another free 'show' is the dive into the **aquarium** for maintenance and feeding, which takes place several times a day. Inside are sharks and schools of coral-reef fish. Or you can enter the **Heavens Room** to experience the **Race for Atlantis** motion simulator IMAX 3-D experience, which costs from $6.95 to $9.50 depending on age. You'll be given electronic headsets that are loaded on to one of the four passenger simulator bases before the Race for Atlantis takes you on a hi-tech chariot ride through a surrealistic landscape. The sound and visual effects combined with fog really do make you feel as if you're perched on a cloud! When you get back down to earth you can try another heavenly experience – this time the **Caviarteria**, Las Vegas' first caviar, champagne, vodka and martini bar. Caviarteria is America's oldest and biggest distributor of gourmet delicacies and if you're in the mood, you can try anything from smoked salmon to Icelandic gravadlax salmon, foie gras and a host of champagnes and vodkas. Afterwards, if you can still walk, wander around the mega **Virgin Megastore**, which has its own café, have a pudding at the **Cheesecake Factory** and see what **Niketown** has on offer for your tootsies.

What's more, you can do any or all of the above between 1pm and 11pm from Sunday to Thursday or until midnight on Friday and Saturday. To make life even easier, you can either park in the Caesars Palace free covered car park or make use of the valet parking in the underground traffic tunnel at Caesars Boulevard.

Showcase Mall

Following in the footsteps of the Forum Shops' retail and entertainment formula is this 280,000-square-foot centre at the southern end of the Strip, just north of the MGM Grand, which opened at the end of 1996. It houses the **World of Coca-Cola**, the **Official Allstar Café, Sega Gameworks**, the **Ethel M Chocolate** store and the **M&M World** retail store.

What stands out a mile, though, is the 100-foot-tall giant Coca-Cola bottle that houses two lifts made out of glass, while the logo consists of half-a-mile's worth of neon lighting. To reach the World of Coca-Cola, you take the see-through lifts to the fourth floor and as you rise you hear sounds of crackling ice, pouring soda and old Coca-Cola jingles. The first thing you see is the **Time Walk**, in which entertainers, dressed in fashions from different periods of Coca-Cola's history, walk out of scenes to tell stories and answer questions about life in each decade. Some of the scenes include a bank in Atlanta in 1886, which was home to the secret formula, a 1907 advertising studio, 1930s soda fountain and a 1960s hot-rod garage.

Then there is **Santa's Toy Store**, where you'll find out how the modern-day image of Santa Claus was created for a special Coca-Cola advertising campaign. The **Fantastic Fountain** is a 25-foot-high soda fountain with stacks of screens filled with images of people enjoying Coca-Cola around the world. At the **Tastes of the World**, a 25-foot-long soda fountain-style counter, you can taste the different mixes of Coca-Cola that are sold all around the world, including Guarana Tai, a mixed fruit flavour from Brazil, Simba Pina, a pineapple-flavoured drink from Paraguay, and Krest, a ginger ale from Thailand. In the **Salute to Folk Art**, there are amazing exhibits of works of art that have been created using Coca-Cola bottles! Finally, you arrive at the shop where you'll find

interactive displays, Coca-Cola bears, limited-edition collectables, clothing, toys, six-packs, coolers, vending machines and even delivery trucks! Entrance: Adults $4.75, under 12s £2.50, under 6s free.

Don't try too many Colas, though, or you won't have enough room left to try out Andre Agassi's **Allstar Café**. The arena-style café, which is laid out on three floors, is co-owned with Shaquille O'Neal, Joe Montana and Monica Seles among others and is a great fun place to taste traditional American food.

Chocolate lovers will be in heaven at Ethel M's flagship store on the ground floor of the Showcase. Here you can custom-make your own assortment from more than 67 different varieties of chocolates, all made at the firm's factory 12 miles east of Las Vegas in Henderson. The second and fourth floors house the M&M World retail store and an Ethel M Chocolates Dessert Bar.

Fashion Show Mall

This is the shopping centre to go to for clothes and is home to top stores including **Neiman-Marcus, Saks Fifth Avenue, Macy's, Dillard's** and **Robinson's-May Co.**, along with more than 140 boutiques including **bébé, Louis Vuitton** and **El Portal**. It also houses four top-notch restaurants **Chin's, Sfuzzi** and **Morton's** of Chicago and is home to Steven Spielberg's fabulous **Dive!** where you eat in a nautical adventure wonderland.

When you arrive, park in the **underground car park** and take the escalators to the shopping level. There is also **complimentary valet parking** available at three points around the mall. Throughout there are **automatic teller machines** and **phone booths** where you can use your pre-paid phone card, plus a **foreign currency exchange centre**.

The **Concierge Desk** can supply directions, concert tickets and show reservations, multilingual brochures,

7

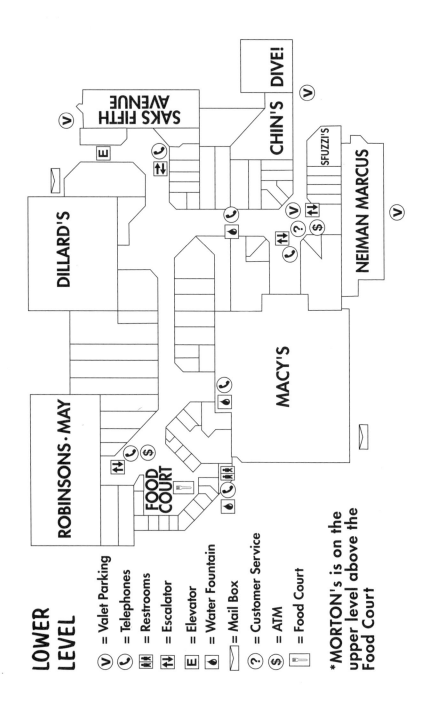

golf tee times and special event information.

★ Look out for the Fashion Show
★ Mall's new Shopping Spree Value
★ Books for great deals and offers.

Before you start to browse around the shops, join the **Premier Shopper Club** by going to the **Customer Service Center** and filling out the form or using the **Smart Shopper Pavilion** touch screen. Once you have been accepted you can browse through the Internet site and pick up money-saving coupons from the stores. You will also find out about all the latest promotions and activities going on at each of the stores. As a member of the Club, you will automatically be entered into free prize draws simply by swiping your card at the Smart Shopper Pavilion! There are many other bonuses, but most are really aimed at people living in America.

In addition to the restaurants, the food court on the ground floor has every kind of fast food. Other food outlets include **Ethel M Chocolates, Starbucks** coffee shop, the **Sweet Factory** and **Mrs Field's Cookies**. Open from 10am to 9pm Monday to Friday, 10am to 7pm Saturday and 12 noon to 6pm on Sunday.

Factory outlet district

Just a short trip south of the MGM Grand along the Strip is the district of factory shops where many famous brand names are sold at 20–70% discounts. First stop is the **Belz Factory Outlet World** at the corner of Las Vegas Boulevard South and Warm Springs Road. Here, the 625,000-square-foot mall is home to a **permanent laser show** plus 140 outlet

stores that include **Nike, OshKosh, Off 5th, Saks Fifth Avenue** and **Levi's**.

A mile further south is the open-air **Las Vegas Factory Outlet Stores of America** that include a huge range of shops from men's and women's clothing to bookstores and shoe shops. Both are open from 10am to 8pm Monday to Saturday and from 10am to 6pm on Sunday.

★ If you can't bear to be without
★ your English newspaper a day
★ longer, you'll find the biggest
★ selection of the dailies from
★ around the globe at the
★ International News-stand at
★ 3900 Paradise Road.

Chinatown Plaza

This specialist plaza – the equivalent of Las Vegas' Chinatown – has been designed to reflect a Tong Dynasty plaza, complete with golden-yellow ceramic roof tiles. Here you'll find products from the Orient and Asia, including jewellery, herbs, music, arts and hand-crafted furniture, plus seven Asian restaurants including a Japanese sushi bar.

There are also several festivals held here each year including a **New Year Celebration**, the **Chinese New Year Celebration** and an **Oriental Food Festival**. The Plaza is also home to the **Long Fung Wedding Temple**, which has three different settings from a Chinese Buddhist Temple to an elegant non-denominational chapel and an outdoor garden wedding chapel. You'll find the Plaza on the Spring Mountain Road about one and a half miles east of the Strip and there is a free shuttle bus service from the Strip throughout the day. Phone 702-222 0590 for details of bus times.

7

A–Z of shopping outlets

Belz Factory Outlet World:
7400 Las Vegas Boulevard South, 702-896 5599.

Boulevard Mall
3528 South Maryland Parkway, 702-735 8268. This is Nevada's largest shopping mall and houses the Panorama Food Court Cafés.

Forum Shops at Caesars
3570 Las Vegas Boulevard South, 702-893 4800.

Chinatown Plaza
4225 Spring Mountain Road, 702-221 8448.

Fashion Show Mall
3200 Las Vegas Boulevard South, 702-369 8382.

Las Vegas Factory Outlet Stores
9155 Las Vegas Boulevard South, 702-897 9090.

The Meadows Mall
4300 Meadows Lane, 702-878 4849.
Contains 140 stores, a food shop and carousel.

Red Rooster Antique and Gift Mall
1109 Western Avenue, 702-362 0067.

Red Rooster Antique and Gift Mall

Bargain-hunters should head off to this mall, which is the oldest in Las Vegas and now has shops selling one-of-a-kind collectables. Here you'll also find Patricia Schell's Victorian tea room, called **Tricia's Teas**, where you can dress up in an amazing array of Victorian hats, boas, shawls and antique jewellery before beginning the two-hour afternoon tea party. In true Mary Poppins style, Patricia tells guests how to hold their cups, the correct response when offered sugar and the proper way to spread jam on scones as you tuck into a traditional afternoon tea. The cost is from $12.50 to $20, depending on what you have.

The mall is open from 10am to 6pm Monday to Saturday and from 12 noon to 5pm on Sunday. You'll find it on Western Avenue at the corner of West Charleston.

Hotel shopping

Most hotels offer souvenirs to reflect the theme of the hotel, but not to be missed are the fun souvenirs you can pick up at the Luxor, Treasure Island and MGM Grand. If it's clothes, shoes and CDs you want, you should stick to the major shopping malls, though the new **Exclusive** clothes shop at the Luxor is an exception to this rule.

Aladdin Hotel: On the Strip. Due to open in Spring 2000, the new resort hotel will have shopping and entertainment in a Middle Eastern-style setting.

Atrium Shopping: Tropicana on the Strip, 702-739 2222. Includes a selection of shops and services such as shoeshines and boutiques.

Bally's Las Vegas: Bally's Hotel on the Strip, 702-739 4111. More than

40 stores from jewellery to fashion, plus men's and women's hair salons, ice-cream parlour and a place to have your photo taken in costumes from the 1800s.

Bellagio: On the Strip, 702-693 7111. In keeping with the overall theme of 'only the best' at this resort hotel, Via Bellagio is all about sophisticated shopping at its finest. Here you can browse through world-renowned designer shops including Giorgio Armani, Prada, Chanel, Tiffany & Co., Moschino, Hermes and Gucci. If you don't want to give the bank manager a heart attack, leave your credit cards in the hotel safe!

Circus Circus Shops: On the Strip, 702-734 0410. Includes a newsagent plus gift and souvenir shops, a clown shop selling limited-edition collectors' items, clown dolls and figurines, a candy store, novelty photo booth, shoeshine, hair salon and the Grand Slam Trading Post souvenir shop.

Excalibur Hotel: On the Strip, 702-597 7777. Fantasy shops on the medieval theme include the Excalibur Shoppe, Castle Souvenirs, Gifts of the Kingdom, Spirit Shoppe, Dragon's Lair and Desert Shoppe, which sell everything from swords and suits of armour to Excalibur merchandise.

Las Vegas Hilton: Paradise Road, 702-732 5111. Don't forget to pick up your *Star Trek* souvenir merchandise and other goodies at the Hilton shops.

Luxor: On the Strip, 702-262 4444. **Exclusive** is the exciting women's clothing store which has everything from business outfits to cutting-edge designer gear. Another recent addition to the Luxor is the **Giza Galleria,** which contains 18 shops selling everything from King Tut's souvenirs to ice cream and sweets. Other shops include the **Scarab Shop** for hieroglyphic T-shirts and sweatshirts, **Innerspace** for limited-

edition Egyptian collections, and the **Logo Shop** selling everything from Luxor key-chains to stuffed animals and glassware.

Mandalay Bay: On the Strip, 702-632 7777. Has a selection of tropically-themed shops to match the hotel's own theme selling everything from Bali art to fine cigars, children's and designer clothes.

Monte Carlo: On the Strip, 702-730 7777. Shops include a small convenience store, sweet shop, flower shop and the **Lance Burton Magic Shop** with demonstrator shows.

The Shopping Promenade: Treasure Island on the Strip, 702-894 7111. Includes fun souvenir shops and boutiques on the Treasure Island theme.

Paris Las Vegas: On the Strip, 702-967 4611. Newly opened in the autumn of 1999, the new luxury resort of Paris Las Vegas has posh French shops in their own Rue de la Paix district. Here quaint cobblestone streets and winding alleyways lead you to French boutiques selling wine and cheese, flowers and designer clothes.

The Street of Shops: The Mirage on the Strip, 702-791 7111. Includes designer and leisure wear boutiques, gift shops and those selling souvenirs from *Siegfried and Roy* and **Cirque du Soleil**.

The Venetian: On the Strip, 702-733 5404. Cobbled walkways, a reproduction of Venice's Grand Canal and a replica of St Mark's Square are the setting for the Venetian's Grand Canal Shoppes. There are 90 shops and boutiques along a quarter-mile stretch of a Venetian street, while Warner Brothers has its own attraction called Soundstage 24. A mixture of shops, food and movie-theme entertainment, all the staff are decked out in movie-character costumes.

7

8 GOING TO THE CHAPEL

How to get married in the wedding capital of America

So you've seen the resort hotels, tried your luck on the casino tables and shopped till you dropped. All there is left for you to do is tie the knot – but don't worry, it's not an essential part of your visit! All the same, if you're with the right person and the mood takes you, then Las Vegas has more chapels per square mile and more options on how you tie the knot than any other city in the world – and it's all so easy.

Liberal state laws mean that Nevada is one of the few states that does not require a blood test and to get you quickly on your way to the altar, the Marriage License Bureau is open from 8am to midnight – and 24 hours a day on Friday and Saturday.

If you do decide to go ahead, you'll be in star-studded company – this is where Elvis wed Priscilla, Frank Sinatra wed Mia Farrow, Jane Fonda wed Roger Vadim and Paul Newman wed Joanne Woodward. Others include Bruce Willis and Demi Moore, while Brigitte Bardot, Joan Collins, Bing Crosby, Joan Crawford and Judy Garland all said 'I do' at a chapel in Las Vegas.

It's so easy that 280 couples get married every day in Las Vegas – an amazing 110,000 a year. The most popular day is Valentine's Day, closely followed by New Year's Eve.

And you can do it all in such style. Dress up as a medieval prince and princess at the Canterbury Chapel in the Excalibur, allow an Elvis impersonator to wed you at Graceland Wedding Chapel or try any of the other themes available from *Star Trek* to gangsters and rock 'n' roll. Then again, you could decide to say your vows before diving off a bungee-jump platform, soaring high above everything in a hot-air balloon or taking a flight over the Grand Canyon. You can even stay in your car at the world's first ever drive-up wedding chapel or try the new Tunnel of Love chapel at A Little White Chapel on the Strip.

★★★★ **INSIDE TRACK** ★★★
★ ★
★ Avoid Valentine's Day unless you ★
★ want to queue for four hours to ★
★ get your licence! ★
★★★★★★★★★★★★★★★★★★★

It costs $35 to get your licence and $35 for the ceremony. A very basic package starts at $100, but the sky's the limit depending on where you wed, what you do and the accessories you choose.

Ceremonies

Like every other aspect of Las Vegas, the business of helping people to tie the knot is booming – and more and more hotels are determined to cash in. Their ceremonies tend to be more ostentatious than those at ordinary chapels, but they have prices to match, too! Like the lucky bride who won the opening wedding at Caesars Palace's Neptune Villa, you could be carried on a velvet sedan chair by four Centurions to the fountain entrance of Caesars Palace to be greeted by Caesar and Cleopatra before being escorted to the chapel. The décor is amazing, featuring a two-story double balustrade staircase encircling a koi pond and rising to a wood-panelled foyer that is framed by exotic fish in a saltwater aquarium. Inside the chapel, the ceremony area is draped with sheer white chiffon and the walls feature a hand-painted mural of ancient Roman ruins under beautiful blue skies. No doubt about it, here you'll get all the pomp and

The rules

Both parties must go to the *Marriage License Bureau*. You'll find it on the 1st Floor, Clark County Courthouse, 200 South Third Street (702-455 4415) and it's open from 8am to midnight Monday to Thursday and continuously from 8am on Friday until midnight on Sunday. (Once the licence has been issued it is valid for one year.)
Minimum age for adults is 18. Those aged 16–17 must have either a parent present at the time the licence is issued or a notarised affidavit.
You will need your passport.
If you have been divorced, you will need to specify the date and place when it became final.

circumstance of the old Roman Empire – and all for the simple price of $5,000.

Not quite as expensive, but definitely unusual are the packages being offered at the MGM Grand in addition to the ceremonies at their two chapels, the Legacy and the Cherish. The first allows couples to take their vows at the top of the 250-foot Sky Screamer before descending into a 100-foot freefall dive at speeds of up to 70mph. The second is having your wedding ceremony in the trendy Studio 54 nightclub set to the sounds of the 70s. The third is to get wed on the set of the stage spectacular *EFX* near a mystical waterfall with Merlin presiding as minister.

The most famous chapels in town are those owned by **Charolette Richards**, dubbed the 'Wedding Queen of the West'. In her time she has married celebs like Joan Collins, Patty Duke and Bruce Willis.

Her ever-growing empire of chapels includes **A Little White Chapel**, the **Drive-Up Wedding Window**, **A Little White Chapel in the Sky** for balloon weddings, the **We've Only Just Begun Wedding Chapel** in the Imperial Palace Hotel and the **Chapel by the Courthouse**. She also owns two of the newest in town – the **Tunnel of Love** drive-through chapel

at A Little White Chapel on the Strip and the **Speedway to Love Wedding Chapel** for those wishing to get married at the Speedway.

In 1991 Charolette noticed a handicapped couple having difficulty getting out of their car to go into her chapel so she hit upon the idea of a drive-up window. It became such a novelty that all kinds of couples began queueing up for the drive-through wedding. They come on motorcycles, rollerskates, in cars, limos, trucks, taxis, removal vans and even boats!

Now it includes a **Tunnel of Love** in which couples are surrounded by floating cherubs, twinkling stars, birds on ribbons and signs everywhere saying 'I love you, I want you, I need you and I can't live without you' as you drive through the 14-foot-high tunnel. You have been warned!

Charolette also has a **Braveheart-theme** wedding ceremony in which couples can tie the knot in secluded woodland in a re-creation of the film scene when Mel Gibson's Wallace married Murron. It is a night-time service conducted in the moonlight with couples dressed in costume.

At **A Little White Chapel** you pay anything from $139 for the **Economy** package that includes a candlelight ceremony, music, four photographs and corsage and buttonhole to $499 for the **Joan Collins Special**, which includes the candlelight ceremony, music, photographs, bridal bouquets, corsages, buttonholes, garter, champagne glasses, lithograph marriage certificate, video recording, wedding cake and an etched marriage scroll. All the packages include a courtesy limousine service from your hotel to the Marriage License Bureau, on to A Little White Chapel and back to your hotel. The chapel fee is $45, drive-up weddings cost $25, gazebo weddings $25, hot-air balloon weddings start at $500 and helicopter weddings start at $195. You can also arrange for a video recording at $39, photos at $59 and gown and tuxedo rentals from $50.

Another great place to try is the **Divine Madness Fantasy Wedding Chapel**, recently opened by a Californian designer who has made customised clothes for 22 years. Here you can choose to get married in costume as Tarzan and Jane, Caesar and Cleopatra, Romeo and Juliet or Rhett Butler and Scarlet O'Hara among others. Costume rental, complete with jewellery, headdress and other accessories, costs between $60 and $225 per person.

At the **Excalibur** you can choose to get married in the gazebo of the **Canterbury Wedding Chapel**. Here a renewal wedding package costs $199 for the ceremony, music, one red rose, photo and bottle of champagne, while the wedding packages go from $250 to $780 – the latter including room, dinner and breakfast.

Packages at the **Island Wedding Chapel** at the **Tropicana** start at $250 and rise to $975 including a two-night stay at the hotel, though the rates are better from Monday to Thursday. Ceremonies at the **Flamingo Hilton's Garden Chapel** go from $369 to $1,200, the latter including a mini-suite for one night, pianist for the ceremony, breakfast in bed, dinner

and tickets for the cocktail performance of the Rockettes.

In addition to the chapels there are several very good wedding specialists who can arrange the exact wedding you want.

Coordinators

A Viva Las Vegas Wedding (702-384 0771) arrange an extraordinary number of differently themed weddings from *Star Trek* to Elvis and rock 'n' roll.

With **Stardate**, your special day is presided over by Captain James T Quirk or Captain Schpock in the **Starship Chapel**, surrounded by life-size cut-outs of your favourite characters. The package comes with a Minister Transporter, an illusion entrance, theatrical lighting and lots of fog for $650.

The **Rock 'n' Roll** theme takes place in the **Rock 'n' Roll Chapel**, complete with memorabilia and an electric guitar version of the Wedding March, while a rock star impersonator will sing during the ceremony. $540.

The **Renaissance Fair** theme includes **Merlin** or **King Arthur** as the Minister, while you'll be treated like a king and queen. The basic package costs $590 and includes period music, knights, trumpeters and fair ladies. For an extra $100 you can have a soloist perform your favourite medieval tune.

The **Gambling** package includes showgirls, keno runners, cocktail waitresses, card dealers and a Las Vegas-style singer/minister, plus theatrical lights and fog. It costs $590 and for another $100 you can even have Elvis or Marilyn Monroe at your wedding. Other packages include the **Victorian** ($490), the **Disco** ($550) and the **Beach Party** ($590).

Elvis in Blue Hawaii has an Elvis impersonator and dancers from the Tropicana's *Folies Bergère* at your ceremony, which takes place in the **Elvis Chapel**. In addition to all the Elvis memorabilia, Hawaiian sets, showgirls and hula dancers, there will be theatrical lighting and fog, while 'Elvis' will sing 'Love Me Tender', 'Viva Las Vegas' and 'I Can't Help Faling In Love With You'. $590.

For the **Gangster** theme, you'll step back in time to a 1940s Mafioso shotgun wedding at the **Gangster Chapel** where the Godfather/minister opens the door to wedded bliss accompanied by two bodyguards and a waiter/soloist singing in Italian. $590.

Wedding Dreams of Las Vegas (1-888 2 WED N LV) provide a comprehensive series of packages.

You can get married in the great outdoors of the **Red Rock Canyon** and even have an **Elvis** impersonator to provide the music. The price of $475 includes the minister, photos and flowers, while a limo service and 'Elvis' will cost extra. For $549 you can take a **night flight** over the lights of the Las Vegas strip, have photographs and a video recording of the event as the minister conducts the service in mid-air. Or you can take a **one-hour day flight** over the Grand Canyon with a videographer recording the minister's words for posterity. It'll cost you $1,600 plus tax!

A beautifully romantic high-flying option is the **sunrise balloon flight** with champagne and hors d'oeuvres at $625. If you want a photographer to go up with you that will cost $1,150 and you can have guests at $125 per person. For daredevils, there is the **bungee-jumping** option at $800. You take your vows at the top of the 175-foot tower before taking the plunge. Skydivers will be in heaven with the **New Beginnings** option ($1,200) which includes private use of a passenger jet liner, jump masters, minister, photos and a video of everything.

Romantics may prefer to get married by the four lakes north of the Strip. The basic price of $475

includes minister, photos, bouquets and flowers and optional extras include live music, a video and an Elvis impersonator. For an **intimate** affair, try the private limo wedding in which you'll also get champagne ($250) or get married in the privacy of a hotel room or suite for $375. For another $150 you can have a cake and non-alcoholic champagne reception for 15 people in your room.

Las Vegas Host (2680 Chandler Avenue, Suite 7B, Las Vegas, NV 89120, 702-798 5246) offer a full service for weddings at two different chapels in Las Vegas. There are five packages to choose from at the pretty **Victorian Little Chapel of the Flowers** ranging from $197.95 to $625.95. Here you'll find a cosy atmosphere and pretty setting that includes polished brass chandeliers, etched glass and burnished cherrywood with impressionist paintings.

At the romantic **Candlelight Wedding Chapel**, there are four packages ranging from $180.83 to $533.93. Opened in 1967 (so historic by Las Vegas standards!) this is the only free-standing chapel in the heart of the hotel district on the Strip and is where Whoopi Goldberg, Bette Midler and Michael Caine all got married.

Las Vegas Weddings and Room Coordinators (2770 South Maryland Parkway, Suite 416, Las Vegas, NV 89109, 702-737 6800) can book your rooms and organise every aspect of your wedding. Open 24 hours a day, seven days a week, they arrange flowers, transport, clothes, reception and entertainments. They have 17 chapels and themes include Elvis and nature weddings among others.

Or you can choose to take one of the packages arranged by tour operators from Britain (see Chapter 9).

A–Z of wedding chapels

A Chapel by the Courthouse: 203 East Bridger Avenue, 702-384 9099.

A Las Vegas Wedding Chapel: 727 South 9th, 702-383 5909.

A Little Chapel of Roses: 814 Las Vegas Blvd S, 702-382 9404.

A Little Chapel of the Flowers: 301 Las Vegas Blvd S, 702-382 5943.

A Little White Chapel at the Speedway: North Las Vegas, 702-382 5943.

A Little White Chapel in the Sky: 1301 Las Vegas Blvd S, 702-382 5943.

A Special Memory Wedding Chapel: 800 South Fourth Street and Gass, 702-384 2211.

A San Francisco Sally's Victorian Chapel: 1304 Las Vegas Blvd S, 702-385 7777.

A Wedding on Wheels: 1301 Las Vegas Blvd S, 702-382 5943.

All Religions Wedding Chapel: 2855 Las Vegas Blvd S, 702-735 4179.

Bally's Celebration Wedding Chapel: 3645 Las Vegas Blvd S, 702-894 5222.

Bellagio (The Wedding Chapels at): 3600 Las Vegas Blvd S, 702-791 7111.

Candlelight Wedding Chapel: 2855 Las Vegas Blvd S, 702-735 4179.

Canterbury Weddings: Excalibur Hotel on the Strip, 702-597 7260.

Celebration Wedding Chapel: 3645 Las Vegas Blvd S, 702-892 2222.

Chapel of the Bells: 2233 Las Vegas Blvd S, 702-735 6803.

Chapel of Dreams: 2121 Las Vegas Blvd S, 702-731 5052.

Chapel of Love: 1431 Las Vegas Blvd S, 702-387 0155.

Chapel of the Fountains: Circus Circus Hotel on the Strip, 702-794 3777.

Chaplain at Large: 1301 Las Vegas Blvd S, 702-382 5943.

China Town Wedding Temple: 4215 Spring Mountain Rd, 702-252 0400.

Cupid's Wedding Chapel: 827 Las Vegas Blvd S, 702-598 4444.

Divine Madness Fantasy Wedding Chapel: 1111 Las Vegas Blvd S, Suite H, 702-384 5660 or toll-free on 1-800 717 4734.

Drive Up Wedding Window: 1301 Las Vegas Blvd S, 702-382 5943.

Emerald Gardens: 891 Las Vegas Blvd S, 702-242 5700.

Forever Grand Wedding Chapel at the MGM Grand: 3799 Las Vegas Blvd S, 702-891 7984.

Flamingo Hilton Garden Chapel: 3555 Las Vegas Blvd S, 702-733 3111.

Graceland Wedding Chapel: 6195 Las Vegas Blvd S, 702-474 6655.

Harrah's Las Vegas: The Strip, 702-369 5121.

Hartland Mansion and Café: 525 Park Paseo Drive, 702-387 6700.

Hitching Post Wedding Chapel: 1737 Las Vegas Blvd S, 1-800 572 5530.

8

Island Wedding Chapel: Tropicana Hotel on the Strip, 702-739 2451.

Jet Helicopter Weddings: 3712 Las Vegas Blvd S, 702-736 0013.

L'Amour Chapel: 1901 Las Vegas Blvd S, 702-369 5683.

Las Vegas Helicopters Inc: 3724 Las Vegas Blvd S, 702-736 0013.

Las Vegas Villa: 4982 Shirley Street, 702-795 8119.

Las Vegas Wedding Garden: 200 West Sahara Avenue, 702-387 0123.

Las Vegas Wedding Reservations: 4036 Adelphi Avenue, 702-435 7922.

Little Church of the West: 3960 Las Vegas Blvd S, 702-739 7971.

Long Fung Wedding Temple: 4215 Spring Mountain Rd, 702-252 0400.

Monte Carlo: 3770 Las Vegas Blvd S, 702-730 7777.

Mount Charleston Hotel and Restaurant: 2 Kyle Canyon Road, Mount Charleston, 702-872 5500 or toll-free on 1-800 794 3456.

Neptune's Villa at Caesars Palace: 3570 Las Vegas Blvd S, 702-731 7110.

New York-New York Hotel: 3790 Las Vegas Blvd S, 702-740 6969.

Orleans Hotel and Casino: 4500 West Tropicana, 702-365 7111.

Paris (Wedding Chapels at): 3645 Las Vegas Blvd S, 702-967 4611.

Rainbow Gardens: 4125 West Charleston, 702-878 4646.

Rio Hotel and Casino: 3700 West Flamingo 702-247 7986.

Riviera Wedding Chapel: The Riviera Hotel on the Strip, 702-794 9494.

Scenic Outdoor Weddings: 702-873 8316.

Sherwood Forest: 7768 West Sahara Avenue, 702-256 3202.

Silver Bell Wedding Chapel: 607 Las Vegas Blvd S, 702-382 3726.

Speedway to Love Wedding Chapel: 4243 North Las Vegas Boulevard, 702-644 3000.

The Wedding Chapel: Treasure Island Hotel on the Strip, 702-894 7700 or toll-free on 1-800 866 4748.

The Wedding Room at the Cellar: 3601 West Sahara, 702-362 6712.

Treasure Island at the Mirage: 3300 Las Vegas Blvd S, 702-798 3778.

Tropical Gardens: 3808 East Tropicana Avenue, 702-434 4333.

Tropicana Island Wedding Chapel: 3801 South Las Vegas Boulevard, 702-798 3778.

Valley Outreach Synagogue: 1692 Long Horizon Lane, 702-436 4901.

Victoria's Wedding Chapel: 2800 West Sahara, 702-252 4565.

Wedding Temple: 4215 Spring Mountain Road, 702-252 0400.

Wee Kirk o' the Heather: 231 Las Vegas Blvd S, 702-382 9830.

We've Only Just Begun Wedding Chapel: Imperial Palace on the Strip, 702-733 0011.

WEDDINGS

RIGHT: A MEDIEVAL THEME AT
THE CANTERBURY WEDDING
CHAPEL IN THE EXCALIBUR

BELOW: FOUNTAIN OF GODS

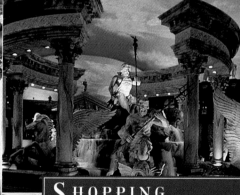

SHOPPING

THE CHEESECAKE FACTORY

ABOVE: ELVIS WEDDING

ABOVE: WORLD OF COCA-COLA

VIA BELLAGIO

VINES IN THE NAPA VALLEY

BIXBY BRIDGE AT BIG SUR

THE NEPTUNE POOL AT HEARST CASTLE™

MONTEREY PENINSULA

GRAND TOUR

SAN FRANCISCO'S NIGHT-TIME SKYLINE

THE GOLDEN GATE BRIDGE,
SAN FRANCISCO

GETTING THERE

The low-down on the tour operators, doing it your own way and specialist holiday planners

So that's the big deal ... now how do you get there? The options are as extensive as the choices open to you when you decide to visit Las Vegas. Do you use the city as a fantastically cheap base for visiting all the natural wonders on its doorstep; head off on a fly-drive tour; or even start in Los Angeles and San Francisco and take in all the wonderful places that you can reasonably visit in the amount of time available to you?

Then there are the other factors, like how many of you are travelling, will you be visiting friends in, say, LA or San Francisco, in which case you could take advantage of the incredibly cheap offers to Las Vegas that are advertised in the local papers. If you have children and teenagers in your party you'll probably be best off with an airline/tour operator that caters well for the family market. You may even want to do a part fly-drive and add on a ranch or golfing holiday or even an adventure trek.

The visitor figures show that Brits tend either to go on a long-weekend package to Las Vegas or to do a combination of any of the above. It is for this reason that if you have ever picked up a brochure on visiting Las Vegas and California there seems to be so much information and so many options to wade through, from multi-centre packages, fly-drives, coach tours, open-jaw flights (see page 142) and so on. It'll take some time to make sense of one brochure, let alone compare a few to see what suits you best. Then there is the other option – to organise your trip totally independently.

To try to make life easier, I've organised this chapter into two sections: the tour operators and independent travel, though even if you are planning to travel totally independently it is wise to read the tour operators section first for the big picture. I apologise if it all seems a little dry, but knowing the nuts and bolts of travel to America is the best way to get a truly fantastic trip and great value for money all at the same time. Paradise or what?!

Specialist tour operators

I don't mean your local travel agents, though they may have a good working knowledge of Las Vegas, Arizona and California, but those who specialise in organising holidays to the region and produce a brochure to display their products. I say this because Las Vegas in particular has quirks all of its own and someone with little 'local' knowledge is unlikely to provide you with the best deals or choice of options.

What's good about the specialist North American tour operators is that the big outfits especially have massive buying power and so can offer the best prices available for both hotels and car-hire services. In many cases you can go for a 'land-only' deal for a nominal charge, which gives you the option to arrange your flights through some of the cheap flight brokers who advertise in *The Sunday Times* (more about that in the independent travel section). Most do not advertise this, though, so you will have to ask.

All the main specialist North American operators provide tailor-made packages, which mean that you can take advantage of any special deals and arrangements they may have with, for instance, hotels, theme parks and local airline companies offering scenic flights round the Grand Canyon area and San Francisco.

The bigger guys – such as **American Connections, Virgin, Kuoni, Jetlife, Premier** and **Getaway Vacations** – can pack in a lot of added-value extras such as room upgrades for honeymoon and anniversary holiday-makers, free transfers to the hotel (generally not part of a North American package), free parking in city-centre hotels (which can be as high as $25 a night in San Francisco), free accommodation and/or free meals for children, extra nights free, free flights to London from regional airports and so on. You may also like to know that of the large tour companies operating in North America, **Virgin Holidays, Kuoni, Travelsphere, Jetsave** and **Page & Moy** did particularly well in the 'would you recommend this tour operator to a friend?' stakes as part of the most recent *Which?* tour operator survey in 1998.

But big is not always best in this market, as good knowledge of the location is very important, along with the operator's determination to provide you with what is best for you (which may involve making alternative suggestions to your own best-laid plans) and offer a generally good level of service. Smaller outfits such as **Just America** do not claim to be the cheapest, but with a high level of return custom and recommendation-to-friends business, they know their emphasis on getting things right for a slightly higher cost means all the difference between an okay holiday and a fantastic one. Their policy is based on not packing too much into one trip so that you travel to see destinations, not see destinations as you travel. Overall, it makes them very good value for money.

Another smaller UK operator, **Funway**, has a sister company in the US which sends more than one million people a year to Las Vegas, so they have tremendously good buying

power and very good access to hotels in Las Vegas. More than 30 hotels are featured in the brochure (the average tends to be about five or six), including all the recently opened resorts like New York-New York and Monte Carlo and even the upmarket Bellagio. In addition to having access to such a huge range of hotels, Funway's relationship with Las Vegas means they are likely to be able to get you into top resort hotels when other tour operators may not. They also provide a whole raft of extras including a Funway fun book, which is full of two-for-one and free admissions to parks and shows and 25% discounts on helicopter tours to the Grand Canyon. Overall, it makes them one of the best operators to Las Vegas.

★ ★ ★ ★ **INSIDE TRACK** ★ ★ ★
★   ★
★   ★
★ When shopping around for flight ★
★ prices, make sure the figure you ★
★ are given includes all taxes and ★
★ airport fees so you can make a ★
★   proper comparison.   ★
★ ★ ★ ★ ★ ★ ★ ★ ★ ★ ★ ★ ★ ★ ★ ★

Using a tour operator is great if you want to get everything sewn up before you go, but remember they're in business to make money and, while their brochures may be in one sense accurate, not all of them always give you the full monty, so to speak. Also, it is always useful to bear in mind that even if something is not included in the brochure, such as open-jaw tickets (see page 142) or air passes (see page 143), you should always ask your preferred operator if they can arrange those for you.

Here's how to take the good, watch out for the bad and reject the downright ugly that tour operators have to offer, followed by an at-a-glance guide. Please bear in mind that any prices quoted are based on the latest prices at the time of going to press.

Scheduled flights

There is really little to be able to compare between charter and scheduled flights in the North American market as only **Unijet** provide charter-only services, but if the European market is anything to go by, this is a good thing as scheduled flights generally provide a far greater degree of satisfaction among customers. For starters, most of the airlines fly every day to a whole range of locations in North America – many at easy-to-catch times of the day – and from a range of regional airports in the UK. Given the way most Brits tend to move around Nevada, Arizona and California during a holiday to the region, this provides the essential flexibility required when organising your trip. What tends to follow on from scheduled services is the ability to make a stop on the way to your final destination (stopover); fly into one city and out from another (open-jaw) and even fly between cities (using multi-centre packages or air-pass vouchers). And if you tend to do a lot of long-haul travelling, you can even arrange it so that you get frequent-flyer points. Most of the operators offer a minimum of three airline prices, some up to six, except for airline-run operators, eg American Holiday (American Airlines); NorthWest Airlines; United Vacations (United Airlines) and Virgin.

Return flight to Los Angeles and Las Vegas

The prices quoted in the guide have been based on a midweek return fare in the 'low-shoulder' season (see The seasons, page 147) of June. Just bear in mind that most prices quoted in brochures are for midweek flights – there is normally a surcharge of around £10–£12 each way per person for flights on Friday and Saturday – and there may be stipulations such as a minimum stay of seven days or one Saturday night with the return flight to be taken within six months. Although I have included these prices as a rough guide, price is not everything, as the more expensive tickets may fly you direct to Los Angeles (there are no direct scheduled services to Las Vegas) rather than drop you off in a 'hub' city where you will more than likely change to a domestic service plane (with no free drinks!). Some tickets may also provide better stopovers and multi-centre deals (see stopovers and multi-centre packages, page 142). For the purpose of the rough price comparisons I have included government and airport taxes to show the full price even where they are shown as extra in the brochure. Certain operators – Key to America, Kuoni and Virgin – do not give flight-only costs, but include accommodation and/or car hire costs. Finally, many of the published prices are subject to change and there may also only be a certain number of tickets available at the cheapest price given, so always check with the tour operator exactly what the price is before working out your holiday expenses.

★ ★ ★ **INSIDE TRACK** ★ ★ ★

Always check around for best flight prices before booking, as there may be good deals on offer.

Airport tax as extra

One word of warning: some of the operators' published prices do not include all the different government and airport taxes and these can vary considerably, in some cases adding nearly £60 on to the cost. As some operators give all-inclusive prices and some don't, you may be fooled into thinking one flight charge is cheaper than the other when, in fact, it may work out to be the same or even more expensive. When asking your agent

9

for flight prices, always ask them to quote you the price with *all* extras included so you can make a better comparison.

Open-jaw flights

Fly into one city and out from another. It's usually very simple to work out the cost – in most cases, you add the cost of flying to one destination to the cost of flying to the other, divide by two and add a £1. This means you don't have to backtrack and it can save you quite a lot of money on a touring trip. These days, though, very few operators advertise open-jaw so you will have to ask whether it can be arranged or shop around until you get the right deal for you.

Multi-centre packages

Fly into one city, look around, fly on to another, look around, fly on to another, look around and then fly home. This kind of package tends to be one of the most popular in the Las Vegas/California holiday market with the trio of Las Vegas, Los Angeles and San Francisco as the leading lights. It's a good idea if you don't want, or don't have, enough time to drive between all the main places you want to see, but it is a more expensive option, generally, than using your full quota of stopovers, or the open-jaw system.

Stopovers

The alternative to the above is to use the stopover system whereby you break your journey at various points. Most of the airlines offer this service, with the first stopover usually free and subsequent stopovers (up to a maximum of three) being charged at around £60 a stop. If you want to use this system you have to ensure that the route you are booking is the correct one for you as the first, free, stopover is usually limited to the 'gateway' city, ie the first place where the plane lands in the United States and where you'll go through American immigration. Watch this as

many of the American airlines use 'hub' cities as their gateway cities, such as Detroit or Minneapolis in the case of NorthWest Airlines, and you may not consider Delta's hub cities of Atlanta or Cincinatti to be as exciting a stopover point as New York or Los Angeles, for instance. With other airlines, such as NorthWest, it may pay to route your trip via Amsterdam so that you get a more interesting 'gateway' city.

★ ★ ★ ★ INSIDE TRACK ★ ★ ★
★   ★
★   ★
★   To make best use of your free   ★
★   stopover, check your 'gateway'   ★
★   city is a reasonable destination,   ★
★   eg New York or Chicago, rather   ★
★   than Cincinatti or Atlanta!   ★
★ ★ ★ ★ ★ ★ ★ ★ ★ ★ ★ ★ ★ ★ ★ ★ ★ ★

Extra stops

Like stopovers, except you'll pay an extra fee, usually £60. If you want to fly to more than one place not covered by your free stopover allowance, or if the place you want to go to isn't on the route, go for an air pass (see page 143).

Child and youth discounts

Most airlines give child discounts (ages 2–11), usually at 50% off the published price during mid and low seasons, and at 40% during peak season. The peak season does vary a little but a rough guide is July–August and the Christmas period which tends to last from around 15–27 December. Very few airlines offer youth discounts for 12–16-year-olds (a paltry 10%, which could be matched by shopping around the flight shops) but your best bets are tour operators with United Airlines and Virgin among their airlines.

Infant fares

The old days of tour operators publishing very cheap infant fares, but then adding on up to £60 of

Frequent-flyer points

Did you know that every time you fly you could be clocking up frequent-flyer mileage points that will eventually give you free air travel or other perks such as last-minute availability, lounge access and free upgrades or discounts off attractions and excursions in the USA? Very often your holiday booking does give you free air miles, but you may not know about it. Even if you do not claim the benefits, your travel agent still has the right to do so and some like to keep this nice little perk under their hats! So, before you go on holiday, register with the airline for their loyalty scheme and keep your booking passes as you will need these to show the flights were taken. Discounted flights may or may not qualify, but it's always worth checking.

Many of the North American specialists will automatically offer frequent-flyer points on American Airlines flights, though you may have to pay an additional £49 for the privilege of collecting them. Having said that, AA give you one Advantage mile for every mile you fly, which is over 10,000 if you're flying from London to Los Angeles – enough to earn you one free ticket to certain European destinations.

If you have a family, it is a good idea to register the whole family in the scheme so each person can build up their points. Some schemes such as the Frequent Virgin Club, expects its economy-class passengers to complete three return economy flights before qualifying, though upper class or premium economy passengers qualify immediately. British Airways offer both air miles and travel points, the latter granting lounge facilities and even free travel insurance with enough credits.

When arranging to join a frequent-flyer programme, ask if there is a bonus for joining at that particular time as different airlines offer bonuses. For instance, not so long ago Virgin was offering a bonus of 2,000 points on joining and Continental a special activation bonus of a whopping 5,000 miles when you take your first Continental Airlines holiday. The scheme offers free upgrades and free tickets.

Finally, in the first deal of its kind, the MGM Grand in Las Vegas has teamed up with American Airlines' frequent-flyer programme. So any time you spend money at the hotel you can earn advantage points.

taxes are, thankfully, mostly gone, though some still continue this practice. A good fully-inclusive price these days is around £70, but do check that the price you have been quoted includes all taxes.

Regional departures

More and more airlines are running routes directly from regional airports in the UK to Las Vegas and California. But neither British Airways nor Virgin does, and in most cases you will have to pay a supplement to fly to London (though Kuoni offers free flights in connection with transatlantic BA and United Airlines flights). In

almost all cases, if you want to fly from Glasgow you will have to pay a supplement of around £45–£50. But United Vacations and US Airtours offer free connections from many regional UK airports.

Air passes

If you plan to visit more than the one city covered by your free stopover or, for whatever reason, are likely to make quite a few flights between certain destinations, then air passes are really the way to go. But you must buy before you go as North American residents are not permitted to buy air passes, so they won't be

9

available once you get to the States.

Sadly, as with most open-jaw tickets, most operators don't advertise these air passes, probably because they are a much cheaper (and more flexible) alternative to the extra stopover system – even Trailfinders have dropped them from their brochure. The only tour operators still advertising air passes are Bon Voyage and Jetset, who use the Freedom USA pass from Southwest Airlines.

There are four passes available: Same or Adjoining State Pass (£45); the Western Pass for travel within the Western time zone – that's from Texas to California inclusive (£69); Central and Eastern Pass for travel anywhere except the Western time zone (£69) and the Anywhere Pass for travel anywhere within Southwest Airlines' route network (£99). Other American airline companies also offer these passes and if you want one it would be possible for your tour operator to arrange one for you, so just ask!

★ ★ ★ ★ ★ **INSIDE TRACK** ★ ★ ★
★   ★
★   ★
★ When booking flights be sure to ★
★ claim your free air miles or find ★
★   out about the airline's loyalty ★
★ scheme before you go to be on ★
★ track for free air travel or other ★
★ benefits such as priority booking, ★
★ lounge facilities and upgrades.   ★
★ ★ ★ ★ ★ ★ ★ ★ ★ ★ ★ ★ ★ ★ ★ ★ ★

Weekend breaks

Unijet, charter specialists to Las Vegas, have been known to advertise long weekends to Las Vegas for as little as £400 during the low-season winter months. If that sounds like fun to you, keep your eyes peeled for those newspaper ads! In addition, more and more tour operators are offering weekend breaks.

Fly-drive and tailor-made tours

These have to go hand-in-hand in the North American market as there are so many options it would be daft for any tour company to force people into taking one particular tour (that's what coach trips are for!). However, Chapter 11 is devoted to my ideal tour of Nevada, Arizona and California, which can be shortened depending on the amount of time you have available, and which gives you comprehensive coverage of the best sights, sounds and towns in this part of America!

Cost of weekly car hire

This has been based on the price of renting a full-size, two-door car in western USA (covering Nevada, Arizona and California) and fully comprehensive insurance to cover all insurance, taxes, airport fees and surcharges you *have* to pay. If you want an additional driver it works out cheaper to take out Alamo Gold so the price for this has also been given, and for hassle-free arrival in USA and car pick-up, being able to pre-rent in the UK really does make life a lot easier. The prices do not include the high-season rental supplement of around £16 a week or £4 a day during the peak seasons of 15 July to 31 August and 20–27 December (though I have shown these separately). A full breakdown of insurance costs and charges is given in the chapter on Driving and Car Rental (see page 159).

Coach and Tauck tours

If you don't want to worry about car hire, driving and all the other arrangements you will need to make, and you don't mind a coachload of people crowding into an attraction at the same time as you, then this could be the way to go. Coach tours are not necessarily all-inclusive, though, and may not include meals so that you have the option of choosing where you want to eat. Tauck tours are the posher version and usually include everything. Run by an American company, the idea is that you will be greeted and treated as an individual, while the tours themselves tend to be shorter so you have more time to relax and explore sights by yourself. In addition, you are put up in first-class hotels with character. Kuoni now also offers Trafalgar tours, which are even posher, with all meals included and first-class accommodation throughout the tour (so definitely no need to bring your sleeping bag!).

Grand Canyon flights

One of the added bonuses of visiting Las Vegas is that you can experience the amazing scenery of Arizona's Canyonlands, plus other natural wonders Bryce Canyon and Zion Park, without the long drive. A whole host of scenic flight operators work out of Las Vegas (details in the Family Fun chapter on pages 113–17), but if you want to make sure of your seat or tie up all loose ends before you go, many of the tour operators are offering these flights. And, again, ask even if they're not advertised as they may be able to arrange a scenic flight for you.

Motorbike hire

Okay, so you fancy yourself as a modern-day cowboy enjoying the ultimate touring experience of travelling along those wide-open roads on anything from a Harley Davidson Electra Glide to a Fat Boy or Road King. You can do that from LA and Las Vegas, but it'll be a lot more expensive than a car! Few operators offer this, but those that do include: American Holidays, Jetlife and North America Travel Services.

Amtrak and Greyhound

Greyhound's International Ameripass means you can go where you want when you want, travelling day or night, from £75 for four days (this cheapest ticket is usually for travel Monday to Thursday), to £340 for 60

days. Trailfinders and Jetset are now the ONLY operators offering these passes. Amtrak rail passes for Western states start at £121 for 15 days of travel (£195 peak season) and go up to £161 for 30 days of travel (£245 peak season). National and other regions are also available. Amtrak covers all the major destinations and sights in California and there is the new non-stop daily service between Los Angeles and Las Vegas for $99 return. The trip takes 5½ hours with trains arriving in Las Vegas at 2pm and departing for LA at 4pm every day. Sadly, few tour operators advertise Amtrak travel, but others may be able to arrange it for you if you ask.

★ ★ ★ ★ **INSIDE TRACK** ★ ★ ★
★ ★
★ ★
★ If you're in Los Angeles check the ★
★ local papers for good deals on ★
★ the new Amtrak rail service ★
★ between LA and Las Vegas. ★
★ ★ ★ ★ ★ ★ ★ ★ ★ ★ ★ ★ ★ ★ ★ ★

Weddings

See Going to the Chapel, page 131.

Theme park tickets

You can buy these in advance to get a much better deal on standard entrance prices at Disneyland® Park in California, Universal Studios and San Diego Zoo among others. But don't overbook tickets as you may not have time to see all you've paid to see and, especially if you're travelling at off-peak times, you may miss out on cheap deals locally. Full details of the theme park prices and ticket deals are given both in Independent Booking (see page 154) and the Grand Tour (see page 197).

Phonecards

Many operators used to offer these money-saving cards and Jetlife still give you a free one. Call 01703 767793 for more information.

9

Hotel vouchers

There are three basic kinds – the Liberty and TourAmerica Hotel Passes and the North American Guestcheque. In all cases you buy vouchers at a certain price in advance that are valid for one night at a participating hotel. You can book the hotel in advance and the room will accommodate up to four people. It can be a very good way of planning your holiday budget and pre-paying as far as possible. But one major drawback is that if you buy more than you need, there is usually a charge for redeeming any unused vouchers. Often it amounts to the value of one voucher and in some cases it can be one voucher plus an administrative charge of £25.

Another drawback is that you do not benefit from any promotions that participating hotels and motels may run locally. And do bear in mind that these chain hotels are not character-filled and some may even seem a little soulless. Also:

● Purchasing the vouchers does not automatically give you the right of accommodation, so it is always best to book as far in advance as possible, especially if you intend to travel in the peak seasons (see Seasons, opposite).

● If you intend to arrive after 4pm, you will need a credit card to guarantee your reservation. If it is a hotel/motel in a particularly busy area, such as one of the major sights that is not near a big town or city, I'd recommend you ask them to send or fax the confirmation of your reservation.

● It may seem daft pointing this out but with these chains there are often many in the same town, so it is best to make a note of the full address so you go to the right one!

The Liberty Hotelpass encompasses many of the main hotel and motel chains in America including Days Inn, Howard Johnson, Ramada, Travelodge and Super 8 and you can stay in cities, resorts, near airports and at key touring areas. Most locations have swimming pools, restaurants and facilities for children. Prices per voucher cost between £42 and £45 (including taxes) and you will receive a free directory of participating hotels so you can make advance reservations. In some key touring areas, rooms may require more than one voucher per night, but these are clearly marked in the directory.

The Tour American Hotelpass also includes the main chains of Days Inn, Howard Johnson, Travelodge and Super 8, with over 350 properties along the highways and in major cities, but at £30 a voucher (again for rooms that can accommodate up to four people) it is aimed more at the budget end of the market. As with the Liberty scheme, you will get a directory and some hotels and motels in the key touring areas may require more than one voucher per night.

The North American Guestcheque is solely for use with Best Western hotels and motels and there are two voucher prices: £28 (which equates to $44) and £7 (which equates to $11). All the hotel prices in the directory are listed in denominations of $11 so you can purchase the exact number of vouchers required. Fewer tour operators are offering hotel passes, but if you really want them, ask your preferred operator to arrange some for you.

Other things you need to know

The seasons

There are four: low or off-peak, low shoulder, high shoulder and peak. Basically, the most expensive times to travel are Christmas, July, August, Easter and during the American bank holidays which are: President's Day (George Washington's birthday) – the third Monday in February; Memorial Day – the last Monday in May and the official start of the summer season; Independence Day – 4 July (slap bang in the middle of the high season anyway); Labor Day – the first Monday in September and last holiday of summer; and Thanksgiving – always the fourth Thursday in November. Low or off-peak season tends to be November, then January to the end of April excluding the bank holidays and Easter. May, June and October are low shoulder and all other times are high shoulder.

★★★★ **INSIDE TRACK** ★★★
★ Don't try to see too much in too ★
★ short a space of time – you don't ★
★ want to spend your whole ★
★ holiday driving and you may even ★
★ want to leave time for an ★
★ adventure tour or ranch holiday. ★
★★★★★★★★★★★★★★★★★★★

Best times to travel

Without a doubt, Monday to Thursday. Flights are cheaper, airports less crowded for departure and arrival and hotels in Las Vegas, in particular, are far less busy. In fact, the very best days to arrive in Las Vegas are Tuesday to Thursday morning.

The airlines and smoking

One thing you really ought to know is that Virgin and most of the American airlines have a total non-smoking

policy on their transatlantic flights. Even if you do get a transatlantic flight that allows smoking, if you switch to a domestic plane for the final leg of your journey you will not be allowed to smoke on that plane as smoking is banned by law on all American flights. For the moment you can still puff to your heart's content in the smoking sections of BA flights.

Code share

Many airlines now enter into alliances with each other to share routes, which can offer you more choice of routes and fares. It means that your flight is marketed by one airline, with the airline's flight number, but when you board you find the service is operated by a different airline. Some tour operators will inform you in advance, but they may not always know as these alliances are constantly changing. Be careful of this if you have a particular dislike for one airline or know that you definitely want to fly with a certain company. A 1997 *Which?* survey of airlines found that Virgin was among the most highly rated, yet it currently has a code-share alliance with Continental, who came pretty near the bottom of the same report.

Kids stay free

Many operators offer this as an extra, but it is standard policy at many American hotels to allow children to stay free in the same room as an adult. More to the point, if you're NOT being offered this as an option, go elsewhere!

The major operators

Air Vacations
0171 828 1137
Has a very basic brochure with no added extras.

American Connections
London: 01494 473173
Manchester: 0161 835 3655
Glasgow: 0141 332 1311

9

At-a-glance guide

Tour Operator	Air Vacations	Am Connect	Am Holidays	Bon Voyage	Funway	Getaway
Scheduled Flights	Yes	Yes	Yes	Yes	Yes	Yes
Return flight to Los Angeles	£397	£431	£469	£409	£447	£459
Return flight to Las Vegas	£397	£431	£469	£409	£447	£459
Taxes charged separately	Yes	Yes	No	No	No	No
Open-jaw	–	Yes	–	–	Yes	–
Multi-centres	Yes	Yes	Yes	–	Yes	Yes
Free stopover	Yes	Yes	Yes	Yes	Yes	Yes
Extra stops (per stop)	–	£60	£60	£60	£60	£60
Child discount (2–11 yrs)	–	50%	40%	40%	50%	50%
Infant fare (under 2 yrs)	–	£61	Ask	£75	£99	£100
Regional departures	Yes	Yes	Yes	Yes	Yes	Yes
Frequent-flyer points	Ask	Ask	Yes	Ask	Yes	Ask
Air passes	–	–	–	Yes	–	–
Weekend breaks	–	–	Yes	–	Yes	–
Fly-drive tours	Yes	Yes	Yes	Yes	Yes	Yes
Tailor-made holidays	Yes	Yes	Yes	Yes	Yes	Yes
Car hire firm	Hertz	Alamo	Alamo	Alamo	Alamo	Alamo
Cost of weekly car hire inclusive of comprehensive car insurance	£199	£212	£210	£212	£212	£212
High season extra per week	£15	£15	None	£17	£16	£16
Alamo Gold cost per week	n/a	£12	£14	£12	£6	£10
Free one-way rental	–	–	–	–	Yes	–
Pre-rent in UK	–	Yes	Yes	–	Yes	Yes
Escorted coach tours	–	Yes	Yes	–	Yes	Yes
Tauck tours	–	–	Yes	Yes	–	–
Rail tours	–	–	–	–	–	–
Grand Canyon flights	Yes	Yes	Yes	–	–	Yes
Motorbike hire	–	–	Yes	–	–	–
Amtrak/Greyhound	–	–	Yes	Yes	–	–
Weddings	–	–	Yes	–	Yes	–
Theme park tickets	–	–	Yes	Yes	Yes	Yes
Hotel vouchers	–	–	Yes	–	–	–

At-a-glance guide

Tour Operator	Jetlife	Jetset	Just America	Key to America	Kuoni	North America
Scheduled Flights	Yes	Yes	Yes	Yes	Yes	Yes
Return flight to Los Angeles	£456	£440	£421	n/a	n/a	£455
Return flight to Las Vegas	£456	£440	£421	n/a	n/a	£455
Taxes charged separately	No	No	Yes	No	No	Yes
Open-jaw	–	–	–	–	–	–
Multi-centres	Yes	–	Yes	Yes	Yes	–
Free stopover	Yes	–	Yes	Yes	–	Ask
Extra stops (per stop)	£60	–	£50	–	–	–
Child discount (2–11 yrs)	50%	33%	50%	50%	50%	Ask
Infant fare (under 2 yrs)	£69	Ask	£97	Ask	Ask	Ask
Regional departures	Yes	–	Yes	Yes	Yes	Ask
Frequent-flyer points	Ask	Ask	Ask	Ask	Ask	Ask
Air passes	–	Yes	–	–	–	–
Weekend breaks	Yes	Yes	Yes	–	Yes	–
Fly-drive tours	Yes	Yes	Yes	Yes	Yes	Yes
Tailor-made holidays	Yes	–	Yes	–	Yes	Yes
Car hire firm	Alamo	Alamo	Alamo	Alamo	Alamo	Alamo
Cost of weekly car hire inclusive of comprehensive car insurance	£210	£266	£196	£205	£213	£233
High season extra per week	£16	£16	£13	£15	£14	£16
Alamo Gold cost per week	£14	n/a	All inc.	£12	£14	All inc.
Free one-way rental	–	n/a	Yes	–	–	–
Pre-rent in UK	Yes	n/a	Yes	–	–	Yes
Escorted coach tours	–	Yes	Yes	Yes	Yes	Yes
Tauck tours	–	–	–	Yes	–	Yes
Rail tours	Yes	–	–	–	–	–
Grand Canyon flights	Yes	Yes	Yes	Yes	Yes	Yes
Motorbike hire	Yes	Yes	–	–	–	Yes
Amtrak/Greyhound	–	Yes	–	–	–	–
Weddings	Yes	Yes	–	–	Yes	–
Theme park tickets	Yes	Yes	Ask	Yes	Yes	Yes
Hotel vouchers	Yes	Yes	Ask	–	Yes	–

9

At-a-glance guide

Tour Operator	Northwest Air	Premier	Trailfinder	United Vacations	US Airtours	Virgin
Scheduled Flights	Yes	Yes	Yes	Yes	Yes	Yes
Return flight to Los Angeles	£432	£442	n/a	£414	n/a	n/a
Return flight to Las Vegas	£432	£442	n/a	£437	n/a	n/a
Taxes charged separately	No	No	n/a	No	No	Ask
Open-jaw	–	–	n/a	–	–	–
Multi-centres	Yes	Yes	n/a	Yes	Yes	Yes
Free stopover	Yes	Yes	n/a	Yes	Yes	Ask
Extra stops (per stop)	£58	£63	n/a	Ask	£50	–
Child discount (2–11 yrs)	50%	50%	n/a	40%	40%	50%
Infant fare (under 2 yrs)	£67	£62	n/a	£80	Ask	£100
Regional departures	Yes	Yes	n/a	–	Yes	No
Frequent-flyer points	Ask	Ask	Ask	Yes	Ask	Yes
Air passes	–	–	–	–	–	–
Weekend breaks	–	–	Yes	Yes	Yes	–
Fly-drive tours	Yes	Yes	Yes	Yes	Yes	Yes
Tailor-made holidays	Yes	Yes	Yes	Yes	Yes	Yes
Car hire firm	Alamo	Alamo	Alamo	Alamo	Alamo	Dollar
Cost of weekly car hire inclusive of comprehensive car insurance	£198	£231	£195	£217	£210	£227
High season extra per week	£16	£21	£15	£16	£16	£28
Alamo Gold cost per week	£14	n/a	£10	All inc.	£11	–
Free one-way rental	–	Yes	–	Yes	–	Yes
Pre-rent in UK	–	Yes	–	–	Yes	–
Escorted coach tours	–	Yes	Yes	Yes	–	Yes
Tauck tours	–	–	Yes	–	–	–
Rail tours	–	Yes	–	–	–	–
Grand Canyon flights	–	–	Yes	Yes	Yes	Yes
Motorbike hire	–	–	–	–	–	–
Amtrak/Greyhound	–	–	Yes	–	–	–
Weddings	–	–	–	–	–	Yes
Theme park tickets	–	Yes	–	Yes	Yes	Yes
Hotel vouchers	Yes	–	–	Yes	Yes	Yes

Offer a very good 'land-only' section of hotels; also do ranches and has a special brochure purely for Las Vegas.

The American Holiday
0870 605 0506
Do 'land-only' deals for a £30 fee, plus free maps and shuttle services at certain destinations. Also offer adventure holidays, horse riding, dude ranching and motorbike hire.

Bon Voyage
01703 330332
One of the bigger operators, but surprisingly, offers very few extras.

Funway
0181 466 0222
Bonus offers at certain locations: free meals and breakfasts for children, free cocktails for adults and fun books, packed with money-saving deals on sightseeing trips, attractions, shows, shopping and dining. Funway's sister company in America is very big in Las Vegas. It has its own car rental and sightseeing options that can be reserved on its website at: www.funwayholidays.co.uk.

Getaway Vacations
0181 313 0550
On self-drive bookings: a free Rand McNally Road Map/Travel Planner.

Jetlife
01322 614200
If you fly with Continental Airlines to the western states, you will get a free car upgrade.

Jetset
0990 555757
Free accommodation for children at certain hotels. Offers Greyhound Ameripass and Air Passes. However, does not give clear details of the 'fully inclusive' insurance and car hire prices, so check the package DOES include everything you want.

Just America
01730 266588
Has the best value, easiest-to-use arrangements for car hire. Also specialise in a highly-personalised, tailor-made service.

Key to America
01784 248777
Bonus scheme at certain hotels: free children's meals, free activities, room upgrades, dining discounts, free breakfasts and fifth night free.

Kuoni
Reservations: 01306 742888
Brochure line: 07000 458664
Extra nights free, room upgrades, free sports, meals and drinks and food discounts. Special deals for honeymooners and those celebrating 25th or 50th wedding anniversaries (though you'll have to take a copy of your marriage certificate with you!).

North America Travel Service
0171 938 3737
Specialises in fly-drives but very little information about flights and availability of open-jaw and stopovers. Some free night deals at certain hotels. Has separate brochures for coach, Tauck and adventure tours.

NorthWest Airlines
01424 224400
Offers flight discounts for teenagers.

Premier Holidays
01223 516688
'Premier Plus' offers include extra nights free at certain hotels; free transport to attractions, breakfasts, upgrades for honeymooners, tea and coffee and use of health clubs.

Trailfinders
0171 937 5400
Specialises in low-cost flights (only with United Airlines), but no details given. One of the few tour operators still offering Amtrak passes and the only company that still does the Greyhound Ameripass.

9

Unijet

0990 114114

United Vacations

0181 313 0999

No regional departures, unless you fly via Amsterdam, but free connecting flights from regional airports during off-peak times. Books of vouchers for cheaper dining and attraction entrance fees.

USAirtours

0990 280067

Free drinks, breakfasts, shuttle to the Strip in Las Vegas, and free extra nights at certain hotels.

Virgin

01293 617181

Free kids' funpack on flights, free breakfasts, free meals for children and extras for honeymoons and anniversaries at certain hotels. Don't forget to join the frequent-flyer programme if you qualify. Plus $50 discount at Virgin Megastores and better deals for single parents.

Escorted tours only

APT International Tours

0181 879 7444

Discounts if you have travelled with APT before, and a travel bag.

Jetsave

01342 313033

For groups of 15 or more, there are 'generous' discounts plus free places, depending on numbers travelling. No supplements for single travellers if prepared to share a room.

Page & Moy

0116 250 7676

Is consistently rated highly by repeat-visit travellers.

Travelsphere

01858 410818

National Express pick-ups to point of departure for £5; savings on hotel airports and regional departures.

McCarran International Airport, Las Vegas

Just one mile from the Strip and five miles from downtown, McCarran International Airport is one of the slickest, most modern and easy-to-use airports in America. In a recent passenger survey of 36 major airports – which looked at speed of baggage delivery, ease of reaching gates, available ground transportation, cleanliness, quality of restaurants, attractiveness, closeness of parking and ease of following signs – McCarran came sixth.

The airport is among the ten busiest airports in the world and deals with 800 flights a day and around 30.5 million passengers a year. A new runway – opened recently at a cost of $80.5 million – will give the airport the capacity to handle 60 million passengers a year in the future. It has direct flights to 62 US airports and nine international destinations and more than 5,000 cars a day use the parking facilities.

Like many other aspects of life in Las Vegas, the airport also has the very latest technology. There is no need for departing passengers with tickets to go to ticket counters inside the terminals – they can check in their luggage at the ticketing/departure kerb. And it is the first airport in America to use Common Use Terminal Equipment (CUTE). CUTE allows airlines to use any gate as needed, which will allow more efficient scheduling of gates and mean faster boarding for passengers. In addition, all facilities are accessible to the disabled and there are amplified phone sets throughout the terminal.

McCARRAN INTERNATIONAL AIRPORT

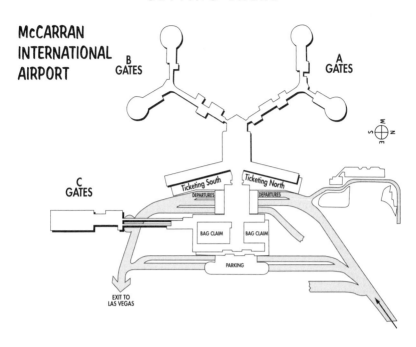

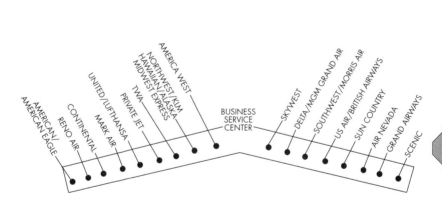

B Gates:	America West, Sun Country.
C Gates:	American, Morris Air, Private Jet Expeditions, Southwest, United/Lufthansa.
Charter/International Terminal:	Aeroexo, Aero Mexico, AeroMonterrey, Air Canada, Air TransAT, Allegro, American Trans Air, Canada 3000, Canadian International, Canadian Regional, Carnival, Empire, Express One, Great American Airways, Leisure, Mexicana, Miami Air International, Rich International, SAM, Viscount.

153

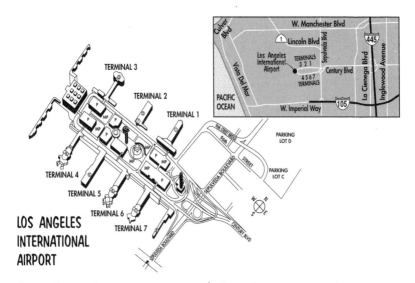

**LOS ANGELES
INTERNATIONAL
AIRPORT**

Los Angeles International Airport

If you are planning a tour holiday or perhaps an open-jaw flight, you may want to come into or out of Los Angeles airport, which is a major international airport with all the best facilities.

Independent booking

There may be many different reasons why you want to organise all or part of your trip independently. Some people (jammy dodgers I call them!) fly to San Francisco or Los Angeles to visit friends and then decide to go off to Las Vegas and other parts of California or Arizona on little trips. But by nature we Brits are an independent lot and one of the most appealing ideas for us is just to fly to the west coast of America and hit the open road. Whatever the reason, the following tips will help you to save money in all the right places so you have more to spend on enjoying the sights and buying those essential pairs of Nikes etc.!

Flights

Competition in the transatlantic flight market is fierce, which is good news

for us the customers. It also means that it makes sense to shop around for the best deal you can get. I recommend that you read all the notes in the Tour Operator section (see page 139) of this chapter first so you can acquaint yourself with all the terms and deals available from non-stop to stopovers and open-jaw to multi-centre. Once you have worked out what your priorities are, then you have a pretty good chance of beating the prices quoted in the brochures by phoning round the transatlantic flight bookers who advertise in the Sunday papers. *The Sunday Times* is particularly good for this. Remember, too, that the tour operators specialising in the North American market also have access to deals being offered by the airlines from time to time so can often beat their own published prices! Low and low shoulder (see The seasons, page 147) are particularly good for brilliant deals, such as flights to Las Vegas or Los Angeles for £200.

You can even go for a totally no-frills, mega-cheap flight with what are known as 'consolidated' fares. These are the old-style bucket-shop fares which have now been legalised. The travel agent negotiates deals on your part, so you get very cheap fares and they're happy, too, as they earn better commission rates. The main restriction with these fares is that you can only use one airline and sometimes it may involve flying via that airline's 'home' country, for instance, somewhere in Europe. Also you won't get free stopovers and extra stopovers, but you can get around this by buying air passes for internal flights (see page 143). But remember, these air passes are not available in the States so you need to buy them before you go.

Hotels

Off-the-cuff: If you're happy touring around Nevada, Arizona and California staying in the rather soulless chains such as Days Inn, Ramada and so on, you could take advantage of many of the special deals that are advertised in local papers and find your night's stay on an ad hoc basis. Generally this is no problem at all in cities and towns, but it may be worth booking a few days in advance for rooms at major sightseeing destinations, such as the Grand Canyon or Furnace Creek in Death Valley. Even if you'd prefer accommodation with a little more character, you can still find cheap deals through agents once you are in America – the numbers are given on page 157.

Las Vegas: This is one of the weirdest cities on earth for hotel prices. In most cities around the world, hotels tend to be busy during the week and offer incentives to fill their rooms at weekends. With Las Vegas the reverse is true. So many Americans from Salt Lake City to Phoenix and Los Angeles use Las Vegas as a weekend destination that occupancy rates are a staggering 96% on Friday and Saturday nights (all the more amazing considering they have nearly 120,000 rooms to fill). On top of that, the city hosts huge conventions and special events such as rodeos and prize fights that tie up hotels, restaurants, transportation,

showrooms and traffic for a week at a time. For these reasons, although Las Vegas hotels have their rack (standard) room rates, prices vary wildly above or below that rate according to how busy it is and how much they think they can get away with! Having said that, the price of accommodation is probably cheaper than anywhere else in North America and given the class and quality of facilities on offer, you can live like a king or queen very cheaply at top resorts in Las Vegas. Here's how.

★ ★ ★ ★ **INSIDE TRACK** ★ ★ ★
★ ★
★ ★
★ Most hotels will allow children ★
★ under a certain age to sleep for ★
★ free if sharing a room paid for ★
★ by two adults. ★
★ ★
★ ★ ★ ★ ★ ★ ★ ★ ★ ★ ★ ★ ★ ★ ★ ★ ★ ★

Cheap deals: If you happen to be in southern California in December or January and pick up a local paper, then you may see promotional offers direct from Las Vegas hotels in which the rooms are practically given away. On the basis that an empty room is a liability, they will be happy to do this just to get your foot in the door – and their casino! The deals often include not only incredibly cheap rooms, but also free shows and meals.

In addition, the travel sections of the Sunday papers just about anywhere in the States – and at just about any time of year – are good for picking up fantastic deals to Las Vegas. But by far the best places to buy good Las Vegas deals from are southern California (Los Angeles and San Diego), Phoenix, Denver or Chicago. The package usually includes room, transport and possibly rental car and shows. Even if you've already got your transportation sorted (ie car, air-pass etc.) you can still take advantage of the special deals by asking for the 'land only' part of the deal – everything on offer without the transportation.

9

In almost all cases you will get a better deal on Las Vegas hotels once you are in the States (with the possible exception of Funway, which has access to so many hotels at great prices), especially if you are travelling at low or shoulder seasons.

In the unlikely event that you can't find deals for Las Vegas in the *LA Times* or other local papers, contact airline tour companies such as American Airlines Fly-Away and Delta Dream Vacations and ask if they have special deals at particular hotels.

Good American agents to use include the National Reservation Bureau on toll-free number: 1-800 461 0124 (but don't phone from a hotel room as you'll be charged the hotel phone rates). Prices will vary according to the time of year but when I looked they had rooms at Circus Circus from $46 (approx £28 at $1.60 to the £ or £14 a head for two adults) at the Excalibur from $55 (£17 a head for two) and at the Luxor from $65 (£20 a head for two) among many others. And in all cases the price included free show tickets.

★ Bear in mind that hotel prices in ★
★ America are for accommodation ★
★ only and do not include the cost ★
of breakfast.

Other Las Vegas agents that will help not just with the price of a room, but actually get you in at the inn, so to speak, include: Las Vegas Travel, again toll-free on: 1-800 286 9195 and Las Vegas Hotels Directory, toll-free on: 1-800 732 1191; Accommodations Xpress 609-391 210; Las Vegas Rooms, toll-free on: 1-800 233 5594 (they can also organise weddings and car rentals); Las Vegas Backpackers Hostel and Adventure Center, toll-free on: 1-800 550 8958; and Gold Reservations, toll-free on: 1-800 627 4465.

Remember, most hotels in America work on a per-room price basis, though there may be a maximum number of adults allowed. In addition, the room usually consists of a double or two double beds – the latter can't be guaranteed, but can be requested. In some cases there may be a small extra charge if there are more than two adults, but this won't be much.
No room at the inn: It is also worth using one of the agents mentioned above if you're having trouble booking yourself into one of the top resort hotels as they are more likely to have rooms. You may phone the Luxor, for instance, to be told there are no rooms available – even when the hotel is not full. The reason for this is that agents are given blocks of rooms to sell, so as far as the reservations manager is concerned, those rooms are not available.

When making your own accommodation arrangements, guaranteeing your hotel room is essential, especially if you intend to arrive after 4pm. You will have to give your credit card details, but it is always best to get a written confirmation from the hotel.

One word of warning: If booking a hotel yourself, always guarantee your first night with a credit card (even if you do not plan to arrive late). Send a deposit if needed and try to get written confirmation of your reservation. If you're staying in a hotel in San Francisco or LA when booking your hotel in Las Vegas, for instance, they're sure to have a fax you can use to receive a written confirmation. Keep this with you in case you have problems on arrival. Armed with such evidence of your reservation the hotel cannot turn you away. They must find you a room of at least the same rate and standard or better than the one you reserved.

The Internet

Take care when making bookings via the Internet. As with all independent travel arrangements, you do not have a tour operator to complain to (and, possibly, get money back from) if things go wrong. Stick to bigger hotels and car-hire firms if you are pre-booking some time in advance as you are not covered if the company goes bust before you arrive for your holiday.

Probably the biggest drawback to Internet bookings though, is that there have been concerns about the security of sending credit card details over the Internet. A good way to do it would be to take details from the Internet and make arrangements via the phone, fax or by letter.

The specialists

So you've seen the bright lights of the big cities, taken in the amazing natural wonders of the West and had a flutter in Las Vegas – what more could you want? Well, the truth is that we Brits not only have an independent spirit, we also have romantic notions of the rugged outdoors and cowboy lifestyle. The chances are that if you've gone all the way to the West, you'll want to add on a ranch holiday or 'soft' adventure tour including rafting, cycling, climbing and motorbiking or perhaps go horse riding, bird watching, play a little golf, do the

jazz thing or get a real taste of California wines. I have included details of all these options at the appropriate places in the Grand Tour chapter (see page 165) but here are the companies offering those services and their phone numbers.

Adventure
Hemmingways: 01737 842735.
Outlaw Trails: 01293 529345.
Ranch America: 01923 671831.
Trailfinders: 0171 938 3939.
Trek America: 01295 256777.

Bird watching
Ornitholidays: 01423 821230.

Golf
Destination Golf USA: 0181 891 5151.
The American Golf Holiday: 01703 465885.

Horses
Equitor/Peregrine Holidays Ltd: 01865 511642.

Jazz
Ashley Tours: 01886 888335.

Ranching specialists
American Round-Up: 01404 881777.
North American Representatives: 01344 890525.
Ranch America: 0181 868 2970.

Major tour operators also offering a few ranching holidays.
American Connections: 01494 473173.
Getaway Vacations: 0181 313 0550.
Jetlife: 01322 614200.
Kuoni: 07000 458664.
United Vacations: 0181 313 0999.
Virgin: 01293 601530.

Wine
Arblaster and Clarke: 01730 893344.
Winetrails: 01306 712111.

9

DRIVING AND CAR RENTAL

How to get out on the open road

It's the grand dream, isn't it – driving along the American highway, the only car on a stretch of road that goes on for so long you only lose it on the horizon, music blasting, shades on and not a care in the world. Believe me, it truly is an experience not to be missed. You cannot help but get a sense of being so much closer to nature when all around you is space, space, space on an unbelievable scale. And if there is not much of interest to see in some places (as is the case!), the skies are likely to provide some spectacular sights of their own from multi-coloured sunsets to heavenly blue skies and massive rainfalls that you can see from miles away. I once spent a whole day driving on a straight open road surrounded by Arizona desert landscape, with blue skies each side and a monumentally large downpour from the skies straight ahead – and not a drop fell on me until the night (when my tent almost got washed away in the downpour!), which shows just how big the country is.

I tell you all this to help convey the scale of what you will encounter on a touring trip round the west of America and the moral of the story is: unless you particularly want to spend your entire holiday driving, don't try to see too much on a two-week holiday.

The other point is that while you may have some reservations about your ability to drive on the wrong side of the road in a foreign country, it really is not a problem in America. Recently a friend was planning a trip to Los Angeles but she and her boyfriend were so worried about driving round the city and up to San Francisco that they weren't sure if they should go, even though they really wanted to (I might hasten to add

that they were jammy dodgers with friends in LA!). I pointed out that driving in America is not only a lot easier than driving in Britain, but a great deal more fun too, and that, while I have no understanding of why, the whole system of getting on and off freeways and turning left and right is so much easier when driving on the right-hand side of the road. After returning from a wonderful trip in which they hired a car and ventured off to San Francisco, taking in the fantastic vistas provided by the Pacific Coast Highway, my friend told me she was so pleased I had encouraged them to go. And this is my advice for all of you – if you want to do it, just do it and you'll have the trip of a lifetime.

Car rental

Of course you'll need a car and this is where the rental firms come into play. Most of the tour operators have special deals going with Alamo, though one or two use Avis, Budget or Dollar. Included in the At-a-glance Guide in the previous chapter (see pages 148–50) is the price of a two-door, full-size car for one week off-peak, including insurance, surcharges, taxes and unlimited mileage. The prices have become pretty standardised since last year, but by far the best deal is through Just America, which offers many extras included in the price – and at a lower rate than any other operator.

Charges and deals

Many of the tour operators give the price of hiring the car separately from what it will actually cost you to walk away from the rental desk with your car keys, though some, such as Air Vacations, Bon Voyage, Jetset, Just America, Key to America and

Trailfinders, show all-inclusive prices. This makes sense as these are charges you *must* pay in addition to the car hire fees: LIS, CDW, airport user fee, state local surcharges and taxes, cash deposit, additional driver fees, under-age driver fees, child seat (if you need one) and deposit. In any case, when checking the price of hiring a car, make sure you look at the right area and right dates, as prices vary from place to place. Florida and California are cheaper than Western USA prices, which cover Arizona and Nevada.

Liability insurance supplement (LIS): This is $11.99 per day ($9.99 in California). Theoretically it is optional, but as basic car rental includes third party liability up to just $50,000 and as many Americans are great at suing your pants off, this essential insurance gives you cover up to $1 million. Take it and sleep soundly at night.

Uninsured motorist protection: A lot of Americans do not have any or enough insurance and if they caused the accident, you would have no one to sue for damage to your property or for personal injury (the car is covered by CDW, see below). This new type of insurance is sometimes called **extended protection** (EP) in the brochures as it covers LIS (see above) plus a further $1 million for personal damage or injury caused by a third party, and does not cost more – hey, a bargain, for once! In other cases it is not listed separately, but comes under LIS, in which case you need to check that your tour operator's comprehensive package includes this uninsured motorist protection as opposed to LIS alone.

Collision damage waiver (CDW): This costs $16.99 per day. It covers you for $10,000–$50,000 worth of damage to your hire car regardless of the cause, plus theft or loss.

Airport user fee: This will cost you up to 10% of the total charge.

State/local surcharges and taxes: 5–15% of total cost (though as high as 26% in Phoenix, Arizona).

Cash deposit: This tends to be around $100 per week. In addition, you will often be asked to provide a credit card in the driver's name to cover any incidentals such as the deposit or under-age driver charges. If you want to leave a cash deposit you'll probably be asked to show three forms of identification, for instance passport, driving licence and airline tickets.

Additional driver fees: $5 per driver per day.

Under-age driver fees: All the UK deals are for drivers with a minimum age of 25 and drivers under 25 will have to pay a further $15 per day.

Child seat and deposit: Children up to the age of five must, by law, travel in a child seat in America, and you should book these in advance. The cost will be $4–$5 per day plus $50 deposit.

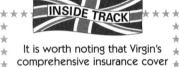

★ ★ ★ **INSIDE TRACK** ★ ★ ★ ★
★   ★
★   It is worth noting that Virgin's   ★
★   comprehensive insurance cover   ★
★   (car hire with Dollar) includes all ★
★   the extras covered by Alamo   ★
★   Gold, ie additional drivers and   ★
★   child seat.   ★
★ ★ ★ ★ ★ ★ ★ ★ ★ ★ ★ ★ ★ ★ ★ ★

Comprehensive Alamo rentals: The all-inclusive packages and comprehensive insurance cover schemes you take out in advance in the UK tend to cost around £20 a day in Western USA and £15 to £17 a day in California. They include extended protection, CDW, airport user fee and state/local surcharges and taxes, and generally work out cheaper (by about £60 per week) than paying for all the above on arrival (and save a lot of time when you go to collect your car).

Alamo Gold: Many of the tour operators now offer an Alamo Gold scheme which, for a fee of around £10 to £15 a week, includes three additional drivers and gives you a free tankful of petrol, worth around $15 to $25 depending on the size of the car hired (though additional driver fees are not payable in California or Nevada).

Alamo Gold as standard: Some operators, such as Just America and North America Travel Services, automatically give you the extras of Alamo Gold without any extra charges.

Hertz comprehensive package: This includes EP, CDW, airport user fee and state/local surcharges and taxes, but does not include extra drivers or petrol.

One-way drop-off fees: Most companies charge if you want to pick up your car in one location and drop it off in another, which can easily add $100 to your rental costs. The exceptions tend to be if you pick up and drop off in California, though always check. Some tour operators have negotiated free drop-offs between California, Arizona and Nevada (see the At-a-glance guide on page 148 for details). In addition, one-way rentals are only available on cars above a certain size and need to be booked in advance.

Virgin's Dollar all-inclusive package: Includes all your insurance and taxes. For a further £38.50 per week you are also covered for your first tank of petrol, under-25 drivers, additional drivers and baby seats – so it is more expensive than Alamo Gold, but a more comprehensive package, too!

Limits: In most cases you will not be allowed to drive your hire car in Mexico or off-road in America.

Documents: You will need a UK driving licence or a driving licence from your country of residence. You do not need an international driving licence, nor is it acceptable.

Pre-rental: Some tour operators are now offering you the chance to fill out all the necessary paperwork before you leave home so when you arrive you can just pick up your car keys and go. Not only does this save you

time, but it also means you can bypass efforts by the counter staff at American car-hire firms to give you the upgrade hard sell! In any case, you will generally get a better deal for bigger cars if you arrange this in advance. The possible exception is in Las Vegas where they practically give away upgrades on a quiet week. But be warned, if you arrive in Las Vegas when the town is packed, expecting to pick up a car of your choice, you may find it is nigh-on impossible!

About the cars

Sorry, but size _is_ an issue!: Where your flight includes car rental, it will normally be for a small, economy-size car, which probably won't be much good for an extensive tour even if there are only two of you. An Economy is usually something like a Geo Metro, which equates to a Fiesta-sized hatchback; a Compact may be a Chevrolet Cavalier – an Escort-sized car; an Intermediate may be a Pontiac Grand AM – a small family saloon such as an Orion; a Full Size may be a Chevrolet Lumina – a more spacious Vectra. You can even go up to a Premium (eg Buick Le Sabre), Luxury (eg Cadillac Sedan de Ville), Convertible (eg Chevrolet Cavalier), Luxury Minivan (eg Pontiac Transport) and Four-wheel Drive (eg Chevy Blazer). Because the boot sizes of all American cars are much smaller than their European equivalents, I chose a full size car for my example price comparison in Chapter 9's At-a-glance Guide.

10

★ ★ ★ ★ **INSIDE TRACK** ★ ★ ★

★   ★
★ If you do decide to stick to an ★
★ economy-size car, you may find ★
★ that it has trouble getting up ★
★ steep hills with the air ★
★ conditioning on, in which case ★
★ you should turn it off until you ★
★ get to the top! ★
★ ★ ★ ★ ★ ★ ★ ★ ★ ★ ★ ★ ★ ★ ★ ★

Automatics: All American hire cars will be automatics. Some things may confuse you at first, such as you won't be able to drive until you put the car into D for drive and you probably won't be able to take the keys out of the ignition until you have put the car into P for park. D1 and D2 are extra gears which you only need to use when going up steep hills. Some larger cars have cruise control, which lets you set the speed at which you want to travel and then take your foot off the gas pedal (the accelerator to you and me!). There are usually two buttons on the steering wheel for cruise control, one to switch it on and the other to set your speed. You take off cruise control by pressing the on button again or by simply accelerating or braking. In some cases the handbrake may also be a bit different. Some cars have an extra foot pedal to the left of the brake, which you need to press to engage the handbrake. Pull a tab just above it to release or press the main brake pedal.

Air conditioning: There's none of this having to roll down all the windows, getting windswept hair and sticky hands when driving around in the heat in America, as all cars come with air conditioning. But you must keep the windows closed to make it work and sometimes you will have to switch on the car's fan first to make the A/C or air button work.

Fuel/gas: You've hit the highway and need to fill up, but just bear in mind that for the most part Interstates (the main roads) do not have gas stations

– you will have to get off and drive to a station, though they are not usually too far away. Generally there are two prices: one for self-service and another if the attendant fills up your car. They may also clean your windows (you'll find that essential on long trips, thanks to the myriad of flying insects) and would expect a tip for this, but there will be equipment for you to do this yourself.

Driving in the US

No speeding, please!: The speed limits on the main Interstates are well signposted and tend to be between 55 and 70mph (75mph on some lonesome stretches in Nevada), while the MINIMUM allowed is 40mph. In Los Angeles this information is probably surplus to requirements as there is so much traffic you'll probably be going at the same speed as on some parts of our M25! Also, in built-up areas, the speed limit may be as low as 15 to 20mph.

Be warned, the Americans take their speed limits very seriously. Self-confessed 'gullible traveller' Bob Maddams was on a 65mph stretch of endless road between Nevada and Utah when boredom set in. He'd not passed a single car for two hours and there was nothing for miles in front or behind him so he decided to put his foot down.

He says: 'Less than a minute later the needle was nudging 95 and less than 30 seconds after that a cop car, siren wailing and lights flashing, was waving me down. Where the hell he came from I will never know.'

Facing the prospect of a hefty $200 fine, Bob put on his best Hugh Grant accent, hoping to win over the police officer. But Mr Dark Shades was having none of it and said: 'Are you aware that I am empowered to enforce an immediate jail term for the degree of this offence?' After that Bob was highly delighted to get off with the $200 fine – even if it meant not being able to afford to eat for the next week!

Restrictions: Flashing orange lights suspended over the road indicate a school zone ahead, so go slowly. School buses cannot be overtaken in either direction while they are unloading and have their hazard lights flashing. U-turns are forbidden in built-up areas and where a solid line runs down the middle of the road. It is also illegal to park within 10 feet of a fire hydrant or a lowered kerb and you should never stop in front of a yellow-painted kerb – they are for emergency vehicles and you will get towed away! Never park on a kerb either. Seat belts are compulsory for all front-seat passengers. It is worth bearing in mind that the legal limit for blood alcohol in America is lower than in Britain and the police are very hot on drink-drivers. It is also illegal to carry open containers of alcohol in the car itself.

Accidents and emergencies: If you have even a minor accident, the police must be contacted before the cars can be moved. The car-hire firm will also expect a full police report for the insurance paperwork. In the case of a breakdown there should be an emergency number for the hire company among the paperwork they gave you. Always have your driving licence with you (remember an international driving licence is not valid) and your car-hire agreement forms in case you are stopped by the police at any time. If you are pulled over, keep your hands on the wheel and always be polite. If they find out you're British you could just get away with a ticking off for a minor offence (but not for speeding at 95mph!).

Signposts and junctions: One of the most confusing aspects of driving around towns in America is the way they hang up road names underneath the traffic lights at every junction. The road name given is not for the road you are actually on, but the one you are crossing. Another thing to be wary of is that there is very little advance notice of junctions, and road names can be hard to read as you approach them, especially at night. So keep your speed down if you think you are close to your turn-off so you can get in the right lane. If you do miss your turning, don't panic, as nearly all roads in American towns are arranged in a simple grid system so it will be relatively easy to work your way back.

Sometimes you will meet a crossroads where there is no obvious right of way. This is a 'four-way stop' and the way it works is that priority goes in order of arrival. When it is your turn, pull out slowly. At red lights, it is possible to turn right providing there is no traffic coming from the left and no pedestrian crossing unless specified by a sign saying 'No turn on red'. A green arrow gives you the right of way when turning left, but when it is a solid green light, you must give way to traffic coming from the other direction.

Hiring cars locally: You may not wish to hire a car for the entire time of your trip, but can easily arrange this when you arrive. You'll find phone numbers for all the major car-hire firms in a local phone directory, but bear in mind that the prices they quote you will *not* include all the extras outlined earlier in the chapter, so be sure to include those when you do your calculations. (I have given the names of car-hire companies in Chapter 1, see page 12.)

10

11 THE GRAND TOUR

The ideal trip to see everything you want in the West

San Francisco (including Napa Valley); Monterey Peninsula; Big Sur; Hearst Castle and the Pacific Coast; Los Angeles; Long Beach; San Diego; Palm Springs; Grand Canyon; Monument Valley; Lake Powell; Las Vegas; Death Valley; Mammoth Lakes; Yosemite; Lake Tahoe; San Francisco.

It's highly unlikely that you'll want to travel all the way to Las Vegas (fantastic though it is) without taking in some of the other great sites the West has to offer. The brochures are full of suggested itineraries, but may not explain that staying at Furnace Creek in Death Valley for two nights, say, is not something you'd really want to do. What I have done here is to include the places you might want to visit, indicating travel times between locations, but I've also suggested alternative routes in case time does not permit you to do everything. It is advisable to read the chapter on Driving and Car Rental (see page 159) before making your final decision, too, as this helps to explain the sheer size of the States – in many parts of America, cities are at least 200 to 300 miles apart, so do bear that in mind before heading off into the sunset.

I have started with San Francisco for two main reasons: you can fly direct to the city and it is probably the one city – apart from Las Vegas – where you are better off without a car. Parking in San Francisco is a nightmare and walking around it is easy, so why waste money on car rental and insurance when you don't need it? The alternative is to fly direct to Los Angeles, start your tour from there and finish in San Francisco, using the 'open-jaw' option (see page 142) that is available through most transatlantic airlines. This way you will be able to hand over your car once you arrive in San Francisco and, again, save car-rental fees. To comfortably see everything included in the Grand Tour, I would advise allowing yourself three weeks. Alternatively, you can opt just to do sections of it, but either way the idea is that you should have enough information to make a considered decision on what is best for you.

San Francisco

Surrounded on three sides by the Pacific Ocean and San Francisco Bay, the city has one of the world's greatest natural harbours and is joined to the mainland by two masterpieces of bridge design – the Golden Gate Bridge and Oakland Bay Bridge. Its 46-square-mile area is home to more than 700,000 people, making it one of the most compact cities in America, with one of the densest populations.

Everything about the city makes it a treat to visit and, mostly, a place to 'experience' rather than 'see'. The weather is 11°C/20°F cooler than elsewhere in California during the summer, providing a blessed relief to the otherwise sweltering summer heat of the rest of the state; it rarely goes below 4°C/40°F or above 21°C/70°F, though you'll need a cardigan or light jacket even for summer evenings. You'd be hard-pressed to find a restaurant that dishes up a poor-quality meal and the

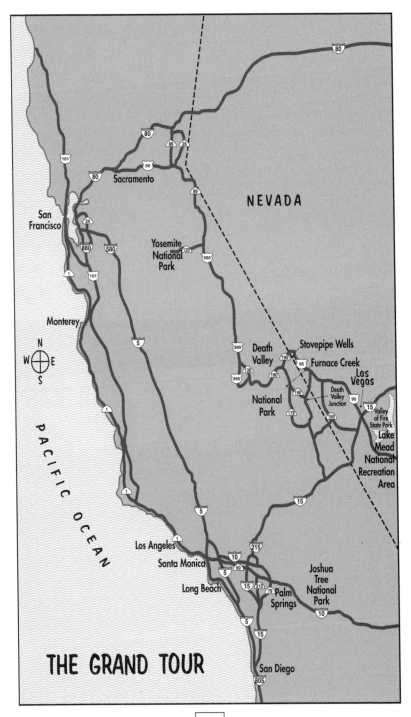

THE GRAND TOUR

San Franciscans are a happy, hospitable lot who, without realising it, provide plenty of entertainment for visiting Brits! If you want to do the tourist thing, I've included the major sights, as well as describing the different fun and trendy areas.

Getting about

If nothing else, *The Streets of San Francisco* and numerous movies have all taught us that the city is filled with hills that are great for filming car chases with leaping automobiles! In fact, there are 42 hills ranging from 200 feet to 938 feet and the favourite sport of locals when showing around visitors is to take you up the 'scariest' hills. The ten steepest are clustered around Russian and Nob Hills and Pacific, Dolores and Buena Vista Heights. At the bottom are yellow 'Hill' or 'Grade' signs, which mean: 'Don't even think about it unless you've had your brakes checked recently'. In some cases, these city signs have even been amended from 'Hill' to 'Cliff' by locals. Get the picture? Incidentally, most runaways tend to be removal vans from out of town and if you want to tackle one of these hills, bear in mind that even the locals accept they're not Steve McQueen in *Bullitt*. Also, just *walking* these streets is difficult and many of the sidewalks are edged with steps, while locals have learnt that brand new leather-soled shoes are to the pavements what skis are to snow!

The best advice when in San Francisco is to park your car (if you have one) and get about by Muni (municipal railway or Muni Metro), taxi, cable car or on foot. Unlike most other American cities, San Francisco is quite compact and you will find it surprisingly easy to walk around. If you use public transport, make sure you have the correct fare for the Muni – $1 – as no change is given. The cable car fare is $2. Muni passports ($6 for one day, $10 for three days and $15 for seven days) give unlimited rides and even discounts to some attractions. The Muni information line is 415-673 6864. For travelling further afield, use the Bay Area Rapid Transit (BART). Phone 415-992 2278 for schedules and routes or pick up a schedule from the Visitor and Information Center on Powell and Market Streets.

★ ★ ★ **INSIDE TRACK** ★ ★ ★
★   ★
★   You can get your bearings by   ★
★ hopping on and off the Gray Line ★
★ narrated tour of San Francisco at ★
★   either Union Square, Pier 39 or   ★
★   the Embarcadero Center. It lasts ★
★   1½ hours and costs $16.   ★
★ ★ ★ ★ ★ ★ ★ ★ ★ ★ ★ ★ ★ ★ ★ ★

If you must drive, remember cable cars and pedestrians always have the right of way.
Parking: Always respect parking zones, as indicated on the kerbside. Red means no stopping or parking; yellow a half-hour limit for commercial loading vehicles; green, yellow and black are taxi zones (though you can park in yellow zones after 6pm); and blue are for disabled placard holders only.

★ ★ ★ **INSIDE TRACK** ★ ★ ★
★   ★
★   Parking's a nightmare and if you ★
★ leave your car in the wrong place ★
★   it *will* get towed away!   ★
★ ★ ★ ★ ★ ★ ★ ★ ★ ★ ★ ★ ★ ★ ★ ★

On certain streets, parking is forbidden during morning and evening commuter hours. If you do find a meter, check how long you can stay and follow the city code – always turn the tyres toward the street when facing uphill, and towards the kerb when facing downhill. This way you use the kerb as an extra brake. Many of the neighbourhoods also only allow parking by permit, so if

11

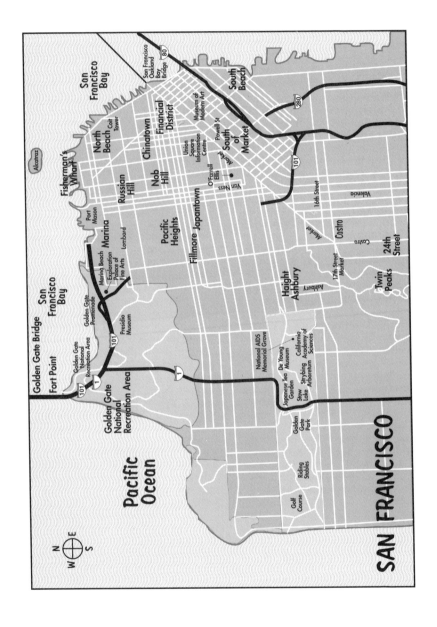

you park in the wrong place you could face fines of $20, plus a towing fee of $100 and daily storage fees. If you park in a bus zone or a place marked for wheelchair access, you face fines of $250; in spaces marked handicapped, it's $275.

Parking garages: These can be found at 665 Beach at Hyde, Fisherman's Wharf (415-673 5197); 255 Third Street (415-777 2782); Museum Parc on Third at Folsom (415-543 4533); 833 Mission Street, Downtown (415-982 8522); 766 Vallejo Street, North Beach (415-558 9147); 1910 Laguna (415-563 9820) and 2055 Lombard Street (415-495 3772) for Union Street; 433 Kearny Street (415-956 8106) and 733 Kearny Street (415-982 6353) for Chinatown. Phone ahead for rates, availability and hours.

Top sights

Golden Gate Bridge: The world's most beautiful suspension bridge, linking the city to Marin Country and the area north, opened in 1957 at a cost of $35 million and 11 lives. It is 1.7 miles long and crews work non-stop to sandblast off rust and repaint it, using 45,460 litres or 10,000 gallons of orange paint each year. Auto toll ($3) collected southbound, pedestrians free (but who'd walk it?)

San Francisco–Oakland Bay Bridge: One of the world's longest steel bridges (over eight miles). Toll collected westbound. For a spectacular view, take the Treasure Island exit and continue to the naval base entry gate.

Golden Gate National Recreation Area: Running along the north bay coast is Golden Gate Promenade, a Mecca for joggers, cyclists and romantics wishing to see panoramic views of Alcatraz, Angel Island, the Marine Shoreline and East Bay. Here you will also find the **Palace of Fine Arts**, built for the 1915 Panama-Pacific International Exposition and now returned to its former glory. It also contains the **Exploratorium** science museum and a theatre.

Marina: To the right of the Recreation Area is the Marina and **Marina Green**, which was developed on the site of the 1915 Panama-Pacific International Exposition and is used by kite-fliers, joggers and sunbathers. You can chill out at **Greens** (Building A, Fort Mason Center, 415-771 6222) which serves up fine vegetarian cuisine with some of the best views of the Marina and Golden Gate Bridge.

Golden Gate Park: South of the Recreation Area. Originally 1,017 acres of sand dunes, it now has miles of drives, green lawns, playing fields, bridle paths, lakes and flowers. It contains the **Japanese Tea Garden** (Tea Garden Drive, 415-668 0909), an authentic Japanese garden, dating back to 1894, and a tea house that serves tea and fortune cookies, plus a pagoda, ponds, bridges and bonsai. Best time to see it is in the spring, when cherry blossoms and flowering shrubs create a rare floral spectacle. Admission is $2 for adults or $1 for children under 12, but tours are free. The 'living library' **Strybing Arboretum** (Ninth Avenue and Lincoln Way, 415-661 1316) nurtures more than 6,000 species of plants and is open 8am to 4.30pm weekdays, 10am to 5pm weekends and holidays. Entrance is free. **MH de Young Memorial Museum** (Tea Garden Drive, 415-750 3600) exhibits fine American art with special galleries devoted to objects from Greece, Egypt, Rome, Africa, Oceana and the Americas. Open 9.30am to 4.45pm daily except Mondays and Tuesdays. Entrance: $6 adults, $4 12–17s and under 12s free. First Wednesday of each month is free. In the same building is the **Asian Art Museum** (415-379 8800), acclaimed for its jades, porcelains, bronzes and ceramics. Open 9.30am to 5pm Wednesday to Sunday (closed Monday and Tuesday). Adults $6, 12–17s $4, under 12s free, and the first Wednesday of each month is free. The **California Academy of**

Sciences (Music Concourse, 415-750 7145) is open daily from 10am to 5pm. Admission adults $7, 12–17s $4, under 6s free. Free on the first Wednesday of each month. There are also plenty of sports including a nine-hole **golf** course (415-751 8987), **tennis** courts (415-753 7101), daily **boat** rentals on Stow Lake (415-752 0347) and **riding** lessons (415-668 7360). If you want to cycle, rollerblade or skate, you can rent the gear from **Golden Gate Park Skate and Bike** (3038 Fulton Street and Sixth Avenue, 415-668 1117).

Museum and attraction passes: If you plan to visit the Museum of Modern Art, the Exploratorium, MH de Young Memorial Museum, San Francisco Zoo, California Palace of the Legion of Honor and California Academy of Sciences, and take a Blue & Gold Fleet Bay Cruise, then buy a San Francisco City Pass. For $29.95 for adults and $17.95 for 12–17s, it will save you more than 50% off the gate admission prices, as long as you see everything within a seven-day period. The ticket booklets can be bought at any of the participating attractions.

Fisherman's Wharf: Apparently 84% of visitors to the city visit this tourist spot, but when Brits talk about places not to see in San Francisco, this is the only place on the list! If anyone tells you you must see it, just nod politely – the whole thing is just one big tourist spot filled with tacky T-shirts and fast-food outlets. Not really what San Francisco is about, is it? If you insist on going, **Lou's Pier 47 Club** (300 Jefferson Street at Taylor, 415-771 0377) offers cheap meals with live music daily from 6am to midnight.

★ ★ ★ ★ INSIDE TRACK ★ ★ ★
★　　　　　　　　　　　　　　★
★　　　　　　　　　　　　　　★
★　　Alcatraz has now been　★
★　designated a National Park and　★
★　the number of visitors per day　★
★　has been limited so it is best to　★
★　　　pre-book your ferry.　　★
★ ★ ★ ★ ★ ★ ★ ★ ★ ★ ★ ★ ★ ★ ★

Alcatraz: One of your must-see sights; the views from the cruise boats to the island 1½ miles north of Fisherman's Wharf are spectacular – Golden Gate Bridge to your left, Bay Bridge to the east and the Downtown skyline with its landmark Transamerica Pyramid behind. Phased out as a federal penitentiary in 1963 (Al Capone being its most famous inmate), it was

★ ★ ★ ★ INSIDE TRACK ★ ★ ★
★　　　　　　　　　　　　　　★
★　　Hopping on a cable car from　★
★　Powell Street to Fisherman's　★
★　Wharf (return fare $4) is a good　★
★　way to get the traditional tourist　★
★　spot out of the way. The end of　★
★　the line also drops you off in an　★
★　excellent location for a good　★
★　photo of San Francisco Bay.　★
★ ★ ★ ★ ★ ★ ★ ★ ★ ★ ★ ★ ★ ★ ★

opened to the public ten years later. Surrounded by freezing waters, buffeted by cold and constant sea breezes, it is now derelict and falling to pieces (seen Sean Connery's *The Rock*?). On-island activities include trail walks, ranger-led tours and audio-cassette tours narrated by former inmates and guards who give you an excellent idea of why no inmate ever managed to escape! Warm clothing and walking shoes are essential. **Blue and Gold Fleet** (415-705 5555) run ferries every 30 minutes from Pier 41 for $11. They also have a ticket booth on Pier 39 and their audio tour, which lasts 30 minutes, costs $4. **Red and White Fleet** (415-546 2628) also ferry sightseers to the island.

Top places

Haight-Ashbury: The scene of the original 60s flower-power generation, it is now filled with record shops, thrift stores and cafés. There's a touristy, commercial feel to it and street beggars are not unknown, but it's still

ABOVE AND RIGHT : THE GETTY CENTER

ABOVE: PACIFIC PARK IN SANTA MONICA
BELOW: MELROSE AVENUE

3RD STREET PROMENADE
AT SANTA MONICA

GRAND TOUR

BEVERLY HILLS

JURASSIC PARK™ AT UNIVERSAL STUDIOS

THE MULAN PARADE AT
DISNEYLAND® RESORT
IN CALIFORNIA

THE *QUEEN MARY* AT
LONG BEACH

A GONDOLA RIDE AT
NAPLES IN LONG BEAC

'IT'S A SMALL WORLD'
AT DISNEYLAND®
RESORT IN CALIFORNI

GRAND TOUR

UNIVERSAL CITY WALK

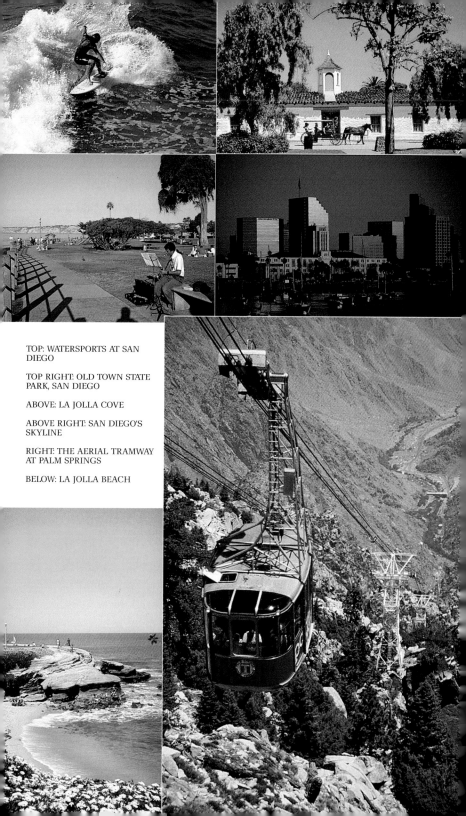

TOP: WATERSPORTS AT SAN DIEGO

TOP RIGHT: OLD TOWN STATE PARK, SAN DIEGO

ABOVE: LA JOLLA COVE

ABOVE RIGHT: SAN DIEGO'S SKYLINE

RIGHT: THE AERIAL TRAMWAY AT PALM SPRINGS

BELOW: LA JOLLA BEACH

GRAND TOUR

TOP: WHITEWATER RAFTING ON
THE COLORADO

CENTRE: HIKING DOWN THE
GRAND CANYON

ABOVE: THE GRAND CANYON

LEFT: JEEP TOUR IN THE DESERT

fun to visit and you get great views of the city from Buena Vista Park. You can see where the Grateful Dead lived at 170 Ashbury and Janis Joplin's home at 112 Lyon Street. Two of the best-known second-hand shops are the **Buffalo Exchange** (1555 Haight Street, 415-431 7733), where you can pick up some great items at remarkable prices, and **Forever After Books** (1475 Haight Street, 415-431 8299), heaven for spirituality, psychology, history, health and fiction fans. There are plenty of places to eat but three that stand out for fun people-watching are the trendy **Squat & Gobble Café** (1428 Haight, 415-864 8484), **Crêperies** (237 Fillmore Street, 415-487 0551) and **Just Desserts** (1000 Cole Street, 415-664 8947), a full espresso bar with a wide selection of freshly baked desserts and breads. **The Castro:** Steep streets and brightly painted Victorian houses provide a pretty environment for San Francisco's gay quarter. Filled with imaginative boutiques, bookstores and bars, it is one of the most fun districts of the city. For a full insight into the history of the area, it's worth booking yourself on **Cruisin' the Castro**, a historical walking tour of Castro Street by Ms Trevor Hailey. It begins at 10am sharp and you must book in advance (415-550 8110) as there is a four-person minimum, 16-person maximum. $35 including brunch. In any case, you won't want to miss the **Castro Theater** (429 Castro Street). Built in 1922, it is one of the last grand movie palaces left in America and features camp revivals with hilarious pre-film, audience-participation concerts on the Mighty Wurlitzer. The **Names Project** (2362 Market) houses the AIDS memorial quilt, a powerful reminder of the dreadful toll of AIDS, and each June the Lesbian, Gay, Bisexual, Transgender Pride Celebration Parade attracts crowds of up to 500,000. One of the trendiest stores in the district has to be **Rolo San Francisco Inc** (450 Castro, 415-626 7171),

which sells 'upscale' fashion clothes and accessories. **Under One Roof** (2362 B Market Street, 415-252 9430) is a famous speciality gift shop that supports many AIDS charities and is open daily from 11am. A great pitstop during the day and a comedy club seven nights a week, is **Josie's Cabaret and Juice Joint** (3583 16th Street, 415-861 7933). It serves vegetarian food and features stand-up female impersonation and music. **Shopping: Market Street** (stretching from the Castro north to Gough Street and Van Ness in Downtown) is *the* district for art deco and antiques. **Golden Gate Antiques** (1564 Market), **Another Time** (1586), **Design For Living** (1612), **Decodence** (1684) and **Centrium Furnishings** (2166) offer an amazing selection of funky and fun art deco and twentieth-century 'antiques'. In nearby Gough Street, **The Other Shop** (112), **Deco to 50s** (149), **Modern Era Decor** (149) and **Vintage Modern** (182) offer everything from affordable collectables to furniture, lighting and jewellery. On your way up Market, you'll come across **Norstrom** (865), a speciality store filled with clothes, shoes, accessories and four restaurants – where you can get a much needed coffee! – and **House of Blue Jeans** (1059), which has one of the biggest selections of Levis in San Francisco. It'll be hard work taking it all in but you can make a pit stop at the 1950s (an almost superfluous description as just about everywhere seems to have that 50s feel!) diner **It's Tops Fountain Coffee Shop** (1801, 415-431 6395), which opens for breakfast and lunch daily and has late nights (until 3am) from Wednesday to Saturday. Alternatively, if you reach Market and Van Ness it's just a short stroll to the **Hard Rock Café** (1699 Van Ness Avenue, 415-885 1699) where quintessential American food is dished up in the usual rock 'n' roll environment. **Valencia** and 16th is also good for smaller-scale shopping with **Upstairs**

11

Downstairs (890 Valencia, 415-647 4211), San Francisco's vintage department store for art deco, a leading light locally. The myriad of cafés, bars, restaurants and music venues to hang out and eat in make it a lively evening area. Try the **Slanted Door** (544 Valencia, 415-861 8032) for authentic Vietnamese cuisine. Another good evening haunt is **Café du Nord** (2170 Market Street, 415-861 5016), which provides dining and dancing in a speakeasy environment with top-notch local musicians providing the excellent entertainment.

Noe Valley: Just south of the Castro and 24th Street, this is like a village in the city – a lovely neighbourhood of shops and cafés.

Twin Peaks: Take a scenic drive to the 910-foot peaks for spectacular views of the city and beyond. It's even more amazing at night when the city is all lit up.

North Beach: Between Russian Hill and Telegraph Hill, this is the home of the Beat generation and the literary capital of California, with its hub at the **City Lights Bookstore** (open until midnight) on Columbus and Jack Kerouac Lane. If you go in around 11pm, it'll be full of people who are completely stoned conducting the most amazingly esoteric conversations – an entertainment in itself! The area is also rich in Italian heritage, so you'll find a staggering array of Italian restaurants, bakeries and delis in less than a square mile. Try **Calzone** (430 Columbus Avenue at Broadway, 415-397 3600) for pizzas in the heart of the Italian quarter, while **Fior d'Italia** (601 Union Street, 415-986 1886), just minutes away from Chinatown, is America's oldest Italian restaurant. At night, North Beach is home to the neon-studded 'strip' of cabaret and jazz clubs, strip joints, coffee bars and restaurants, all clustered around Broadway and Columbus. At **Finocchio's** (506 Broadway, 415-982 9388), a local institution since 1936, you can see

'fabulous female impersonators' (drag queens, please!) in three revues starting at 8.30pm Thursday to Saturday. **Roaring 20s** (552 Broadway, 415-788 6765) is one of the city's most famous nude nightclubs. Go if you must, but be warned, you'll definitely not find any parking nearby so take a cab.

Coit Tower: On Telegraph Hill in North Beach district. This is the highest point on Telegraph Hill and was built as a monument to San Francisco's firefighters. The hills are so steep here you'll see cars parked at right angles to the kerb to stop them rolling away. Open daily from 10am to 6pm ($3), the tower has breathtaking views of the bay and city below and you'll even be able to make out the twists and turns of San Francisco's most famous road, **Lombard Street**, to the east.

Nob Hill: One of the poshest districts of the city, it takes its name from a contraction of the Hindu word 'nabob' – a person, especially European, who has made a large fortune in India or another country of the East. In this case, the 'nobs' made their fortunes in the West of the mid-1800s in gold, silver and the Central Pacific Railroad. This is where the mega-rich built their huge, over-the-top mansions that had lowlanders coming from far and wide just to stare at them. But the steep streets were a bit too much to handle, so the millionaire hill-dwellers installed their own cable car line, which still operates today! These days one of the top attractions is the **Fairmont Hotel** (950 Mason Street, 415-772 5000), where a penthouse suite with butler, maid and limousine service goes for $6,000 a day. See how the other half live and take the (free!) glass elevator ride to the 24th storey **Crown Room** for spectacular views of the city and bay. Then treat yourself to one of the best Sunday brunches in the city at the top. The hotel is also home to the intimate **New Orleans Room** (Lobby Level, 415-772 5259), a Mecca for jazz musicians and fans from the world over. You may like to know that the nearby Huntington Hotel's secluded suites have provided the perfect hideaway for royals (Prince Charles, Princess Margaret and Princess Grace) and stars (Pavarotti, Lauren Bacall and Alistair Cooke) alike.

Chinatown: You enter the 24 blocks of hustle, bustle, exotic shops, restaurants, food markets, temples and museums through Dragon's Gate at Grant Avenue and Bush Street. This is the biggest Chinatown outside Asia and immigrants keep on arriving. It's the complete opposite to all things American – the streets are narrow, crowded and alive. Grant Avenue is usually considered the most important street, though for the *real* Chinatown, take a walk down Stockton Street, while Portsmouth Square at Clay and Kearny Streets is considered the centre of life – this is where the locals gather for board games, discussions and t'ai chi rituals. Stroll around the herb shops that sell ancient potions to cure everything from rheumatism to sex problems, enjoy some dim sum for lunch and watch fortune cookies being made. If you're visiting San Francisco in February, then don't miss the Chinese New Year celebrations when a week-long festival culminates in a huge Downtown parade including a block-long Golden Dragon.

Union Square and Powell Street: By day, a chic stretch of boutiques, antique stores, gourmet shops, delicatessens and classy restaurants. In a Knightsbridge-style setting you'll find the fun Nike Town plus Armani, Cartier, Hermes, Gucci, Nieman-Marcus and Macy's around Maiden Lane and Stockton Street. Powell Street is home to Saks Fifth Avenue and the trendy **Urban Outfitters** (80 Powell). Take a break for brunch at **Sears** – the 1950s setting is just perfect for eggs over easy and constant coffee. At night, the singles bars are the main attraction.

Lori's Diner (336 Mason Street, 415-392 8646) serves up good old-fashioned food in a 50s Americana setting, while movie memorabilia, state-of-the-art video and audio entertainment are the hallmark of **Planet Hollywood** (2 Stockton Street, 415-421 7827).

A little further south is the **South of Market** district, where you'll find plenty of evening entertainment. The **Cadillac Bar** (1 Holland Court, 415-543 8226) has live guitar music under ceiling fans in an authentic Mexican setting. **Za Spot** (371 11th Street, 451-552 5599) is good for people-watching as tasty pastas, pizzas and salads at good-value prices are served up in a fun environment. **Cyberworld** (528 Folsom Street, 451-278 9669) is the place to web-watch or just relax and sip a caffe latte with a twirl of raspberry while taking in panoramic views of the bay and bridge. One of the most famous bars in the Bay area is **Holy Cow** (1531 Folsom Street, 415-621 6087), where tourists rub shoulders with locals and regulars and the DJs spin hits from the 70s, 80s and 90s.

Not far away is the **Museum of Modern Art** (151 3rd Street, 415-357 4000), which houses a pretty good collection in a nice building and has a café that's great for tea in comfy leather chairs.

Restaurants

Pick a restaurant, any restaurant, in San Francisco and you'll get a good meal, but here are a selection of favourites. **Fog City Diner** (1300 Battery Street, 415-982 2000) is an upscale restaurant which dishes up innovative food with fresh shellfish daily and take-outs (doggy bags) on all items. **42 Degrees** (235 16th Street, 415-777 5588) is a trendy, upmarket restaurant, that serves Californian cuisine. **Infusion** (555 Second Street, 415-543 2282) is a casual but classy bar and restaurant with live acoustic music and vodka infusion bar. The **Vertigo Restaurant and Bar** (600

11

Montgomery Street, 415-433 7250) at the base of the Transamerica pyramid in the financial district, is a favourite haunt of movers and shakers. Delicious food and live music.

Hotels

I've lost count of the number of times people have told me: 'I've just got back from visiting friends in San Francisco'. But for all those of you who aren't in that lucky position of having accommodation on tap, here are a selection of hotels, ranging from budget to deluxe. The **Hotel Griffin** (155 Stewart Street, 415-495 2100) offers comp breakfasts, parking and stylish rooms from from $145 a double. At Nob Hill, the **Fairmont Hotel** (950 Mason Street, 415-772 5000), which has appeared in many movies – from Hitchcock's *Vertigo* to *Towering Inferno, The Rock* and *Sudden Impact* – will set you back around $230 a night for a double room. The **Ramada Plaza Hotel** (590 Bay Street, 415-885 4700) is within walking distance of Pier 41 and ferries to Alcatraz. Doubles from $150. **Ocean Park** (2690 46th Avenue, 415-566 7020) offers doubles from $47 depending on the season and is just minutes from Golden Gate Park. Downtown is the **Hotel Nikko** (222 Mason Street at O'Farrell, 415-394 1111) where doubles start at $280. Just steps from Union Square and the theatre district, like its sister hotel in Los Angeles, the Nikko offers fine dining and the very latest technology in all rooms.

Wine country

Before leaving San Francisco, take a day trip to the Napa and Sonoma Valleys, one hour north, that are home to California's vineyards (Americans call them wineries) and a favourite weekend retreat for wealthy San Franciscans. Route 12 winds its way between the two valleys which lie either side of the Mayacamas Mountains, where you'll see row upon row of vines in rolling, fertile

countryside. Most of the vineyards are open to the public and offer tours explaining the wine-making process that culminate in the all-important tasting (usually for little or no charge). If you plan to do an *Abolutely Fabulous* re-creation of Eddie and Patsy's visit to a French vineyard, make sure someone else is driving! One of my favourites in the Napa Valley is the nineteenth-century monastery and vineyards of the **Christian Brothers**, who produce very good Chardonnay (or was that because it was about the fifth vineyard I'd been to in a day?). For a more European vineyard look, try the Sonoma Valley where many of the buildings resemble Tuscan villas, Spanish haciendas or even French châteaux. The **Viansa** at the southern end of Sonoma Valley would be perfectly at home in Tuscany and even has an Italian marketplace next door where a huge cellar is packed with sauces, antipasti, oils and nibbles for you to try. Buy a selection of cheeses and breads and retire to the stone terrace with some of the vineyard's Chardonnay or Cabernet Sauvignon for a delicious lunch in an idyllic setting.

For a complete one-day printed excursion itinerary to some of Napa Valley's vineyards, shops, restaurants and health resorts, including time of tours and discounts, contact **Wine Country in a Day Itinerary** (60 Park Street, 415-550 8025). The **Napa Valley Wine Train** (from the station at 1275 McKinstry Street, Napa, 800-427 4124) takes you on a non-stop, three-hour trip through the Napa Valley on board a lovingly restored 1915 Pullman car. It runs every day year-round, but reservations are necessary. You can opt for brunch, lunch or dinner. For those wine-lovers among you who would like to spend more time in the valleys and vineyards, **Arblaster and Clarke Wine Tours Ltd** (01730 893344) organise week-long tours to the region.

South of San Francisco, three routes lead to the stunning Monterey Peninsula: Highway One, the coastal highway, goes via Half Moon Bay, Santa Cruz and Monterey Bay; Highway 280, a scenic freeway connects with US 101 at San José; and Highway 101, the Bayshore Freeway. It's about 2½ hours' drive to the Peninsula, so leave early in the morning – that way you will be able to fit in all the sights on your way to your final destination of the day: the fabulous Madonna Inn (more about that later). Incidentally, before you start your tour you can get a complete B&B directory of California, from CABBI, 2715 Porter Street, Soquel, CA, 95073, enclosing $4 for postage. The guide lists members of the California Association of Bed and Breakfast Inns (CABBI) by city and in alphabetical order with distances to major attractions.

The Monterey Peninsula

The **Monterey Peninsula** is known for the historic towns of Monterey and Carmel. The pretty villages – a true rarity in America – are incredibly popular and sit either side of the Peninsula, which forms the not-to-be-missed 17-mile drive past Pebble Beach Championship Golf Course and colonies of elephant seals and otters.

At the fishing village of **Monterey** you'll find that the old canneries (fish-canning companies) immortalised by Steinbeck, have been converted into shops, bars and an aquarium. Fisherman's Wharf, a tourist trap if ever you saw one, is worth a visit if only to lunch out at one of the many bars and restaurants that are famous for free jazz. If you want to stay in the peninsula area a little longer, then the top attraction is the **Monterey Bay Aquarium** (886 Cannery Row, Monterey, 408-648 4888). A new exhibit called *The Inside Story* shows you everything from who fixes the meals each day for all the fish and what's involved in raising an orphaned sea otter pup. Ahhh!

One of the most important things that Clint Eastwood did for **Carmel** during his time as mayor was to help preserve its heritage so it retains its pretty (quaint by American standards) cottages covered in flowers and beautiful views of the sea. He gave up his mayorship a while ago, but still has an interest in the Hog's Breath Bar and Mission Ranch. You'll find most of the shops and restaurants in the Central Square.

After brunch at Carmel, follow Highway One down to the coastline past the *Big Sur* and spectacular *Brixby Bridge* for the two-hour trip to Hearst Castle in San Simeon.

Hearst Castle™: 100 Hearst Castle Road, San Simeon, 1-800 444 4445. One of the last great estates produced by America's Gilded Age, this was the famous home of the intriguing and complex American billionaire William Randolph Hearst before it was handed over to the American public. Designed and built from 1919 to 1947, the estate consists of 165 rooms filled with fine and decorative art collections, and 127 acres of gardens, terraces and

11

walkways. Four daytime tours lasting one hour and 45 minutes run daily except certain holidays (adults $14, 6–12s $8, under 6s free), plus evening tours in the spring and autumn (adults $25, 6–12s $13, under 6s free). The big new 'attraction' is the 40-minute large-format film experience, which gives a fascinating insight into the building of the castle and considerable care that was taken over the most minute details. *Hearst Castle – Building the Dream* is shown at the Hearst Castle Theater every hour at half past the hour and costs $6 for adults, $4 for juniors. Reservations can be made in advance by calling 1-800 444 4445 between 8am and 5pm any day of the week.

If you check your timings carefully, you should just about be able to squeeze in a tour and watch the film before moving on to your hotel for the evening, the fabulous Madonna Inn. To get there follow the Pacific Coast Highway south to San Luis Obispo, join the 101 going south and take the Madonna Road exit just south of the town.

Madonna Inn: (100 Madonna Rd, San Luis Obispo, 805-543 3000 for information or 805-543 9666 for reservations). One of the most sumptuous hotels – in the over-the-top, camp Liberace style – that you will ever come across, this inn is well worth a visit if not an overnight stay! Built by the architect husband and interior designer wife team of Alex and Phyllis Madonna, the 109 rooms are all individually decorated to their own theme from the Old West to Spanish, the Caveman and the luxurious Austrian Suite. There is no room more ornate, elaborate or laden with sumptuousness from the cosy, deep-pink, round chairs to the wood-carvings, copper and brass accent and custom-etched glass than the Gold Rush Dining Room, where delicious seafood and steak dinners are served and live entertainment is provided for dancing. Truly unmissable!

From here it's about two hours' drive south to Los Angeles, straight down Highway 101 or a little longer if you insist on seeing the fantastic views from the Pacific Coast Highway.

Los Angeles

Welcome to la-la land, lotus land or El Lay – the place where you don't need to go to a theme park to see some extraordinary sights; the land of fast cars and freeways, nose jobs and every other kind of plastic surgery known to man; of movie stars and trophy wives, fantastic weather and superb beaches filled to the brim with beautiful people just doing their thing. This is not only a place to see but, like San Francisco, a city to experience – and it'll take you some time because it's huge – covering a massive 467 square miles with a population of 3.7 million people. Los Angeles county is in a desert basin (winter temperatures of 15–21°C/60–70°F, summer 25–30°C/80–90°F with an average of 329 days of sunshine a year) surrounded by the San Gabriel Mountains and divided by the Santa Monica Mountains. It includes 160 miles of coastline with altitudes ranging from nine feet below sea level to 10,080 feet above.

La-la land was born on 4 September 1781 when a handful of Spaniards, Native Americans, blacks and mestizos (people of mixed race) first settled in what is now known as Downtown. It was named El Pueblo de Nuestra Señora la Reina

LOS ANGELES

de los Angeles – the town of our Queen of the Angels – and was a territory of Spain. After it changed hands to Mexico in 1835, Los Angeles was declared a city. In 1846, American soldiers entered LA and the Stars and Stripes have flown over the city since January 1847. That was just one year before the famous Gold Rush, when the precious metal was found in Coloma Valley.

Since then it has become home to the American film industry, Disneyland® Resort in California and Universal Studios®. Our fascination with stars and the whole celebrity lifestyle means that nearly a million Brits are visiting California every year and, with incredibly cheap transatlantic airfares now on offer, that figure is sure to rise.

Packed with restaurants, hotels, theme parks, beaches and a whole host of shopping opportunities, it is impossible for me, in this mini tour, to provide you with the most comprehensive listings of everything on offer. So I've stuck to the important things – the places that make LA tick, where you're most likely to see the stars, where you can do heavy-duty damage to your credit cards while shopping and finally, how to just relax and enjoy yourself with all the beaches and water sports. This is my high-lighted tour within the Grand Tour of places you mustn't miss out on in LA.

As with all things American, it's location, location, location, darling – and in LA that means avoiding the eastside (crummy). Think westside – Beverly Hills, Sunset Boulevard, Melrose Avenue, Malibu and Santa Monica. That's where the beautiful people go to see and be seen. If you want to go east, venture no further than Los Feliz, the funky, kitsch, up-and-coming neighbourhood near Hollywood, or Silver Lake district.

The top attractions are: Disneyland® Resort in California, Universal Studios®, the Walk of Fame, Rodeo ('ro-day-o', darlink!) Drive, Venice Beach, Mann's Chinese

Theater, Sunset Boulevard, Santa Monica, Knott's Berry Farm®, Marina del Rey and the Queen Mary in Long Beach.

Getting about

Given its size and the myriad of freeways – 500 miles of them criss-crossing greater LA – you'll need to know how to get about. First off, each Southern California freeway has both a number and a name, usually called after its final destination as viewed from Downtown. Thus the stretch of Interstate 10 between Downtown and Santa Monica is called the Santa Monica Freeway, and the stretch heading east out of Downtown is known as the San Bernardino Freeway because that's the place where the road once ended.

★ ★ ★ ★ **INSIDE TRACK** ★ ★ ★ ★
★   ★
★   When getting on and off   ★
★   freeways, the signs may say   ★
★   something like Sacramento,   ★
★   which is more than 400 miles   ★
★   away from LA. Remember, signs   ★
★   are based on a big city in the   ★
★ general direction of the traffic so ★
★ always think 'big picture' when it ★
★ comes to LA road signs and have ★
★   your map handy!   ★
★ ★ ★ ★ ★ ★ ★ ★ ★ ★ ★ ★ ★ ★ ★ ★ ★ ★

Highway 110 heading south is Harbor Freeway, heading north it's Pasadena Freeway. Highway 60 is the Pomona. Interstate 5 heading south is the Santa Ana Freeway, heading north it's the Golden State. Highway 1, the Pacific Coast Highway, is known as PCH to locals. In addition, regardless of what the maps may call these roads, Angelenos have their own rules regarding names and numbers. The Santa Monica Freeway is only ever called the Ten and the San Diego Freeway, the 405. Others, though, are only ever referred to by their

LOS ANGELES AREA

SAN GABRIEL MOUNTAINS

San Fernando Valley

San Gabriel Valley

Pasadena

Burbank

North Hollywood

Universal Studios

Los Feliz

Silver Lake

LOS ANGELES

Downtown

Monterey Park

Long Beach

Alamitos Bay

Knott's Berry Farm

Anaheim

Disneyland

Hollywood

West Hollywood

Beverley Hills

Rodeo Drive Shopping

Bel Air

Getty Center

Brentwood

Santa Monica

Venice

Marina del Rey

Manhattan Beach

Hermosa Beach

Redondo Beach

Sunset Blvd.

Montana Ave.

3rd Street Promenade

Malibu

PACIFIC OCEAN

N
W E
S

name, such as the Hollywood
Freeway, which is the segment of the
101 that runs north-west to south-east.
Other sections of the 101 are called
the Pasadena Freeway, but are only
ever referred to by their number. But
the Ventura Freeway is referred to by
name, not number. So you've got all
that now, yes?!

Angelenos love their cars and
love to drive them fast and frequently.
Out of nine million people living in LA
county, there are seven million
vehicles – with an average of 3.3 car
trips a day per vehicle. All ten of the
nation's most heavily travelled
interchanges are in southern
California. At peak times – 6 to
10am and 4 to 7pm – you'll need
your wits about you and probably
won't go anywhere fast. At other
times, many of the freeways will still
be pretty crowded, so always allow
plenty of time to get to your final
destination. Some freeways have
specific lanes for car pools which can
only be used when two or more
people are travelling in the same car.
If you travel in them alone, you face
fines of up to $300. It is also a
ticketable offence to be stuck in the
middle of a busy intersection once the
light turns red, so make sure you can
clear the intersection before driving
into heavy traffic. There are also stiff
fines for not wearing a seat belt.

★ ★ ★ **INSIDE TRACK** ★ ★ ★
★   ★
★   ★
★ Parking is a nightmare in LA but ★
★ always keep a good supply of   ★
★ change for when you do spot a   ★
★ meter!   ★
★ ★ ★ ★ ★ ★ ★ ★ ★ ★ ★ ★ ★ ★ ★ ★

So now you know how to get
around, where do you go first? To
make life simpler, I've divided up the
areas and put in where to go, what to
see, where to shop, eat, drink and be
merry, in that zone. No doubt about
it, Hollywood will probably be top of
your list, so why not start there?

Hollywood

Home to **Mann's Chinese Theater**
(6925 Hollywood, 213-464 8111)
and the **Walk of Fame**, which runs all
the way down both sides of
Hollywood Boulevard between La
Brea and Argyle and even goes up
into Vine Street, this area is actually
well on the seedy side now, but is a
good starting point for all the tours
that show you everything you want to
know about Hollywood.

The **Clarion Hollywood Roosevelt
Hotel** (7000 Hollywood Boulevard,
213-466 7000) suffers from faded
grandeur but is full of history. It was
once home to Charlie Chaplin and
Douglas Fairbanks. The Presidential
Suite retains original furnishings from
the time when Carole Lombard and
Clark Gable played away from home
there, and has a picture-perfect view
of the famous Hollywood signpost
(built in 1923 to promote a real
estate development called
Hollywoodland, it lost its last four
letters over the years, but gained
status as *the* Hollywood logo) and all
the other Hollywood landmarks.
Despite major renovations, the
paintwork is a bit tatty, the wallpaper
is peeling off the servants' quarters
and a night at the two-storey
apartment would set you back
$1,500 plus tax (14% for hotels).
Still, other rooms start at $110 and
you can stay in the swimming pool
area, where Marilyn Monroe stayed,
from around $130 a night.

After David Hockney was
commissioned to paint the swimming
pool (blue with fish) it had to be
designated a work of art to get
around local laws that all pools have
to be painted white.

The hotel was the first built in
Hollywood and hosted the first ever
Oscar ceremony in 1929, but it's a
spooky place that enjoys its
association with ghosts and ghoulies
from the 30s and 40s Golden Era.
Ask to see the mirror where Marilyn's
ghost was once spotted and the
ballroom that is now home to a

ghostly cold patch. Stars still stay at the hotel after they have been inaugurated into the Walk of Fame or had their hands and feet cast for the concrete slabs outside Mann's Chinese Theater, which is more or less opposite the hotel. Just north of Hollywood Boulevard on Vine is the HQ of **Capitol Records** (1750 Vine), a gloriously purple, circular building designed to look like a stack of records, and with a mural to celebrate the golden era of jazz.

Museums: The recently-opened **Hollywood Entertainment Museum** (7021 Hollywood Boulevard, 213-465 7900) gives you the behind-the-scenes low-down on movies, TV, radio and recording. You can see restored sets, hi-tech interactive stations, multimedia exhibits and memorabilia. You can even add sound effects to a film and learn other trade secrets. After beaming up in the *Star Trek* transporter, supping a beer at the *Cheers* bar will get you back down to earth nicely! **Frederick's of Hollywood** (6608 Hollywood Boulevard, 213-466 8506), a retro exhibit of stars' undies, opened in 1946 and has everything from Joan Crawford's petticoats to bras worn by Madonna, Cher and Natalie Wood.

Tours: Try **Graveline Tours** (213-469 4149 or 1-800 797 DEAD) for a 2½-hour tour in a hearse of Hollywood's best-known deaths and scandals. Daily except Monday at 9.30am from Hollywood Boulevard. For $40, you get a memorial folder with maps. **Starline Tours** (213-463 3333) promises to show you at least 50 to 60 star homes in a two-hour tour of Beverly Hills and Bel Air that leaves daily from the Chinese Theater ($29). The **Los Angeles Nighthawks** (310-392 1500) specialise in VIP nights on the town by limousine or luxury bus. Customised itineraries include live music, cabaret, comedy or dance clubs. Prices start at $250 for four hours for a minimum of two people and get cheaper depending on the number of people in your

group (limos hold 12 people). Daytime music history tours are also available.

Eating: Pinot Hollywood (1448 North Gower Street, 213-461 8800) is one of celeb-chef Joachim Splichal's less pricey restaurants but the star of the show in the area is beyond a doubt the Japanese palace of **Yamashiro** (1999 North Sycamore Avenue, 213-466 5125), which serves excellent Japanese cuisine in a great setting with a great view.

Evenings: The place to get into in the area is the **Magic Castle**, the famous magician's club on Sycamore Avenue just behind Yamashiro, for dinner with a showcase by a top illusionist. Strictly speaking, it's not open to members of the general public, but a good hotel concierge (try the Roosevelt) should be able to get you in for the right kind of tip! The **Palace** (1735 North Vine Street, 213-462 3000) a 1,200-capacity bi-level club that plays host to major gigs, recently reopened after a million dollars' worth of renovations. Star acts have included Nirvana, Smashing Pumpkins and Nine Inch Nails.

East Hollywood

The Silver Lake District (known to locals as Swish Alps because of its large gay community) is a funky neighbourhood around Sunset and Vermont Avenue, which is frequented by celebs, young people and world-class designers. This area is the Carnaby Street of LA, filled with hand-beaded cardies, retro 60s clothing, alligator handbags and chunky necklaces. **Soap Plant**, for instance, sells everything from soaps to body oils and cards. The area borders **Los Feliz** in North Vermont and Hollywood, a drab but fairly funky zone populated by up-and-coming wannabees, music people (Herb Alpert has his studios on La Brea, as do A&M Studios) and home to trendy boutiques and street vendors. You can sip coffee in 50s café **Onyx Sequel** (1804 North Vermont) before

11

California lingo

PLACES

The Bev Cen	The Beverly Center shopping centre.
BH	Beverly Hills.
The Boo	Malibu, also the 'Bu.
Bortsch belt	The Fairfax district (because of the heavily Jewish, elderly population).
Boys' Town	West Hollywood (because of its large gay population).
Bronzeville	East Los Angeles (due to the largely Latino population).
Eastside	The eastside of the city that consists of mostly lower-income families, immigrants and *real* artists.
Flats	The flat streets of Beverly Hills below Sunset Boulevard.
Ghost town	Downtown LA.
The Hills	Hollywood Hills.
The Motherland	South Central Los Angeles.
The Nickel	Skid row, Downtown.
NoHo	North Hollywood.
No-man's-land	The eastern area of Downtown, where the artists' lofts are.
Over the hill	Valley talk for LA or Beverly Hills or Hollywood talk for Burbank where many of the TV studios are.
The Palisades	Pacific Palisades, also Pali.
Smurf Village	Any White middle-class suburb.
So Paz	South Pasadena.
Swish Alps	Silver Lake (due to its large gay community).
Valley	Often a disparaging term for the San Fernando Valley and its towns. Also, valley girl, val speak and vals.
WeHo	West Hollywood.
Westside	The affluent, mostly white sections of the west side of LA, eg West Hollywood, Beverly Hills, Bel Air.

MONEY

Century	100 dollar bill, *also* C-note
Dead presidents	Folding money, bills, *also* Presidents.
Deuce	Two dollars.
Dime	Five-dollar bill, also fin, finski, five-spot, fiver.
Jacks	Dollars.

Moolah	Money, also dinero (Spanish), ducats, bucks, green, paper, government art collection.

EVERYDAY

Action	Used to intensify nouns, eg 'Major traffic action on Sunset', or can be used in the context of (getting) sex.
As if	No way!
ATM	A generous, wealthy father – automatic teller machine.
Barhopper	Person who hangs out at bars (any Brit!).
Beam me up, Scotty	From *Star Trek*, used to indicate that someone needs a reality check.
Bike dyke	Female motorcycle cop.
BK lounger	Burger King.
Brain fart	A clumsy error or careless remark.
Burly	Exceptionally cold (anything below 7°C/45°F in California!).
Buy 'n' die	A Hyundai.
Caddie	Cadillac.
Confuser	A computer to anyone over the age of 30!
Cooked	Drunk or stoned.
Cyclist	Psychiatrist (short for trick cyclist).
Don't go there	A subject best left unmentioned.
Earth to ...	Used with a person's name, implies they are out of touch with reality.
Fat pockets	Rich.
Get out	I can't believe it, also get out of here (as in Eddie Murphy's favourite phrase in *Beverly Hills Cop*).
Hel-lo	That's obvious, *or* Wake up and smell the coffee: 'Hel-lo, that was a red light you just went through!'
Hi-didge	Expensive (from high digits).
Hondo	A tourist (you!).
'Hood	Neighbourhood.
Honeywagon	Female toilet – originally the trailer used as a women's toilet on set.
I don't THINK so	No way, no chance.
Joe six-pack	An average guy.
Kickin'	Great, happening.
Limo lock	Gridlock at a celeb-heavy event.
Mickey D's	McDonald's, also Mac's, Mick D's.

11

Oil spill	Visit from a rich relative who pays for everything.
Open the lunch box	Pass wind.
Park the love Porsche	Have sex.
Passion boat	Big, luxurious car, usually something a pimp would drive.
Retail action	Shopping.
Shade	A suntan.
Sighting	Spotting a celebrity.
Squeeze the lemon	Hurry up to make a yellow light. *Also,* Punch the sun.
Somebody needs a nap	Indicates someone's getting irritable.
Tag the lawn	Urinate in public.
Thank you for sharing that	Oh do shut up.
The 411	Information. 'What's the 411 on Robert?'
To attend class	Watch TV.
To be comped	To be treated, have the tab picked up (originally Las Vegas speak).
To breathe blue	Stay calm, based on New Age speak for the colour of the calm aura.
To dish	Gossip.
To fade	Ignore or snub someone.
To have a hard on	Be very enthusiastic about something.
To have a heat on	To be drunk.
To make a collect call	Get someone else to pay for something, such as dinner!
Tree hugger	An environmental activist
TV parking	Parking that's too good to be true – close, immediate and legal (taken from the unrealistic ease with which cars are parked on TV).
Video moment	A special, cherished moment.
Whistle bait	An attractive person.

The Elvis tour

Here are ten places where the King used to go. If you plan to visit them all, allow at least half a day.

1. **The lake shrine of the Self-Realization Fellowship** (17190 Sunset). The Pacific Palisades shrine where Elvis went to relax and meditate.
2. **Pacific Coast Highway.** He loved to ride his motorbike between Sunset Boulevard and Malibu.
3. **The Perugia Way House** (500 block in Perugia Way). His first home in LA, a Bel Air rental, and the place where Elvis met the Beatles.
4. **De Neve Park on Beverly Glen Boulevard** (just north of Sunset Boulevard), where he played football with his pals on Sunday afternoons.
5. **1100 block of Hillcrest Road in Beverly Hills:** site of the home he bought for Priscilla and Lisa Marie.
6. **Beverly Wilshire Hotel** (9500 Wilshire Boulevard). He stayed here when he first moved West until he was kicked out for playing one too many pranks.
7. **CBS Television City** (7800 Beverly Boulevard). The place where he made his first appearance on The Ed Sullivan Show.
8. **Mann's Chinese Theater** (6925 Hollywood Boulevard). Elvis often used to go to the landmark Hollywood cinema and saw *Patton* there three times.
9. **Red Velvet** (6507 Sunset Boulevard). The club he used to hang out in. Now it's Club Lingerie.
10. **Radio Recorders** (7000 Santa Monica Boulevard). The studio where Elvis recorded many of his hits, including 'Jailhouse Rock'. Incidentally, he recorded more songs in LA than anywhere else in the US.

checking out the Beastie Boys' cool boutique **X-Large & X-Girl Store** (1768 North Vermont).
Evenings: The eccentric, 50s **Tiki Ti** (4427 Sunset) is perfect for cocktails and great chat-up lines, as is the **Good Luck Bar** (1514 Hilhurst). The **Derby** (4500 Los Feliz, 213-663 8979) is a firm favourite with swingers, who strut their stuff in surroundings that hark back to more elegant days. If the queues look too long, you can always head over to The **Dresden Room** (1760 North Vernon, 310-358 1880), an unmissable spot for star-spotting and bizarre cabaret acts.

West Hollywood

(Including Melrose Avenue and La Brea) **Morton's** (8764 Melrose Avenue, 310-276 5205) is famous for power-packed movie-mogul diners on

Mondays. Joachim Splichal, second only to Wolfgang Puck in the chef-star stakes, serves expensive French/Californian food at **Patina** (5955 Melrose, 213-467 1108). Eddie Murphy and Denzel Washington's **Georgia** (7520 Melrose, 213-933 8420) serves up sophisticated Southern dishes. **Campanile** (624 South La Brea, 213-938 1447) is famous for its elegant Californian/Italian food. Investors in **Thunder Roadhouse** (West Hollywood, 213-650 6011) include Dennis Hopper and Peter Fonda and the restaurant, a tribute to the Harley-Davidson lifestyle, was opened by Mickey Rourke, while Whoopi Goldberg, Steven Seagal and Joe Pesci have all put money into **Eclipse** (West Hollywood, 213-933 8420). Then there is **restaurant row** on La Cienega, which boasts fine

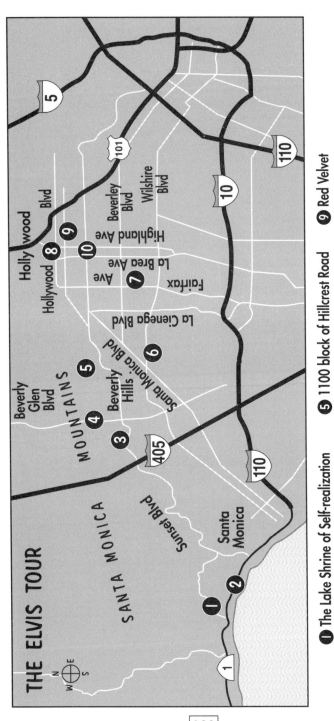

THE ELVIS TOUR

1 The Lake Shrine of Self-realization
2 Pacific Coast Highway
3 500 block of Perugia Way
4 De Neve Park on Beverly Glen Blvd
5 1100 block of Hillcrest Road
6 Beverley Wilshire Hotel
7 CBS Television City
8 Chinese Theater
9 Red Velvet
10 Radio Records

Watch a taping of a show

Tapings are free but you will need patience. Be ready to queue and to be turned away even if you have tickets – studios are small and they tend to overbook to guarantee a full house. Also, be prepared for some wannabe actor 'coaching' you for half an hour beforehand on what you *must* do (when to laugh etc.) and what you *can't* do (eg talk or take photos) during the taping. Humour them as this is probably the closest they'll get to a stage! And do bear in mind that it can take up to four hours to get one 22-minute sitcom episode in the can.

The Tonight Show: Two tickets per person are given out at 8am on the day of the taping at the NBC ticket booth in Burbank (they're usually easy to get) or you can get four tickets if you write in advance (at least two to three weeks) to 3000 West Alameda, Burbank 91523, enclosing an sae. You can call the 24-hour hotline on 818-840 3537 for information on forthcoming guests.

Frasier, In The House and other sitcoms and talk shows filmed at Paramount Studios: You can make reservations by phone five working days before filming and get the latest taping schedules on 213-956 1777. You must reconfirm by phone between 9am and 12 noon on taping day and always queue up earlier than they suggest.

The Price Is Right: Taped at CBS, near Farmers Market. Write for tickets four to six weeks in advance to 7800 Beverly Boulevard, LA 90036, enclosing an sae, or pick them up at the ticket booth up to one week before taping.

Wheel of Fortune: Send an sae to PO Box 3763, Hollywood 90028, with the number of tickets required, allowing at least two weeks (longer from the UK). Tapings are usually Thursdays, Fridays and Saturdays at 2pm and 5pm. Minimum age is eight.

Location shoots: The Entertainment Industry Development Office (7083 Hollywood, 213-957 1000) can provide you with free 'call sheets' of expected location shoots for any given day.

restaurants serving everything from Indian to Japanese, Korean, Jamaican and even the typical American steak! **Comedy and clubbing:** The **Improv** (never call it by its full name, the Improvisation, 8162 Melrose, 213-651 2583) routinely features big-name stand-up comics such as Billy Crystal and Robin Williams. The **Troubadour** (9801 Santa Monica Boulevard, 310-535 0579) is one of the oldest surviving clubs – it opened in 1957 – and has become part of music lore. This is where Elton John made his début in LA.
Shopping: Melrose (kitsch) and La Brea (lined with hip antique shops) are the places to go. At weekends Melrose gets packed with generation X-ers, café patios spill out on to most of the sidewalks (pavements) and the Harley Davidsons outside **Johnny**

Rockets diner are as perfectly aligned as the Rockettes. The whole area is not just good for shopping, but great for star-spotting and people-watching.
Melrose is the HQ of the interior design trade and hundreds of furniture and accessory shops are clustered around Robertson Boulevard and Melrose. At the **Pacific Design Center** (known locally as the Blue Whale or Green Giant), you can stop at the concierge desk to ask for a tour. **Fred Segal** on Melrose is a trendy, expensive clothes store used by the stars, while the kitsch **Yellowstone Clothing** store is on La Brea at Melrose. Running parallel to Melrose is Beverly Boulevard where you'll find **Re-Mix** (7650 Beverly), an unused vintage shoes store, and you can recharge your batteries at the gallery café **Insomnia** (7286 Beverly).

On **La Brea**, 1970s freaks will love **Ragsaver** (819 North La Brea), where you can pick up great gear for as little as $10; **Rag Cie** (La Brea and First) is a fabulous shoe boutique where vintage stock is mixed with contemporary pieces; and **Jet Rag** (825 North La Brea) is filled with fabulous handbags and embroidered Chinese slippers.

Sunset Strip

Sunset Boulevard in West Hollywood is *the* place to be after dusk for everything from cocktails to dinner, comedy to nightclubbing.

Within walking distance from each other on Sunset are the **Whiskey** (8901 Sunset, 310-535 0579), where the Doors, Led Zeppelin and the Kinks played, the **Roxy Theater** (9009 Sunset, 310-276 2222), another landmark showcase, and the **Viper Room** (8852 Sunset, 310-358 1880), Johnny Depp's seedy watering hole where River Phoenix died. Then there is **Billboard Live**, the embodiment of glitz (9039 Sunset, 310-786 1712), a newly opened, $5.5-million state-of-the-art music venue. If you can't get in you can watch the on-stage action on two 108-foot-high video monitors outside. It took $7 million to turn the **House of Blues** (8430 Sunset, 213-650 0476) into a rickety old Southern shack complete with corrugated metal roof and walls, but it is one of the hottest places in town. The brainchild of Dan Aykroyd and Hard Rock Café co-founder Isaac Tigrett, who wanted to nurture live blues as a unique art form, it features daily live performances of established and up-and-coming musicians and a Gospel Brunch on Sundays complete with a buffet of Southern food. Watch out for the opening of the stage from the restaurant when the bar running along the entire width of the house splits in two and is electronically moved to the sides, allowing you to watch the stage while you eat. The **Sky Bar** at the Mondrian Hotel (4440

Sunset, 800 525 8029) is the latest *in* place for stars and is famous for having the most beautiful bell-boys in town. You have to book months in advance for dinner, but you can treat yourself to an iced tea while enjoying a good snoop and checking out the amazing décor. **Spago** (the original at 1114 Horn Ave at Sunset, 310-652 4025) is the place to not just spot stars but also enjoy celebrity chef Wolfgang Puck's fine cuisine. You probably won't get an 8pm table, so go earlier and try lingering over your coffee! Then there is the star-saturated **Le Dôme** (8720 Sunset, 310-659 6919).

Comedy: The **Comedy Store** (8433 Sunset, 213-656 6225) has given many stars their first boost and even when they're famous they come back – Robin Williams once came out and did a 20-minute stand-up routine for people waiting on the street! The **Laugh Factory** (8001 Sunset, 213-656 1336), where Groucho Marx once had an office, now showcases new stars and is still one of the top comedy clubs in LA.

Shopping: Chalet Gourmet (7880 Sunset) is a European deli where Hugh Grant goes to buy British chocolate, and **Book Soup** (8818 Sunset) is a brilliant late-night book store.

Beverly Hills and Westside

Eating: Start the day at the **Westwood Marquis Hotel and Gardens** (930 Hilgard, 310-208 8765). It's famous for its breakfast buffet and lavish Sunday champagne brunch, which you eat in a delightfully airy, floral setting. For star-saturation there is the famous **Ivy** (113 North Robertson Boulevard, 310-274 8303); Wolfgang Puck's **ObaChine** (242 North Beverly Drive, 310-274 4440); the Italian **Pane e Vino** (8265 Beverly, 213-6514600), a gem of a Tuscan villa; and **Chaya Brasserie** (98741 Alden Drive, 310-859 8833), where John Travolta and Danny DeVito lunched in *Get Shorty*. The area is

also home to **Planet Hollywood** (9560 Wilshire Boulevard, 310-275 7828), the first branch of the famous chain owned by Arnie, Bruce, Demi and Sly. Film clips and videos play throughout the restaurant and you can get a close-up of the dress that sparked Robert Redford's *Indecent Proposal* plus Forrest Gump's box of chocolates among other artefacts. **Pangaea Restaurant and Bar** at the Hotel Nikko at Beverly Hills (465 South La Cienega, 310-247 2100) serves up the most wonderfully eclectic dishes in a beautiful setting, with live jazz on a Sunday lunchtime. Steven Spielberg is co-owner of the massive 'sub' (that's an American roll) eaterie **Dive!** (10250 Santa Monica Boulevard, 310-788 3483), which also has an outlet in Las Vegas. And the Beverly Hilton (9876 Wilshire, 310-274 7777) has launched the **Coconut Club**, a supper club celebrating the glory days of old Hollywood.
Shopping: The upscale Beverly Center (known locally as Bev Cen) is the home mall of many celebs. Barbra Streisand loves **Shauna Stein**, but it's unlikely you'll share a changing room with her (girls!) as her personal shopper takes clothes to her. Eddie Murphy is easy to spot – he turns up with two burly bodyguards, but other stars are more discreet – Jerry Seinfeld usually goes shopping in jeans with a baseball cap pulled low in front of his face, for instance. And you can check out the panoramic view of the Hollywood sign from the **Sam Goody** music store on the top floor. Not even London's posh Bond Street can compare with **Rodeo Drive**. This is where *Pretty Woman* Julia Roberts spent oodles of Richard Gere's money and it's worth driving down if only to soak up the posh cars and shops. But it's not for serious shopping unless you enjoy watching trophy wives, helped by snooty sales staff, drench themselves from head to toe in status gear from Cartier to Tiffany, Valentino to Christian Dior,

Louis Vuitton and Giorgio Armani. Someone's got to, I guess!

Malibu

Seriously posh, northern-most area of LA, where Bette Midler and Pierce Brosnan are known for buying their own groceries and often pop into Hughes Market. Paradise Cove beach is the main set for *Babewatch Nights* and the *Rockford Files* trailer. It is also the home of the original John Paul Getty museum, a replica Roman villa based on the elegant Villa dei Papiri, which was destroyed by Mount Vesuvius in AD 79. Currently closed for refurbishment, it is due to reopen in 2001 as the Getty Villa. The core of its exhibits will continue to be its colllection of Greek and Roman antiquities, while the villa itself and view down to the Malibu sea will continue to provide one of the most enjoyable and elegant settings for a museum.
Eating: Johnny Carson is an investor in another of Wolfgang Puck's celebrity haunts, **Granita**, at 23725 West Malibu Road, 310-456 0488.

Santa Monica

Packed with bars, boutiques, nightclubs and restaurants, locals dub it the People's Rebulic of Santa Monica because of its strict rent-control laws (anti-capitalist) and tolerance for street entertainers (anti-establishment)! It's a great place to go to get away from the LA smog and rub shoulders with the stars. The pier has shops and rides at **Pacific Park** – the view of the bay from the top of the ferris wheel is spectacular, while the latest attraction is the Action Ride Theater – arcade games and dancing at free summer twilight concerts, while the carousel is an historic monument. The pier has been used for filming *The Sting, Ruthless People* and *Funny Girl*, and underneath it is the new **UCLA Ocean Discovery Center** (310-393 6149) with aquariums and touch-tanks highlighting marine life in Santa Monica Bay.

Eating: Kick off your daily quest for close encounters with celebrities with breakfast at **Patrick's Roadhouse** (106 Entrada at Pacific Coast Highway, 310-459 4544). Arnie, Patrick Swayze and Johnny Carson have all been spotted at the funky diner. Or **Marmalade** (710 Montana), which is great for bagels and pancake breakfast. Good for lunch is the **Reel Inn** (1220 Third Street, 310-395 5538) a funky seafood restaurant near the water, co-owned by the Grateful Dead's Bob Weir, and the elegant but cool **JiRaffe** (502 Santa Monica, 310-917 6671) where award-winning chefs serve up Franco-Californian dishes to celebrity diners. Or try **Schatzi's** (3110 Main Street, 310-399 4800). Arnie Schwarzenegger contributed sausage recipes as well as the start-up cash along with his wife Maria Shriver and also has his office in the building. For dinner, why not try **Valentino** (3115 Pico Boulevard, near 31st, 310-829 4313). It is considered to be one of the best in LA (and there's some competiton) and owner Piero Selvaggio will make up special meals on request. Alternatively there's the popular **Ocean Park Omelette** parlor (2709 Main Street, 310-392 9025) or Wolfgang Puck's pricey but excellent **Chinois on Main** (2709 Main Street, 310-392 9025).

Shopping: Main and **Montana Avenue** on the city's north side offer upscale, one-off shops and are popular with well-off entertainment industry people and celebs who live in nearby neighbourhoods. **Star Wares** on Main specialises in celeb cast-offs, such as a beaded evening bustier from Cher, while stylish women's clothes can be found on Montana at shops like **Sara and Weathercare** and at **Giselle**. Montana is also home to the aromatherapy oils specialist **Palmetto** and a host of antique and home furnishing shops filled with Mexican silver, sofas, tables and chintz (obviously not everything you drool over will fit in the suitcase!). Closer to the beach is **3rd Street Promenade**, an outdoor pedestrian 'mall' (paved street) near Santa Monica Place, where you can browse, stroll, eat and people-watch. It's not as posh as Montana, but is filled with cinemas, restaurants, bookstores, street performers and shops that stay open so late you really do drop! **Borders** (1415 3rd Street) is filled with discount books and specially priced CDs. Sip on a caffe espresso while waiting for the free gift-wrapping of your groovy purchases.

Venice

Founded by Abbot Kinney in 1990, it is his vision of Venice (the Americans feel the need to explain that's in Italy!), complete with the Doges' Palace and other Venetian buildings. But peeling paint and modern shops in the Camden Market mould have all but overtaken any vestige of elegance. The ocean-front walkway (still referred to as a boardwalk although the original wood has long since been replaced by concrete) and pier are home to tarot tables and tattoo parlours, jugglers, dancers, musicians and skaters in bikinis. One of the most famous 'entertainers' is Harry Parry, a rollerblading guitarist, who almost single-handedly stopped the local council from banning stalls on the ocean-side of the boardwalk, much to the annoyance of the rent-paying shops opposite!

★ ★ ★ **INSIDE TRACK** ★ ★ ★
★   ★
★   ★
★ Don't walk down the cycle and ★
★ rollerblading paths or you'll have ★
★ irate local cyclists to contend ★
★ with! ★
★ ★ ★ ★ ★ ★ ★ ★ ★ ★ ★ ★ ★ ★ ★ ★ ★

Despite a recent $5.5-million renovation project that includes resurfacing the boardwalk and providing more entertainment areas for the street entertainers, it is having difficulty overcoming its seedy and sometimes threatening atmosphere. The presence of the Guardian Angels and regular half-hourly police patrols are both in recognition of the continuing menace caused by the drug and street gangs that were theoretically given the boot a few years ago. Who knows, by the time the new lighting (there is none after the 6pm sunset), pagodas and restrooms arrive, it may seem a little more safe come night-time.

The world-famous **Muscle Beach** draws weightlifters from all over the world to pump iron with the locals, though when I was there, it was the women who appeared to have more going for them in the muscles stakes than any of the male specimens! It is also famous for its basketball courts and was used extensively for filming *White Men Can't Jump*. Despite its seediness, Venice attracts up to 350,000 visitors over the weekend. Get a patio table at the **Sidewalk Café** (1401 Ocean Front Walk, 310-399 5547) to watch the boardwalk scene go by and gaze at the azure-blue sea, or try Dudley Moore's restaurant just off the beach – **72nd Market Street** (at 72nd Market Street, 310-392 8720).

Marina del Rey

One of the world's largest man-made, small-boat harbours, it is famous for whale watching (November to April), boat rentals, fishing trips (bass, barracuda and rock cod) and watersports. **Action Water Sports** (4144 Lincoln Boulevard, 310-306 9539) teach surfing and waterskiing year-round and windsurfing and kayaking in the summer. You can also ride a bike all the way up to Santa Monica on the beach cycle path – a great way to see the coast and pick your beach!

Eating: Start the day off in style with breakfast at the **Terrace Restaurant** in the Ritz-Carlton Hotel (4375 Admiralty Way, 310-823 1700) and take in the sweeping views of the bay.

Hotels

With more than 93,000 hotel rooms on offer, you won't have a hard time getting a room for the night and there is simply not enough space to give an extensive range of options. I have stuck to a few with real star appeal. The **Regal Biltmore** (506 South Grand Avenue, Downtown, 213-624 1011) has provided an elegant backdrop for many a movie including *Independence Day, Up Close and Personal, Forget Paris, True Lies* and *Pretty in Pink*. The nearby **Westin Bonaventure Hotel** (404 South Figueroa Street, 213-624 1000) is one of LA's largest hotels with citywide views from its Top of the Five restaurant on the 35th floor. It was used for filming *Logan's Run* even before it officially opened in 1976 and scenes from *In the Line of Fire, Rain Man, Ruthless People, Lethal Weapon II* and *True Lies* have all been filmed there. The **Plaza Hotel** (3540 South Figueroa Street, 213-748 4141) was used as a set for *The Bodyguard*. (Frighteningly, no current rack rates are available for any of the above!) The **Regent Beverly Wilshire** (9500 Wilshire Boulevard, 310-275 5200) was the perfect setting for *Pretty Woman* as it is right on Rodeo Drive and also featured in *Beverly Hills Cop*. Doubles start at $275. My personal favourite is the **Hotel Nikko** at Beverly Hills (465 South La Cienega, 310-247 0400) where doubles start at around $275. Geared up to movie and record-industry execs, it specialises in providing the very latest high-tech equipment in each of its rooms with large work desks, fax machines, remote control on everything from the TV to the radio and CD player (a selection of CDs is also available). There are speakers for the TV in the marble bathrooms, though not for the CDs, so for the most relaxing moment of the day, slip into the Japanese-style hot tub, which entirely covers you with water, switch the TV on to the classic music channel, pour yourself a large glass of red wine and sip with beautifully ripened Brie (or snack of your choice). You'll only be able to tear yourself away from the luxury of it all by the thought of sitting on the same seat that Denzel Washington sat on during one of the movie junkets that are often held in the hotel lobby or bumping into one of the many stars who frequent the hotel – Kevin Costner (known as the Honeyman because he loves honey with his breakfast), John Travolta, Dustin Hoffman, Denzel and Steven Spielberg have all stayed here. If you ask very, very nicely indeed, you may persuade the staff to let you see the Presidential Suite, where Sharon Stone used that infamous ice pick in *Basic Instinct*, Michael Douglas was set up in *The Game* and Robert Redford made his *Indecent Proposal* to Demi Moore (supposedly in a Las Vegas casino). You'll have no way of getting all the way up to the seventh floor by yourself as the Nikko is so determined to provide a discreet ambience for its celebrity clientèle that it has one of the most sophisticated security systems in place. The lift will only take you as far as the lobby from the underground car park and your special security-card key to your room will only allow you to take the lift to your own floor. Finally, one of the latest haunts of the stars is the **Mondrian** (8440 Sunset Boulevard, 213-650 8999), which has recently been completely refurbished and also houses the famous Sky Bar.

Museums

There are hundreds in LA but if I had to recommend just one it would have to be the **J Paul Getty Museum and Getty Center** in Brentwood Hills, just off the 405 freeway. Opened in December 1997 at a cost of $1 billion to accommodate an arts and cultural campus as well as exhibition space for the museum, the buildings and gardens are themselves a beautiful work of art with a sci-fiesque feel and plenty of curves to keep the feng shui experts happy. You arrive at this futuristic hill-top campus, entirely built out of white travertine stone (specially quarried in Bagni di Tivoli just outside Rome and guillotined for a rough-cut finish) via a tram that wends its way up the three-quarters of a mile ride from the entrance gate, and cannot fail to be struck by its majestic serenity.

The museum itself is a cluster of two-storey pavilions that are bridged by walkways on both levels so you naturally wander indoors and out as you view the works of art collected over a 15-year period of mass acquisition. The most famous is Van Gogh's 'Irises', and sophisticated designs to make the most of daylight will allow you to view the collections of art by Titian, Poussin, Rembrandt, Goya, Turner, Monet and Cézanne, among others, in as natural a setting as possible.

Audioguides, available in English and Spanish, can be picked up for $2 in the entrance hall with its huge glass door, and the Family Room has hands-on activities and games to help children make connections with the works of art displayed in the five galleries. Enjoy snacks and coffees in the beautiful courtyard before wandering off to inspect the gardens.

★ ★ ★ ★ **INSIDE TRACK** ★ ★ ★

★   ★
★   Go midweek and arrive well   ★
★ before opening time as queues ★
★ for the trams to the J Paul Getty ★
★   Museum build up quickly and   ★
★ standing in the boiling Californian ★
★   sun is not fun!   ★
★ ★ ★ ★ ★ ★ ★ ★ ★ ★ ★ ★ ★ ★ ★ ★ ★

Entrance is free, but parking costs $5 and reservations are necessary. You will need to call (310-440 7300) at least a week in advance and longer in summer. If you can't park, go by bus or taxi. It is open from 10am to 6pm at weekends, from 11am to 7pm Tuesdays and Wednesdays and

11am to 9pm on Thursdays and Fridays. It is closed Mondays and major holidays. Be warned, the Getty is one of the top attractions in LA – a Mecca for locals and tourists alike, so the queues do get bad. They do have a landing pad, though, so hiring a helicopter may be one answer!

Other museums worth a visit include The **Geffen Contemporary** (152 North Central Avenue), an innovative and popular exhibition of modern art that was once a temporary gallery, but is now permanently housed in a Little Tokyo warehouse in Downtown. Nearby is **MOCA**, the Museum of Contemporary Art (250 South Grand Avenue). Housed in a dramatic building that was designed by Japanese architect Arata Isozaki, it has a permanent collection of twentieth-century artists. On Thursday evenings there are free outdoor concerts. Hours for both are 11am to 5pm Tuesdays to Sundays (11am to 8pm Thursdays). Closed Mondays and major holidays. Phone 213-626 6222 for information and directions, 213-626 6828 to book.

Miracle Mile, the stretch of Wilshire Boulevard between La Brea and Fairfax, is so dubbed because of its scattering of Art Deco landmarks and grand shops. There are also five museums within walking distance of each other in this area, starting with the biggest of them all, the **Los Angeles County Museum of Art** (LACMA, known locally as the County Museum) at 5905 Wilshire (213-857 6000), which is a complex filled with multi-cultural architecture styles. It opens late on Fridays when free live jazz in the courtyard leaves the galleries pleasantly uncrowded. At the **Petersen Automotive Museum** (6060 Wilshire, 213-930 2277) – a complete history of the automobile – you can sit in an Indy 500 car and drool over Clark Gable's '56 Benz. East is the **Carole and Barry Kaye Museum of Miniatures** (5900 Wilshire, 213-937 6464), which has the largest collection of miniatures in

the world, including a tiny but perfectly formed Zen garden! Take a pit-stop for lunch at the **Farmers Market** (6333 West 3rd, 213-933 9211), which is just a few blocks north. A favourite of the stars, you can satisfy your hunger pangs with Californian cuisine, gumbo and crêpes at this quaint 1930s-built complex of cafés and shops. Then head off to the **George C Page Museum** (5801 Wilshire, 213-936 2230), home to the world's largest collection of Ice Age fossils. The **Craft and Folk Art Museum** (5800 Wilshire, 213-937 5544), right opposite the Page, exhibits fine ethnic and contemporary textiles, pottery and jewellery from all over the world.

Theme parks and attractions

Disneyland® Resort in California

This is the full title that refers to both the Park and its hotel and shopping complex. If going direct to Anaheim from the Los Angeles airport you can pick up the airport bus, which runs 24 hours a day, seven days a week. One way: adults $14, 3–11s $8. Return: adults $22, children $14. Reservations are not necessary, but you can call 714-938 8900 for information.

Disneyland® Park

Numbers after the attractions refer to the map on page 196.

Location: 1313 Harbor Boulevard, Anaheim.

Hours: 8am to midnight or 1am, but times vary throughout the year so check in advance.

Entrance: One-day passport $39 (3–11s $28); two-day passport $72 (3–11s $51); three-day passport $99 (3–11s $75). One-day Senior Fun passport (60+) $37. Under 3s are free. If you are staying at The Disneyland® Resort you can buy a three- or five-day Disneyland® Flex Passport, which gives you one early

11

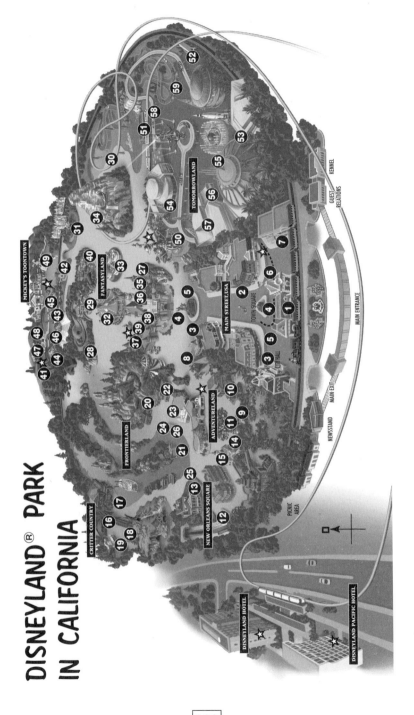

DISNEYLAND® PARK
IN CALIFORNIA

CRITTER COUNTRY

NEW ORLEANS SQUARE

FRONTIERLAND

ADVENTURELAND

MAIN STREET USA

TOWN SQUARE

CITY HALL

MICKEY'S TOONTOWN

FANTASYLAND

TOMORROWLAND

GUEST RELATIONS

KENNEL

MAIN ENTRANCE

MAIN EXIT

NEWSSTAND

PICNIC AREA

DISNEYLAND HOTEL

DISNEYLAND PACIFIC HOTEL

day admission to the Park. You can also buy a Magic Morning Breakfast, which gives you breakfast inside the Park with Disney characters. For details of all the offers phone 714-781 4565.

Guided Tours: $14 (3–11s $12) plus the cost of a passport, or for the Premier Tour, $60 per hour.

Parking: $7.

Advance Information: 714-781 4565.

Lockers: Between the Market House and Disney Clothiers in Main Street. Lockers big enough for suitcases can be found near the Group Sales Window.

Pushchairs (strollers) and wheelchairs: Strollers cost $7 a day, wheelchairs $27 a day, plus $20 deposit in each case, from just inside the Main Entrance.

Top Attractions: Space Mountain; Rocket Rods; Splash Mountain; Star Tours; Pirates of the Caribbean; 'it's a small world'; and Peter Pan – expect queues of at least an hour at peak times.

Don't Miss: Indiana Jones™ Adventure (© Disney/Lucasfilm Ltd) and Honey I Shrunk the Audience.

Entertainment: Parades, night-time shows and other events change all the time depending on the season. For up-to-date schedules stop by City Hall or consult the Disneyland® Today park brochure. The Central Plaza Information Center posts waiting times for many Park attractions as well as show and parade times for the day.

Hidden Costs: Meals cost between $5 and $10 and snacks $2 to $4. Food there includes sales tax, but no alcoholic drinks are served anywhere in the Park – even in the evening.

The Happiest Place on Earth was opened on 17 July 1955, the fulfilment of one of Walt Disney's dreams. Back then it had 18 attractions, now there are more than 60 in eight Lands each one of which represents a different theme. If you've ever been to **Walt Disney World®**

Resort in Florida, then the first thing that will strike you is the size – everything here is so much smaller and more compact. But that, in fact, is part of its attraction as it is so much quicker and easier to work your way around all the Lands, their shops and attractions. And if you expect signs of the age of **Disneyland® Resort**, think again. Annual face-lifts in which more than 20,000 gallons of paint are used, and nightly deep-cleans ensure it maintains Disney's hallmark pristine-clean image.

Main Street USA: After entering the Park, you arrive at this composite of a small-town, turn-of-the-century American high street, packed full of Disney merchandise. Just bear in mind that all prices are exclusive of local sales tax (around 7.75%) and that smoking is banned in all stores, waiting areas, attractions, dining areas, toilets and even in locations designed for watching parades and stage shows, throughout the Park. A Jump, Jive, Boogie Swing Party on Friday (with half-hour dance lesson) and Saturday nights is held at the Plaza Gardens on Main Street. At the top of the Street you can turn left towards Adventureland or head off to the right to the fantastic, new Tomorrowland – guess where I'm going!

Tomorrowland: Reopened in May 1998, it presents the future as a place where technology is an integral part of daily life. The landscaping is based on a garden filled with edible plants from herbs to apple trees and cabbages to spices, to demonstrate a happy world in which nature supports human life. The old **Star Tours** (1), where you board a droid-piloted StarSpeeder for a thrilling and hilarious voyage to the planet Endor (one of my favourite rides), and **Space Mountain** (2), a high-speed rocket flight through deep space, remain, though the latter has been updated with on-board, computer-controlled audio tracks on each seat. The new **Astro Orbitor** (3), located at

11

the entrance to Tomorrowland, gives would-be astronauts the chance to control their altitude as the rockets rotate around the Leonardo da Vinci-inspired mobile of planets and constellations. A fun, but not *thrilling*, ride. Prepare to screech round corners in open-air rockets on the new **Rocket Rods** (4), the Park's fastest and longest high-speed journey. Don't miss **Honey, I Shrunk the Audience** (5) at the Magic Eye Theater in which Wayne Szalinski (the madcap inventor from the hit *Honey* movies) is presented with an Inventor of the Year award before accidentally 'shrinking' you.

Innoventions, at the old Carousel Theater, takes advantage of the building's rotating theatre base for interactive shows that present state-of-the-art technology. Visiting Tomorrowland is sure to be hungry work, so take a break at the galactic **Redd Rockett's Pizza Port** for salads, pastas and pizzas in a retro 50s space-race era setting.

Fantasyland: Then walk through the **Sleeping Beauty Castle** (6) into Fantasyland, an enchantingly happy kingdom that is home to original rides such as **Dumbo the Flying Elephant** (7) and the whirling tea-cups ride **Mad Tea Party** (8). Don't miss one of the Park's favourite attractions, **'it's a small world'** (9), a truly delightful cruise in which 300 'children' from all around the world, dressed in their native costumes, sing and dance. Pretty in pinks, yellows and blues in daylight, it's worth going back in the evening to see it all lit up. **Peter Pan's** (10) **Flight** also has a huge following, but after waiting in lengthy queues, it's disappointingly short. Another favourite is **Matterhorn Bobsleds** (11), in which you careen down slopes past colourful crystal ice caverns and an Abominable Snowman in sleek bobsleds before finally splashing through an alpine lake. It can get very bumpy and I'd advise *not* sitting at the front of the bobsled! You can pay a visit to **Mickey Mouse** (12) and have your photo taken with him at his home in **Mickey's Toontown**, the

topsy-turvy home of Disney's famous characters, before entering the untamed West of America in Frontierland.

Frontierland: Big Thunder Mountain Railroad (13), a runaway mine train ride, and the **Mark Twain Riverboat** (14) to Tom Sawyer Island are the big attractions here.

Adventureland: Here you'll find *the* ride of the Park, the **Indiana Jones™ Adventure: The Temple of the Forbidden Eye** (15). You'll board jeeps (try to get in the front for maximum impact of the events) and revisit the perils of the *Indiana Jones* movies, evading serpents, spiders, explosions and poison darts while travelling on a rickety wooden track over volcanic lava. There are many different permutations of the ride – though they all end with your near decapitation (!) – so it'll be hard to stop yourself from queueing for this ride again and again.

★ ★ ★ ★ **INSIDE TRACK** ★ ★ ★
★   ★
★ When the queue gets close to ★
★ the ride it splits in two. Always ★
★ take the left lane as this moves ★
★ much more quickly (something to ★
★ do with the fact that people ★
★   tend to go right).   ★
★ ★ ★ ★ ★ ★ ★ ★ ★ ★ ★ ★ ★ ★ ★ ★

New Orleans Square provides a taste of Louisiana of 200 years ago when the city was the unchallenged Queen of the Mississippi and apparently home to the world's most daring pirates. You can board bayou bateaux at **Spanish Main** and sail into a great adventure called **Pirates of the Caribbean** (16). This fabulous sailing adventure concludes with a spectacular display of buccaneers plundering and burning a city. Also worth a visit is the **Haunted Mansion** (17) where 999 frighteningly funny ghosts, ghouls and goblins ceaselessly search for the thousandth ghost. Nearby **Critter Country**, a rugged

Practically perfect

One of the highlights of the entire Disneyland® in California experience, particularly for little girls, is tea with Mary Poppins in a recreation of a Victorian parlour and gardens at the Disneyland® Pacific Hotel. The setting is simple but the atmosphere is electric as little girls' dreams are made to come true through meeting their heroine. The world's most famous nanny welcomes guests, entertains, sings and has her photo taken with adoring crowds of youngsters and their parents (usually mums) all dressed up to the nines. Hugs are an essential ingredient, of course, and it is the most touching thing in the world to see beautifully dressed-up little girls (and sometimes boys) queueing for a hug with their screen idol. And here I have a confession to make – when I was there, I made Mary Poppins cry! No, no, it wasn't deliberate – all I asked, after watching tear-jerking scenes as little girls scrunched up their faces for the most heartfelt hug in the world – was: 'What is it like to make little girls' dreams come true?' Mary managed to say: 'Positively nothing can compare' before rushing off tearfully. In my defence, absolutely nobody could fail to be moved by the depth of emotions hovering in the air at this absolutely perfect tea. Practically Perfect Tea consists of scones, sandwiches, sweet surprises and a choice of tea ($18.95 for adults and $12.95 for under 11s).

Space is limited at Practically Perfect Tea, which is held at weekends year round and five days a week during the summer, so make your reservation early on 714-956 6755.

north-west territory, houses **Splash Mountain** (18), where you step into hollowed-out logboats for a watery escapade through the world of Brer Rabbit, Brer Bear and Brer Fox before a thrilling, five-storey drop (the splash!). Small children will enjoy the **Country Bear Playhouse** (19), a musical revue starring 18 comical audio-animatronic bears.
Shows: As previously mentioned, these do change, but it's highly likely that you'll get to see the **Mulan Parade**, which goes from 'it's a small world' to Main Street every day during peak seasons, presenting a series of scenes with characters, settings and tunes from the animated movie.
Hotels: You'll need somewhere to stay and, luckily enough, the Disney fun continues at both the nearby **Disneyland Hotel®** (1150 West Cerritos Avenue, Anaheim 92802, phone 714-778 6600) and **Disneyland® Pacific Hotel** (1717 South West Street, Anaheim, 92802, phone 714-999 0990), all part of the Disneyland® Resort in California. Booking into either will give you early admission to

the Park when you buy a Disneyland® Passport, so you have the opportunity to enter up to an hour and a half before the general public on each specially designated day of your stay (early admission into the Park operates on four to six mornings during the week, depending on the season).

Other benefits include the Resort's Package Express programme where goods bought at any Disneyland® Resort shop are delivered directly to your room, being able to charge purchases to your room, and free use of the resort's swimming pools. There is also direct access to the Park via the Disneyland® transportation system, which has a station-stop right outside the Resort's shopping, dining and travelport area.

Facilities at the hotels include restaurants and lounges, ranging from family-style dining to an award-winning steak house and seafood restaurant, plus a Japanese restaurant and sushi bar.

Rack rates for both are $190 to $225 depending on occupancy and dates; parking is $10 a day for guests or $2 an hour up to a $15 maximum to non-guests. Character breakfasts – where you'll meet characters from Disney movies and see Merlin in action – cost $14.50 at both Disney's PCH Grill in the Disneyland® Pacific Hotel and at Goofy's Kitchen in the Disneyland® Hotel. Standard breakfast is only available at the PCH Grill (from the hotel standpoint) and costs between $5 and $8. Depending on what you order, lunch at both hotels costs $6 to $10 and dinner $10 to $30.

Other theme parks and attractions

Universal Studios® Hollywood: 100 Universal City Plaza, Universal City, 818-622 3801. Established in 1915 by film pioneer Carl Laemmle, the studios have been visited by more than 90 million people since public tours started in 1964. Now it's not just a case of seeing a movie studio,

but spending a day on spine-tingling rides, watching thrilling shows and getting an insight into some awesome stunts and special effects. The thrills start with **Jurassic Park® – The Ride**, when you'll have to hang on for your life as a runaway raft brings you face to fangs with spitters, raptors and the ultimate terror – a ravenous T-Rex. Then Doc Brown will send you screaming through time on **Back to the Future® – The Ride** when you'll have run-ins with a 50-foot tyrannosaurus rex, Ice Age avalanche and molten volcano at the Dawn of Time before being whisked off to the year 2015. You'll see breathtaking action, death-defying stunts and pyrotechnics on the exciting **Waterworld® – A Live Sea War Spectacular** and the newest show is **Totally Nickelodeon**, a 25-minute show featuring stunts and games from some of the channel's top TV shows. Open from 8am to 11pm in the summer and 10am to 6pm at other times every day except Thanksgiving and Christmas. Admission includes all the rides, **Backlot Tram Tour** and live shows. But hours, prices and

Entrance fees

Keith Prowse (01232 232425) and Seligo (0121 643 4321) offer a variety of theme park entrances, ranging from Disneyland® Flex passports to Southern California Valuepasses that include Universal Studios, Hollywood and Sea World in San Diego, plus three-, five- and seven-day LA Funpasses that include entrance to Disneyland® in California, Universal Studios®, Knott's Berry Farm® and money towards dinner at Planet Hollywood or the Allstar Café.

attractions are subject to change, so phone in advance. Over 12s: $39; 3–11s: $29; under 3s free; over 60s: $33. The Celebrity Annual Pass (adults $62, children $53) gives unlimited visits to the park in any one year, plus 15% off for up to six guests per visit, and many other money-saving perks. Parking: $7 cars, $10 RVs.

Universal City Walk: 1,000 Universal Center Drive, Universal City, 818-622 4455. A two-block-long pedestrian promenade with shops, restaurants and clubs. Watch out for a creepy-looking **Beetlejuice** who'll want to have his photo taken with you (no charge)! Also home to **Hard Rock Hollywood** (Universal City Walk, 818-622 7625).

Warner Bros VIP Tour: Main gate at Hollywood Way and Olive, 818-954 1744. Started in 1974, these two-hour tours give the most realistic glimpse into the workings of a modern studio. Knowledgeable guides truck you from the lot's 'jungle' exteriors to eight miles of costume racks, explaining movie-making tricks along the way. You'll see sets used for everything from period pieces to *Blade Runner*, visit production sets for *ER* (sadly, no more George Clooney!) or *Lois and Clark: The New Adventures of Superman* and even *Friends*. Sixty years of history and memorabilia have been crammed into the new museum, which goes big on James Cagney, Errol Flynn and James Dean. The tours start at half-hourly intervals from 9am to 5pm in the summer and hourly from 9am to 3pm in the winter from Mondays to Fridays. Closed weekends and holidays. $29 per person. No children under 10. Reservations are recommended (818-972 TOUR) and free tea and coffee is provided in the waiting area.

Knott's Berry Farm®: 8039 Beach Boulevard, Buena Park, 714-220 5200. This park started life as a berry farm and restaurant in the 1930s when the Knott family decided to entertain waiting customers by

opening an Old West Town. Shops and Montezuma's Revenge followed and you can now pan for gold, hear about Californian history, watch Native Americans dance and learn about their culture. Two of the latest attractions are the Windjammer and Supreme Scream. The **Windjammer** is a surf-inspired, dual roller coaster and America's first major outdoor, dual-track, steel racing coaster. The ride pits two lots of eight passengers in surf-board-style 'jammers' against each other through a series of side-by-side loops, 60-foot drops and twisting turns over water. A different jammer wins each time. **Supreme Scream** propels you more than 250 feet straight up into the air before you plunge back at more than 50 mph in just three seconds, followed by a second, rebound leap halfway up again. Open every day except Christmas, though hours vary so check in advance. Unlimited Tickets cover admission, rides, shows and attractions except for Pan for Gold and special events. Over 12s: $36. 3–11s $26. Pregnant women: $26. After 4pm (when the park is open after 6pm): $16.95 all ages.

Six Flags Magic Mountain: 26101 Magic Mountain Parkway, Santa Clarita, 805-255 4111. Home to **Superman®: The Escape** where you accelerate from nought to 100mph in seven seconds and get 6.5 seconds of weightlessness as you're rocketed to the top of the 41-storey tower before beginning the terrifying backward descent. Spanning 900 feet and looming 415 feet above ground, this is one of the tallest, fastest and most technologically advanced thrill rides ever. The new **Batman: The Ride®** only lasts a minute, but it's a long, gravity-defying, breathtaking one. **Colossus** claims to be the world's largest wooden roller coaster, with loop after loop of traditional thrills. You can also check out other rides from Viper to Psyclone and Flashback for more thrills or watch Gotham City Backlot,

11

the Batman-themed stunt show. Admission is from $17 to $34.

Six Flags Hurricane Harbor: Right next door to Magic Mountain. With a mass of water slides and the tallest enclosed speed slides in southern California, thrill-seekers are sure to get plenty of kicks here. Highlights include **Black Snake Summit**, with winding slides that drop 75 feet, **Lizard Lagoon**, a 3.2-acre activity lagoon with a 7,000-foot pool, **Reptile Ridge**, a three-storey water slide complex with five high-speed slides, and **Bamboo Racer**, a six-lane racing water slide. Entrance is from $17 to $34.

Long Beach

Okay, so you've been there, done that in LA, now it's time to chill out and relax awhile before continuing your travels – and Long Beach is the perfect place to do that. Famous for its long beaches (funny that!), it lies at the southern part of greater LA and has some of the few beaches on the west coast with south-facing sunbathing. It is also home to some of the most beautiful inland waterways on the coast, with excellent facilities for all things to do with sun, sea, sand and water sports. And permanently docked in the harbour is one of LA's big attractions, the *Queen Mary*. You'll also find one of the biggest, newest and most spectacular aquariums in the world here, a new Russian-built submarine museum, a perfectly tranquil Japanese garden, gondola rides, bungee jumping and plenty of restaurants and cafés.

Getting your bearings is quite easy. Running west to east you have

Downtown Long Beach, Long Beach Aquarium of the Pacific in Queensway Bay, the *Queen Mary*, Russian submarine and Shoreline Village on the west; with Belmont Shore, a 15-block beachside neighbourhood of cafés, boutiques, coffee houses and bookstores to the east, behind which is the shopping district of 2nd Street, Gondola Getaway, Naples Island and Alimotos Bay. Further east, just beyond the San Gabriel River is Seal Beach, an up-and-coming movie-making district.

Downtown: Pine Avenue is a bustling Mecca of historical buildings, trendy antique, clothes and home furnishing shops, plus a whole spectrum of restaurants from casual 1950s diners to elegant Italian resturants. To make life even easier, there is even a free Runabout shuttle that covers the whole of Downtown. And if you're in the mood for a bit of art, then there is the **Latin American Art Museum** (628 Alamitos Avenue, 562-437 1689) in the East Village Arts District, America's first museum devoted to contemporary art of the Americas.

Long Beach Aquarium of the Pacific: Next to Shoreline Lagoon in Downtown Long Beach, 562-590 3100. The $117-million aquarium opened in June 1998 as part of a massive project to rejuvenate the waterfront at Queensway Bay. It is now home to 12,000 marine specimens in 21 major exhibit tanks filled with more than a million gallons of sea water. Here you'll get a genuinely close-up view of undersea life from coral reefs to coastal habitats and, as waves crash overhead, you can walk through marine habitats via an underwater tunnel. The 150,000-square-foot aquarium also has 'touch tanks' where you can get close to marine animals such as seals and sea lions.

Queen Mary: 1126 Queens Highway, 562-435 3511. Permanently docked in Long Beach harbour and a major attraction since 1972, this art deco wonderland even appeared in some

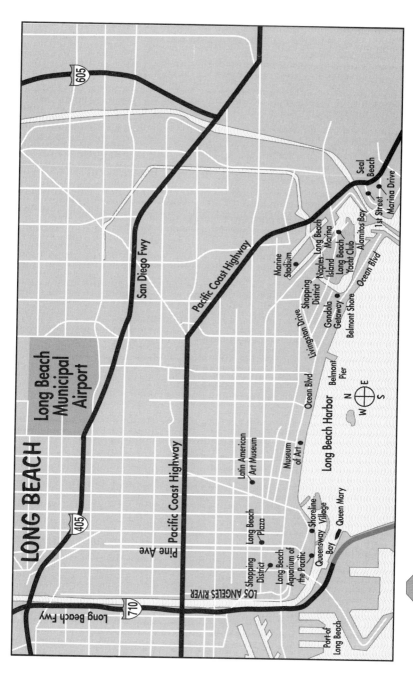

Titanic scenes. It now houses a hotel, museum, excellent restaurants and shopping on the Promenade Deck. Double rooms start at an amazingly good value-for-money $80. A real treat is the champagne Sunday brunch in the Grand Salon, the ship's original first-class restaurant. You'll be entertained by live harp music in a fabulous setting with superb waterfront views. Adults $23.95, under 12s $7.95. A self-guided tour of the museum (\$20 adults, $14 4–11s, under 4s free, 10am to 6pm daily) gives the low-down on ghosts and other things that go bump in the night and *Titanic:* **The Expedition** has a whole array of artefacts from the doomed liner. If the tragedy of it all gets a bit much for you, then throw yourself off the tallest free-standing bungee tower right next door at **Mega Bungee** (1119 Queens Highway, 562-435 1880), or check out the Soviet-built, Foxtrot-class sub **Povodnaya Lodka B-427**, which was built at the height of the Cold War and is now open to public viewing right next to the *Queen Mary*.

Shoreline Village: 401–435 Shoreline Village Drive, 562-435 2668. Home to a waterfront centre of 30 speciality shops in a nineteenth-century seaport village setting with an authentic antique carousel. **Shoreline Village Cruises** (562-495 5884) at the marine and boating centre offer dinner cruises from $29.50 per person and whale-watching cruises from January to April. The village is located next to the new **Rainbow Harbor**, a $650-million renovation project of this part of Long Beach shoreline due to be completed by 2001. It will have a resort-like atmosphere with fishing charters, dinner cruises and water taxis to take you to the Downtown entertainment district and the *Queen Mary*.

Belmont Shore: Another dining and shopping Mecca, it offers some of the city's most upscale shops along 2nd between Livingston and Bayshore drives, plus dozens of restaurants.

Gondola Getaway: 5437 East Ocean, 562-433 9595. Take an hour-long romantic gondola ride around the picturesque waterways of Naples Island and Alamitos Bay. The Italian theme continues as you're serenaded under the Italian-style bridges (by a Kiwi and American of Italian descent!).

Alamitos Bay: Considered to be *the* best beach in greater Los Angeles, its secluded setting means there are no waves – making a perfect beach for children and adults alike.

Seal Beach: Since Aaron Spelling chose Seal Beach for the site of his daytime soap *Sunset Beach*, it is easy-peasy to view filming action at the Seal Beach Pier or quaint Main Street. But Seal Beach is no stranger to filming. Tom Cruise's *Jerry Maguire* was filmed at the Long Beach Marriott and Warner Brothers leased the Spruce Goose Dome for filming *Batman and Robin*.

Earl Burns Miller Japanese Garden: At California State University, 1250 Bellflower Boulevard, 562-985 8885. Take a break and meditate in the tranquillity of this perfect setting for quiet contemplations!

Recreation: At **Alfredo's Beach Rentals** (on the beach in Long Beach, 562-434 6121) you can hire bikes, skates, kayaks, jetskis and boats. If you fancy golf, tennis or other leisure activities, the **City of Long Beach Department of Parks, Recreation & Marine** (2760 Studebaker Road, 562-570 3100) has a full range of facilities and programmes. Rent rollerblades, kayaks and windsurfers from the **Long Beach Windsurf Center** (on East Ocean Boulevard, near Belmont Pier, 562-433 1014). Take a deep-sea fishing trip for anything from half a day to overnight in Coast Guard-approved boats with **Long Beach Sportfishing** (555 Pico Avenue, 562-432 8993). They also do whale watching from January to April. Would-be sailors can charter a yacht from **Marina Sailing Inc** (429 Shoreline Drive, 562-432 4672) for the day or for island vacations.

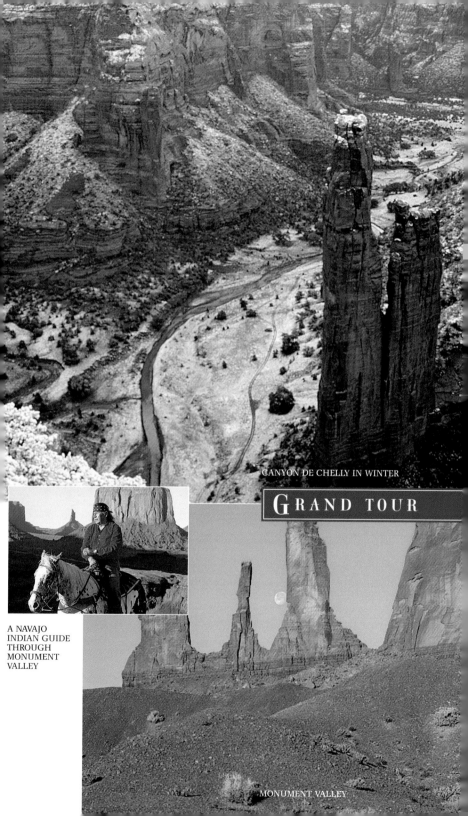

CANYON DE CHELLY IN WINTER

GRAND TOUR

A NAVAJO
INDIAN GUIDE
THROUGH
MONUMENT
VALLEY

MONUMENT VALLEY

RAINBOW BRIDGE AT
LAKE POWELL

YOSEMITE
NATIONAL
PARK

LAKE POWELL

GRAND TOUR

RIGHT: BOAT TRIP ON
LAKE POWELL

You can get a bird's-eye view of the *Queen Mary* and Long Beach by parasailing with **Offshore Watersports** (128 East Shoreline Drive, in Shoreline Village near Parker's Lighthouse, 562-436 1996) or speed along the beachline coast in a jetski or boat. **Scuba Express** (Shoreline Harbor Marina, 562-429 4062) offer open boats and charters for up to 22 divers to the local islands. Steel tanks, soft weights and belts are provided. **Sundiver** (106 Marina Drive, 562-493 1013) are another highly rated scuba-diving charter boat service offering one- and two-day trips to the local islands. Instruction and private charters available.

> From Long Beach take the 405 to Interstate 5 for the 2½-hour drive to San Diego. If you prefer to head straight for Palm Springs, take the 710 north to Interstate 10 for the 2¼-hour drive to the desert resort.

San Diego

Time may be a big factor in your decision to visit California's southern-most city, but the laid-back, resort-like atmosphere and wonderful climate make San Diego a great place to relax while visiting some superb attractions. Just 20 miles from Tijuana in Mexico, this was the birthplace of modern California. Claimed for Spain by explorer Juan Rodriguez Cabrillo in 1542, it has since been governed by the Spanish and Mexicans before becoming part of the United States in 1846.

It may be America's sixth largest city, but it retains a small-town atmosphere and has a collection of communities that each offer their own distinctive flavour: Coronado in the south, La Jolla in the north and Mission Valley in the middle. Overall,

it really is a pretty city, but the best way to experience it is to make the most of all the fantastic watersports and activities: there's everything from scuba diving to whale watching (December to April), surfing to kayaking, jetskiing, waterskiing, deep-sea fishing, harbour tours and private cruises. And qualified divers can even watch and photograph sharks being fed from the 'safety' of a cage. Eat your heart out Jaws! The top attractions are SeaWorld, San Diego Zoo and the Wild Animal Park.

Getting around

Driving around San Diego is a breeze in comparison with Los Angeles, and parking is not too difficult – provided you stick to the rules. The regulations are complex and any transgressions are swiftly dealt with. If you get back to where you parked your car and find it gone, don't assume it's been stolen – call 619-531 2844 first to see if it's been towed away. Your best bet is to always check the kerbside regulations and park within marked spaces. White means you have a three-minute maximum for active loading only (10 minutes at hotels), 24 hours a day unless otherwise specified. But at airports and hospitals, drivers must stay with the car. Green allows short-term parking for the specified time or unlimited time for disabled drivers. Yellow is a 20-minute loading zone for commercial vehicles only, red means no stopping, standing or parking and blue is reserved for disabled drivers from out-of-state with officially issued placards.

★ ★ ★ ★ **INSIDE TRACK** ★ ★ ★ ★
★ ★
★ Any parking spot in San Diego is ★
★ potentially a tow-away zone if ★
★ you park illegally and violations ★
★ are 'vigorously enforced and ★
★ costly'. ★
★ ★ ★ ★ ★ ★ ★ ★ ★ ★ ★ ★ ★ ★ ★ ★

11

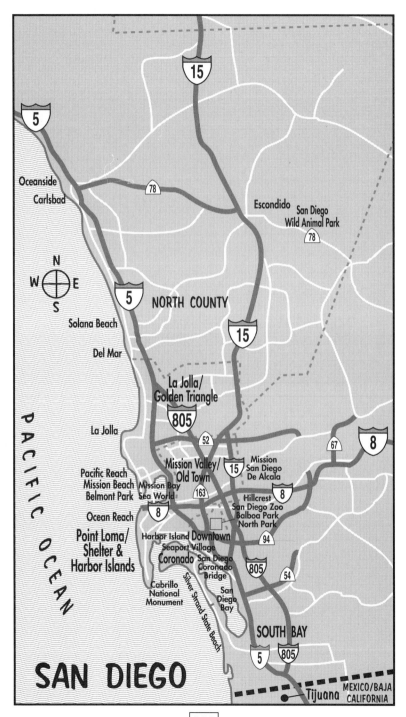

In addition some parking meters only accept quarters. They are enforced Monday to Saturday 8am to 6pm. Meters with yellow poles are also enforced on Sundays.

If you can't face all the parking restrictions, leave the car at your hotel and use public transport, which is clean, easy to use and very cheap. You can buy one-day ($5), two-day ($8), three-day ($10) and four-day ($12) passes for unlimited access to buses and the trolley from the Transit Store at Broadway at 1st. Call 619-233 3004 for information and maps. Otherwise the average fare is $1 to $3 (have exact change ready) for the buses and $1 to $2.25 for the trolley. On average, taxis cost $2 for the first mile and $1.40 for additional miles for up to five people.

If driving across the San Diego–Coronado Bay Bridge there is a charge of $1 for one-passenger vehicles entering Coronado, though it's free if there are two or more of you in the car. The San Diego–Coronado ferry is only open to pedestrians and cyclists and costs $2 each way (50c extra for bikes).

You can take a break from driving and still see the rugged beauty of San Diego's back country on a vintage train ride with the San Diego Railroad Museum. There are four special tours, including a wine-tasting train tour, with standard tickets at $35 for adults or $20 for 6–12s. For dates and times, call 1-888 228 9246.

Seeing things

La Jolla: Pronounced 'lahoya', this is a beautiful coastal community north of Downtown that boasts an Underwater Park, its own bay and expensive houses. This is a place for 'beautiful people' and a refuge for stars wishing to escape from LA. The best thing to do here is enjoy a spot of people-watching on the beach and in the open-air restaurants. Along the ocean, La Jolla Shores is a long, flat beach ideal for bathers and surfers alike, while La Jolla Cove is great for

cliffside coastal walks, romantic strolls and swimming in the sheltered cove. The area is also home to San Diego's **Hard Rock Café** (909 Prospect Drive, 619-454 5101) where John Lennon's Sergeant Pepper and Elton John's Tutti Frutti outfits, and autographed guitars from Duran Duran and ZZ Top are among the memorabilia. If you're getting withdrawal symptoms from a lack of sports, catch up on the latest action at the **Sports City Café and Brewery** (8657 Villa La Jolla Drive, Suite 211, in the La Jolla Village Square shopping centre, 619-450 DINE) where each comfy 'booth' is equipped with its own colour monitor linked to satellite TV, and the food includes pizzas, pastas, ribs, fresh fish and steaks. The Pacific Rim restaurant **Café Japengo** (at the Hyatt Regency, 8960 University Center Lane, 619-450 3355) has a special Sunday Sushi Club where you can try your luck on the wheel of fortune to win free sushi and other prizes and even get free sushi lessons from the chefs. Or try it Monday nights when there is live blues music. Reservations are suggested.

Mission Bay: The world's largest aquatic park with every type of watersport imaginable from boating, fishing, skiing, swimming and board sailing to 27 miles of sun-bleached beaches and six designated swimming areas. Grassy picnic areas are also great for family sports and kite flying, while you can cycle or jog round the miles of paths that wind around the park. You can overdose on free amusements at **Belmont Park** (3156 Mission Boulevard, 619-491 2988), where there is a roller coaster, swimming pool, Pirates Cove family playland, shops, snacks, ocean-front dining and other amusements. It's open daily, but times vary so phone in advance. **SeaWorld of California** (500 SeaWorld Drive, 619-226 3901). This is the third most popular attraction in the whole of California and provides a truly remarkable experience as you see marine animals

11

interact with humans. The show not to miss is **Shamu: World Focus,** a 25-minute, high-energy performance by the killer whale and at the weekends and selected weekdays throughout the year you can experience **Dining with Shamu,** a poolside luncheon, during which Shamu is fed. Altogether there are five major shows and scores of fascinating marine exhibits designed to entertain and educate. At **Wild Arctic®,** board White Thunder, an ultra-modern simulated jet helicopter that flies over the frozen landscape of the Arctic North, giving breathtaking views of rocky glaciers and snowy ice floes. The helicopter barely escapes an avalanche by zooming into a narrow ice cave, but lands safely at Base Station Wild Arctic. Throughout the ride, touch-screens, headsets and video monitors provide 'a total immersion' experience. **Shamu's Happy Harbor®** is a colourful two-acre tropical playland – the perfect place to run, jump, climb, get wet and greet the gentle-giant mammal, Shamu. The most recent attraction is **Manatee Rescue,** which is designed to educate people about these gentle mammals to help prevent their extinction, and which houses America's only West Indian manatee outside of Florida. Open daily from 10am. Call ahead for summer hours. Adults $32.95, 3–11s $24.95, under 3s free.

Parking $5. Prices subject to change. **Mission Valley and Old Town:** If San Diego was the birthplace of California, then the Mission Basilica San Diego de Alcala was the birthplace of San Diego. Founded in 1769 by Father Junipero Serra, the mission and nearby Presidio were the first outposts of the Spanish government and the chain of missions between San Diego and Monterey eventually grew to 21. Today Mission Valley is the place for shopping, eating and entertainment. **Seau's the Restaurant** (Mission Valley Center, 1640 Camino del Rio North, #1376, 619-291 SEAU), owned by San Diego Charger's Lineback Junior Seau, serves up contemporary American fare in a sports-theme setting. For zesty South-western cuisine in a desert-themed setting, try Canyon Café (Mission Valley Center, 619-296 2600). And there's a distinctly tropical feel to the Hawaiian Paradise of the **Islands Restaurant** (2270 Hotel Circle North, Mission Valley, 619-297 1101) where cascading waterfalls and Polynesian decor make the Sunday brunch speciality a superb treat.

Mission Valley also encompasses what is now known as **Old Town State Historic Park,** the original settlement by Europeans. Even after the mission moved up-river in 1774, the soldiers and their families who had been brought in to protect the mission from the Indians remained here and it continued to thrive as the centre of the city until Alonzo Horton built New Town by the harbour. The Old Town was given a new lease of life in 1968 when a major purchasing programme of the six-block centre was undertaken to ensure the history of the area was preserved. The old buildings were restored or reconstructed and now blend with the new **Bazaar del Mundo,** a Mexican-style village that houses fine restaurants and shopping complexes and is the centre for a thriving new community of 10,000 residents.

Cream of the local eateries is the **Casa de Bandini Restaurant** (2660 Calhoun Street, Bazaar del Mundo, 619-297 8211). An award-winning menu of Mexican breakfast, lunch and dinner is served up in a traditional Mexican setting by colourfully costumed waiters.

Downtown: This area includes Balboa Park, San Diego Zoo, the Gaslamp Quarter District and Seaport Village.

Balboa Park: 2125 Park Boulevard. One of America's largest cultural complexes with museums, galleries, theatres and sport – all set in 1,200 acres of rolling parkland. The **San Diego Aerospace Museum** (2001 Pan American Plaza, 619-234 8291) has more than 65 air and space craft and thousands of artefacts to bring to life the history of aviation. (Adults $6, under 17s $2, open 10am to 4pm daily.) Other attractions include the Reuben H Fleet Science Center, the Simon Edison Center for Performing Arts – that includes Old Globe Theater, Cassius Carter Center Stage and Lowell Davies Festival Theater – and Starlight Bowl sporting facilities. It's extemely easy to get around on the free **Balboa Park Tram**, which starts at the Inspiration Point Parking Lot with 11 stops around the park. It operates seven days a week from 9.30am to 5pm in the spring and summer and 10am to 3.30pm in the autumn and winter. The **Balboa Park Visitors' Center** (1549 El Prado, 619-239 0512) has complete listings of exhibits, activities and facilities in the park and elsewhere in San Diego and is open from 9am to 4pm daily. If you plan to see a lot of the sites in the park, the Passport to Balboa Park is the thing to buy. At a cost of $21 ($62 worth) it allows you a week to see the nine museums at the park. Available from the Visitors' Center or any of the museums.

San Diego Zoo®: 2920 Zoo Drive, 619-234 3153. Billed as one of the world's best zoos, it began with the remnants of the world exposition fair and now 3,900 animals representing 800 species live in a 100-acre tropical garden. Many of its occupants are seldom seen in zoos and include a pair of giant pandas from China, furry koalas from Australia, long-billed kiwis from New Zealand, wild horses from Mongolia and playful sun bears from Malaysia. Other attractions include bioclimatic exhibits like the Polar Bear Plunge, Hippo Beach, Gorilla Tropics, Sun Bear Forest and Tiger River, plus a three-mile guided bus tour, a children's petting zoo and baby animal nursery. Adults $15, children $6. Open daily from 9am.

Gaslamp Quarter: 410 Island Avenue, 619-233 5227. The 16½-block Downtown district, once the heart of the 1880s boom, is a charming restoration of San Diego's past and now the scene of the annual Street Scene food and music festival (second weekend in September) and a hub for night-time activity. The whole area has been restored with the old buildings now housing offices, businesses and shops that sell everything from antiques to arts and crafts. A 90-minute audio walking tour provides the historical perspective for $5 or you can take a guided tour at 11am on Saturdays for a $5 donation. You're spoilt for choice when it comes to eating, but a fun diner is **Croce's Top Hat Bar and Grill** (802 Fifth Avenue, 619-233 4355), which serves American South-western cuisine for breakfast, lunch, dinner and late evening with R&B acts every night. **Upstairs at Croce's** is the place to go

INSIDE TRACK

Look out for money-saving coupon books at the Visitor Information Center, 11 Horton Plaza, First and F Street. It's filled with admission discounts for the top attractions, restaurants, museums, tours, the theatre and special hotel rates.

11

for espresso, drinks and desserts. There's authentic Spanish cuisine and tapas at the **Café Sevilla** (555 Fourth Avenue, 619-233 5979), which has the only Flamenco dinner show (every Friday and Saturday night) in the city. Set in one of San Diego's most elegant, turn-of-the-century hotels is **Ida Bailey's Restaurant** (at the Horton Grand Hotel, 311 Island Avenue, 619-544 1866), named after the city's most famous 'madam'. It provides award-winning food in a Victorian setting with cosy 'booths' for romantics. Or you can just pop in for high tea Tuesday to Saturday from 2.30pm to 5pm. A reminder of San Diego's bustling harbour front of 100 years ago, the **Old Spaghetti Factory** (275 Fifth Avenue, 619-233 4323) serves Italian cuisine in a distinctly olde-worlde setting. Phone ahead to see if you can reserve the dining room's authentic electric trolley car seat. If you're in the mood for a bit of Greek dancing, then try **Greek Town Taverna** (431 East Street, 619-232 0461) or the **Athens Market Taverna** (109 West F Street, 619-234 1955). Nearby is the modern **Horton Plaza** (324 Horton Plaza, 619-238 1596), seven city blocks of shopping, dining, entertainment and award-winning architecture; it has more than 140 shops, 20 places to eat and San Diego's branch of **Planet Hollywood** (197 Horton Plaza, 619-702 STAR).
Seaport Village: 849 West Harbor Drive, 619-235 4014. This waterfront dining and shopping complex, a re-creation of the harbourside as it was a century ago, is a picturesque area filled with boutiques, galleries and restaurants. Open daily from 10am to 9pm.
The San Diego Wild Animal Park: 15500 San Pasqual Valley Road, Escondido, 760-796 5621. A 2,200-acre nature reserve with more than 3,000 wild animals and many endangered species allowed to roam freely through the park. You can trek through the African wilderness on a walking safari for close encounters

with cheetahs, warthogs and rhinoceroses, and even feed giraffes. Or take the monorail past vast savannahs, Nairobi Village and Mombasa Lagoon, an interactive play area. Adults $18.95, children $11.95, under 3s free. Parking $3. Open daily at 9am.

★★★★ INSIDE TRACK ★★★

Go to the top of the Cabrillo National Monument for spectacular views of the harbour and coastline and grey whale watching during the migration season (January to April).

★★★★★★★★★★★★★★★★★

San Diego Bay: South of Mission Bay, this natural harbour is home to thousands of pleasure craft, sport fishing boats, and an increasing number of cruise ships. One of the best ways to see the harbour is from the water and you can take a tour, lunch or dinner cruise with **San Diego Harbor Excursions** (619-234 4111) at various times any day of the week. Next to the Broadway pier is the **Maritime Museum** (1306 North Harbor Drive, 619-234 9153), which includes a stately 100-year-old windjammer, the *Star of India*, the *Berkeley* steam ferry and the 1904 steam yacht, *Medea*. Try a spot of lunch at the 'authentic' British-style pub, the **Elephant & Castle Pub and Restaurant** (1355 North Harbor Drive, at the Holiday Inn, 619-232 3861). 'Merrie olde Englande' dishes include roast beef and Yorkshire pud, shepherd's pies and burgers and the 65-foot mahogany bar (a tribute to the Brit's ability to drink!) is the longest of its kind in San Diego. Then take the San Diego–Coronado Bay Ferry (it runs hourly for pedestrians and cyclists) on the 15-minute trip across the bay to Coronado. There you will find the famous **Hotel del Coronada** (1500 Orange Avenue, 619-435 6611), which was built almost entirely of wood in 1888 and was reputedly the largest structure outside of New York to be electrically lighted, with supervision of the project reportedly carried out by Thomas Edison himself. Since then it has appeared in *Some Like It Hot* with Marilyn Monroe, and Peter O'Toole's *The Stuntman*. You can take a guided tour of 'the Del', as it is known locally, see where the Duke of Windsor stayed in 1920 when he was Prince of Wales, and experience a bit of upper-crust life as you watch the world go by and sip afternoon tea. For a knockout view of the San Diego skyline, don't miss the Hawaiian-style **Peohe** (1201 First Street, 619-437 4474).

Doing things

Experience air combat in an open cockpit biplane with **Biplane Rides and Aerial Dogfights** (6743 Montia Court, Carlsbad, 760-438 7680) – not for the faint-hearted! Or sailplane with **Sky Sailing** (31930 California Highway 79, Warner Springs, 760-782 0404). The more sedate alternative is a balloon ride at sunrise or sunset with **A Balloon Adventure by California Dreamin'** (162 South Rancho Santa Fe Road, 760-438 3344) or **A Skysurfer Balloon Co** (1221 Camino Del Mar, Del Mar, 619-481 6800), complete with champagne and hors d'oeuvres. For bikes, surfboards, boogie boards and in-line skates, try **Aquarius Surf 'n' Skate** (747 Pacific Beach Drive, 619-488 9733), **Bikes and Beyond** (1201 First Street, Coronado, 619-435 7180) or **Hamel's Action Sports Center** (704 Ventura Place, Mission Beach, 619-488 8889). There is no shortage of companies offering everything from day/evening/chartered cruises to whale watching, diving, sports fishing, speedboats and jetskis. A few of them include **Club Nautico San Diego** (333 West Harbor Drive, 619-233 9311) for power boats, whale watching (December to April), skiing, fishing and diving; **Discover Sailing** (955

Harbor Island Drive, 619-297 7426) for hands-on sailing or simple relaxation in classy, clean yachts with food and drink; **Lee Palm Sportfishers** (2801 Emerson Street, 619-224 3857) for long-range sports fishing trips from two to 18 days; **Point Loma Sportfishing** (1403 Scott Street, 619-223 1627) for deep-sea fishing trips lasting from six hours to 17 days; **San Diego Yacht Charters** (1880 Harbor Island Drive, 619-297 4555) can provide bareboat or skippered sail and power boats; and **Seaforth Boat Rental** (1641 Quivira Road, 619-223 9588) everything from skiing, sailing, fishing, diving and cruising plus jetskis and speedboats. Try **Blue Escape Dive & Charter Inc** (1617 Quivira Road, 619-223 3483) for scuba-diving; **California Water Sports** (4215 Harrison Street, Carlsbad, 760-434 3089) for jetskis, kayaks, canoes and waverunners; while **Mission Bay Sportcenter** (1010 Santa Clara Place, 619-488 1004) is a complete watersports facility including rentals and instruction in sailing, windsurfing, waterskiing, jetskiing, surfing and kayaking. You can see and photograph sharks from an underwater cage with **San Diego Shark Diving** (PO Box 881037, San Diego 92168-1037, 619-299 8560); for certificated divers only. Wetsuits, surfboards and surfing instruction is provided for those who want to ride the waves with **San Diego Surfing Academy** (PO Box 99938, San Diego 92169-1938, 619-565 6892).

★ ★ ★ ★ ★ ★ ★ ★ ★ ★

★ If you do decide to visit Tijuana, ★ just remember that your hire car ★ conditions will usually exclude ★ taking it into Mexico. You can ★ take the San Diego Trolley to the ★ border and walk across. Once in ★ Mexico, bear in mind that ★ drinking on public streets is ★ generally prohibited. ★

★ ★ ★ ★ ★ ★ ★ ★ ★ ★ ★ ★ ★ ★ ★ ★

11

All that jazz

The San Diego Thanksgiving Jazz Festival is a Mecca for world-class musicians and jazz aficionados alike. Also part of the jazz-lover's circuit in California is the sea-cruise Dixieland Jazz Festival, which runs for four nights from Los Angeles to San Diego in November. Jazz is played on deck while balmy ocean breezes keep you toe-tappingly cool! Ashley Tours (01886 888335) can organise trips to both festivals.

Hotels

For the best rates at more than 300 hotels, you won't go far wrong with **San Diego's Central Hotel Reservations** company (1-800 434 7894). They can also provide discounts for SeaWorld, San Diego Zoo, the Wild Animal Park, Old Town Trolley Tour and harbour tours and dinner cruises. Or you can try the **Comfort Inn** in the SeaWorld area (4610 De Soto Street, 619-483 9800) if you fancy a budget hotel. Rooms from $39. Also in the Sea World area, near the beach, golf, tennis and sports fishing, is the **Quality Inn Airport by the Harbor** (2901 Nimitz Boulevard, 619-224 3655) with rooms from $54. The **Holiday Inn Express** in the zoo area of La Mesa (9550 Murray Drive, La Mesa, 619-466 0200) is conveniently located and has rooms from $50. For a posher life you can stay at **La Valencia Hotel** (1132 Prospect Street, La Jolla, 619-454 0771) from around $150 a night. Here you get to choose between garden, village, patio or ocean views. For an historical perspective of the city, you could stay at the **US Grant Hotel** (326

Broadway, 619-232 3121) from $185 a night for a double. Built by Ulysses Grant Jnr in honour of his father and completely renovated in 1985, US presidents Woodrow Wilson and Franklin D Roosevelt have both stayed there. The **Gaslamp Plaza Suites** in the historic Gaslamp Quarter, was once a jewellery exchange and is now recognised in America's National Register of Historic Sites. Or try another Victorian-era hotel in the Gaslamp Quarter, the **Horton Grand** (311 Island Avenue, 619-544 1886), which has doubles from $140. It was originally built in 1886 and restored 100 years later. Or you can order the *Bed and Breakfast Directory* for San Diego (rates $49 to $350 a night) from PO Box 3292, San Diego 92163, 619-297 3130, for $3.

From San Diego, take Highways 15 and 215 north to Interstate 60 going east and join Interstate 10 for the 3½-hour trip to Palm Springs.

Palm Springs desert resorts

Palm Springs, the place where the stars go to play, is at the heart of the Palm Springs desert resorts, eight distinctly different cities that are Cathedral City, Desert Hot Springs, Indian Wells, Indio, La Quinta, Palm Desert, Palm Springs and Rancho Mirage, which stretch 40 miles east to west and 20 miles north to south. Oh yes, and there are an estimated 10,000 palms! With 350 days of sunshine a year, 91 golf courses, 600 tennis courts and 30,000 swimming pools, it's a perfect setting for a bit of rest and relaxation. Palm Springs was born when the Agua Caliente band of Cahuilla Indians spotted 'Se-Khi' (boiling water) bubbling out of the desert and built a bathhouse that led

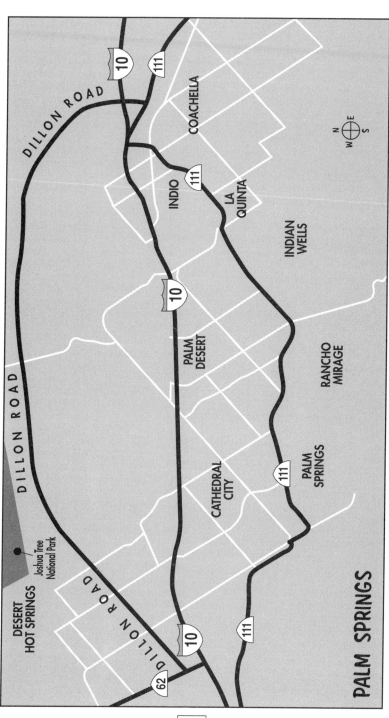

PALM SPRINGS

to a full-on spa resort. Now jeep eco-tours, the Living Desert Wildlife Park, covered wagon tours, 'dude' ranches, riding, rock climbing, hiking, the Palm, Murray and Tahquitz Canyons and Joshua Tree National Park provide exciting daytime entertainment. In the evening, the myriad of restaurants, bars, nightclubs and theatres provide plenty of action.

The **Aerial Tramway** (760-325 1391) climbs the 5,516 foot San Jacinto Mountains, where you can go hiking in the summer, cross-country skiing in the winter and experience some spectacular views in a much cooler environment (about 15°C/30°F cooler than in the city!). Main attractions include the **Oasis Waterpark** (760-327 0499), an amusement park with water slides, wave pool, lazy river, health spa and café; **Palm Springs Desert Museum** (760-837 0777), a world-famous museum for art and natural sciences that is open year-round; and the **Living Desert** (760-346 5694), a 1,200-acre wildlife botanical park that is home to cheetahs, warthogs and mountain lions. The **Indian Canyons** (760-325 5673) of the Andreas, Murray and Palm Canyons provide spectacular scenery, while the trading post, picnic grounds, hiking and horse trails are open from 8am to 6pm year round. At the **Joshua Tree National Park** (Highway 62 through Yucca Valley to the main HQ in Twentynine Palms or the east entrance off 1–10 at Cottonwood Springs Road, 45 minutes from Indio; call 760-367 7511), at the junction of the Mojave and lower Colorado deserts, there is a wildlife sanctuary, campgrounds, horse and hiking trails. **Fun things to do:** Go on a sunrise or sunset ballooning adventure with **Dream Flights** (760-321 5154); make a freefall tandem jump with **Parachutes over Palm Springs** (760-346 9888); or take a sailplane ride with **Sailplane Enterprises** (1-800 586 7627). Hire a bike from **Adventure Bike Tours** (760-328 2089) or with a

guide from **Bighorn Bicycles** (760-325 3367). **Palm Springs Desert Museum** (760-325 7186) organise custom hikes; **Desert Safari Tour Guides and Outfitters** (760-776 6087) offer spectacular eco-tours of the Indian Canyons lasting from one hour to a full day and even full-moon hikes. The **Uprising Rock Climbing Center** (760-320 6630) is the largest open-air facility of its kind in America and has three separate climbing towers. Go orienteering and learn wilderness skills with the **Living Desert** (760-346 5694). You can hire a horse from **Smoke Tree Stables** (760-327 1372) and go riding in Palm Springs or see the beautiful palm oasis and streams of Indian Canyons. For free-wheeling fun, **Offroad Rentals** (760-325 0376) provide all-terrain vehicles, safety equipment and instruction. Or you can be an easy rider by renting a motorbike for a half day, full day or week from **Route 66 Harley Rental** (760-324 9755). **Tours:** For a guided group bike tour, try **Adventure Bike Tours** (760-328 2089) and for guided jeep eco-tours, **Desert Adventures** (760-324 JEEP). For more traditional tours, you can see the sights and celebrity homes with **Celebrity Tours of Palm Springs** (760-770 2700) or do the Western thing on a **Covered Wagon Tours Inc** (760-347 2161) which includes a desert tour in a covered wagon (funny that!) with dinner and country music. **Golf:** There is simply not enough space to list all the golf courses that Palm Springs is famous for. You can either get a list from the **Convention and Visitors' Bureau** (The Atrium, 69-930 Highway 111, Suite 201, Rancho Mirage) or try two specialist tour operators. **Destination Golf USA** (0181 891 5151) arrange golfing holidays for as long as you like in Palm Springs, San Diego, Carmel and the Napa Valley in California and Phoenix and Scottsdale in Arizona. In Arizona, the **Wigwam Resort** doesn't just have a fabulous name but is set in the beautiful 75-acre oasis of orange trees, flowers and palms. The Las Vegas, California and Arizona Classic Pro-ams feature heavily in the **American Golf Holiday** (01703 465885), but will also organise tailor-made golfing holidays to fit in with your plans and will arrange everything for you – right down to tee-time reservations!

Mad dogs and Englishmen: The Americans are too sensible to go to the desert in the heat of the summer, but that makes Palm Springs a very-good-value destination for us Brits, who don't tend to be put off by silly little things like blistering heat. It is becoming a bit of a regular summer occurrence for the Visitors' Bureau to arrange special rates for everything from golf, to shopping, dining and other leisure activities. And hotel rates tend to be 30–50% cheaper. Even during July and August it is possible to play golf and tennis, though only in the early morning and late evening, and any time is good for cooling off in one of the many pools! To find out what the latest offers are and receive a **Vacation Planner** filled with discounts and offers, write to the Palm Springs Desert Resorts Convention and Visitors' Bureau at 69-930 Highway 111, Suite 201, Rancho Mirage, CA 92270. Once in America you can use the toll-free number for requesting the Planner, and make **hotel reservations on** 1-800 41 RELAX or 1-800 417 3529.

> **From Palm Springs, get back on the Ten for the two-hour drive to Arizona.**

Arizona

If it's the people and lifestyle that make California a truly remarkable experience, then it is the history and natural wonders that make Arizona one of the most beautiful and thrilling of all of America's 52 states. It's the land of cowboys and Indians, of gold-mining and ghost towns, of movie-making and centuries-old history and of one of the seven great natural wonders of the world: the Grand Canyon. Without a shadow of a doubt it's well worth a holiday of its own, but I have to be realistic about how much time you have and will stick to the more northerly reaches where you'll find plenty of cowboys and Indians and some of the most spectacular landscapes ever crowded into such a compact area.

Indians: Arizona has the largest American Indian population and more land devoted to Indian reservations than any other state. In addition, the prehistoric Indian tribes, such as the Hohokam of southern Arizona, the Sinagua of central and the Anasazi (ancient ones) of northern Arizona provide some extremely old historical ruins (rare in America) that are a monument to their high degree of sophistication in dry farming, water management, far-flung trade routes and jewellery, pottery and textile-making. And let us not forget, of course, that Arizona was the birthplace of possibly the best known Indian of them all, Geronimo. The Apache Indian warrior engaged nearly three-quarters of the nation's military ground troops during his pursuit after the Civil War and up to 1886 when he surrendered – having never been captured – at Skeleton Canyon!

Ranching: Once you hit **Quartsize**, look out for Highway 60 heading for **Wickenburg**, then head north on Route 89 towards Peeples Valley and Yarnell, named respectively after the rancher and miner who founded them in the late 1800s. Even today mining and ranching are the most important industries of the small communities, with the grasslands a home to a thriving cattle industry that has cowboys still riding the plains. The whole area down to Wickenburg is known as the 'Dude Ranch Capital of the World' because of all the ranches that allow you to visit and participate in the activities. Stay on the 89 to

11

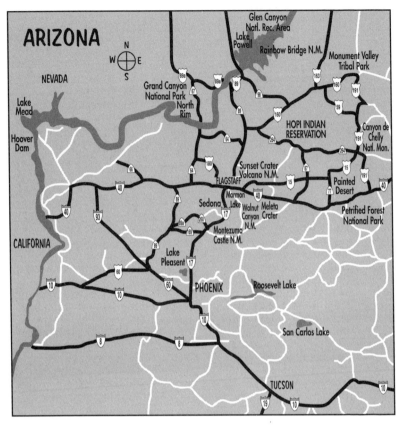

Prescott, the old capital of Arizona, surrounded by Prescott National Forest, the pine-covered Bradshaw Mountains and the Yavapai Indian Reservation, known for its boulder-strewn granite dells and grasslands. Stately Victorian homes are a reminder of its heyday years, while the rowdier side of frontier life is remembered on **Whiskey Row**, where 26 saloons once attracted cowboys from far and wide and where the annual Frontier Days celebration is held at the beginning of July complete with fireworks, dancing, rodeo performances, a parade and cowboy golf tournament.

Further north on 89a is **Jerome**, which sprang up during the gold-mining boom on Cleopatra Hill overlooking the Verde Valley. Once

the ore diminished, it became known as America's largest 'ghost city' and is now home to a colony of artists and visitors who walk the steep, winding streets to see the historic buildings and browse through shops and boutiques. Best historic sites are the town's 'travelling jail', which has moved 225 feet since a 1920s dynamite explosion dislodged it from its foundations, and Jerome State Historic Park, once the mansion of mining developer 'Rawhide' Jimmy Douglas.

To the south east (along Route 260) is **Campe Verde**, established in 1864 as a cavalry outpost to protect Verde River settlers from Indian raids. The old fort still stands in the middle of the town. Just north, along Interstate 17, are the well preserved cliff dwellings at **Montezuma Castle National Monument**, a five-storey, 20-room dwelling built in and under a cliff overlooking Beaver Creek. It was misnamed by early settlers who thought it had been inhabited by Aztecs, but was actually built by Sinagua Indians in the twelfth and thirteenth centuries. Further north is **Clarkdale** where you can see the 100-room pueblo that housed 250 people from the thirteenth century until they mysteriously disappeared some time in the fifteenth century. Clarkdale is home to the scenic Verde Canyon Railroad, a renovated New York Metro Line train that transports passengers along a 40-mile route through cottonwood forests and the base of a desert mesa (table). En route you'll see bald eagles, great blue herons, deer and javelina. Just a little further north is **Flagstaff**, considered to be the gateway to the Grand Canyon, which is about 1½ hours north on Highway 180 through Tusayan or through Desert View on Highway 64, off Route 89.

The Grand Canyon

Two billion years in the making, the majestic spectacle stands from between 4,500 feet to 5,700 feet high for an amazing 277 miles with an average width of ten miles. To geologists, it is like an open book, as they can immediately see that the bottom layer is two billion years old while the top is a mere 200 million years old, with the geologic ages in between represented in its colourful stony strata. Viewing it from one of the many vantage points on the South Rim, you will see the myriad rock formations change colour according to the sun's position throughout the day. The best times to see it (and the quietest) are at sunrise or sunset. But in some ways you can only get a feel for its awesome, breathtaking hugeness by descending thousands of feet by mule. If you don't have the one or two days needed for the trip to spare, you can stop at the new IMAX

theatre at Tusayan and watch the *Grand Canyon – The Hidden Secrets* film.

★ ★ ★ ★ **INSIDE TRACK** ★ ★ ★
★ ★
★ ★
★ To avoid the crowds (five million ★
★ people visit each year) and ★
★ searing heat, go in March, April, ★
★ September or October either ★
★ before 10am or after 2pm. ★
★ ★ ★ ★ ★ ★ ★ ★ ★ ★ ★ ★ ★ ★ ★ ★ ★

Getting the Grand Canyon experience

Entrance: $20 per vehicle, $10 per person arriving by other means. Admission is for seven days. Under 17s free. The park is open 24 hours a day. Free planning guides are available from the National Park Service. For a Trip Planner, Backcountry Trip Planner or Accessibility Guide, write to **Grand Canyon National Park**, PO Box 129, Grand Canyon, AZ 86023.
The film: The IMAX theatre (520-638 2203) at the south entrance in Tusayan has shows at half past the hour from 8.30am to 8.30pm daily on a 70-foot screen with six-track stereo sound. Adults $7.50, under 12s $4.50.
By train: The Grand Canyon Railway (520-773 1976) runs a 1920s Harriman coach steam train from Williams to the South Rim, travelling through 65 miles of beautiful countryside.
By bus: Guided tours to the South Rim from Flagstaff are run by **Nava-Hopi Bus Lines.** Phone 520-774 7715 for times and prices.
By mule: Fred Harvey runs one or two-day inner canyon rides, though you must speak fluent English (to understand instructions), be at least 4ft 7in tall, weigh no more than 200lb and *not* be pregnant. Trips are often booked months in advance, so call 303-297 2757 for information and to make reservations.

11

Staying on the floor of the Canyon:
Phantom Ranch offers ten-bunk dorms
with toilet and shower, plus private
cabins. For reservations, contact
AMFACT Parks and Resorts, 14001
East Iliff Avenue, Ste 600, Aurora,
CO 80014 or call 303-297 2757.
Horseback rides: With the **Apache
Stables** in Tusayan, adjacent to the
park. Write to PO Box 369, Grand
Canyon, AZ 86023 or phone 520-
638 2891.
Rafting the Colorado: Trips include
half-day floating excursions, motor
boat trips and 18-day expeditions on
rowing boats. You need to book at
least six months in advance and
companies include: **ARA Wilderness
River Adventures** at PO Box 717,
Page, AZ 86040 (520-645 3296);
Arizona Raft Adventures at 4050 East
Huntington Drive, Flagstaff, AZ 86004
(520-526 8200); **Arizona River
Runners** at PO Box 47788, Phoenix,
AZ 85068-7788 (602-867 4866);
Canyon Explorations Inc. at PO Box
310, Flagstaff, AZ 86002 (520-774
4559); **Canyoneers Inc** at PO Box
2997, Flagstaff, AZ 86003 (520-526
0924); **Diamond River Adventures** at
PO Box 1300, Page, AZ 86040 (520-
645 8866); **Expeditions Inc/Grand
Canyon Youth Expeditions** at 625
North Beaver Street, Flagstaff, AZ
86001 (520-779 3769); **Hualapai
Tribal River Runners** at PO Box 246,
Peach Springs, AZ 86434-0246 (520-
769 2210); **Outdoors Unlimited** at
6900 Townsend Winona Road,
Flagstaff, AZ 86004 (520-526 4546);
and **Wild and Scenic Inc** at PO Box
460, Flagstaff, AZ 86002 (520-774
7343).
Flightseeing: You can take a flight by
small aircraft or helicopter. Companies
include: **Grand Canyon Airlines** at Box
3038, Grand Canyon, AZ 86023
(520-638 2407); **Air Grand Canyon** at
PO Box 3399, Grand Canyon, AZ
86023 (520-638 2686); **AirStar
Helicopters** at PO Box 3379, Grand
Canyon, AZ 86023 (520-638 2622);
Kenai Helicopters at PO Box 1429,
Grand Canyon, AZ 86023 (520-638

2412); and **Papillon Grand Canyon
Helicopters** at PO Box 455, Grand
Canyon, AZ 86023 (520-638 2419).
Lodging: For full and up-to-date details
of lodges near the rim, write to
AMFACT Parks and Resorts (see left).
North Rim: Through Jacob Lake on
Highway 67, this is a lot quieter than
the South Rim and home to **Canyon
Trail Rides** (801-679 8665), which run
one-hour forest rides, half-day trips into
the Canyon and full-day trips to
Roaring Springs where you can frolick
in the natural pools. Again, you can
get full details of facilities from the
National Park Service. Here you can
stay at the Grand Canyon Lodge from
late May to mid-October. For
reservations, write to AMFACT Parks
and Resorts (see left). The **Kaibab
Lodge**, three miles north of the park, is
also open from late May to mid-
October. For reservations write to
Kaibab Lodge, HC64 Box 30,
Fredonia, AZ 860022 (520-638
2389).
   Once you've been there, done
that at the Grand Canyon, don't miss
out on many other natural and
historical wonders that are well worth
a visit. Leave the South Rim on
Highway 64 and take the 89 south to
**Sunset Crater Volcano National
Monument** (520-556 7042). An
active volcano more than 900 years
ago, it now rises to 1,000 feet and
rangers here offer geology,
seismology and other tours while the
Visitors' Center can provide you with
maps for self-guided trails. Further
south join the Interstate 40 going east
and take in **Walnut Canyon National
Monument** for an awe-inspiring view
of how Sinagua Indians lived in
homes built out of the limestone cliffs.
The **Visitors' Center Museum** (520-
526 3367) displays artefacts that
make it possible to imagine how they
existed. Nearby is **Meteor Crater**,
which dates back 22,000 years when
an enormous meteor travelling at
33,000mph plunged to earth.
Because of its resemblance to the
lunar landscape, the 570-foot-deep

crater was used as a training site for Apollo astronauts and the museum (520-289 2362) displays a 1,406-lb meteorite, the largest found in the area. Further east is the **Petrified Forest National Park** and **Painted Desert Visitors' Center and Museum** (520-524 6228). There are more fossilised trees to be found here than anywhere else in the world. Here you will find million-year-old agate logs lying in profusion on the ground. Then journey north on Route 191 to **Canyon de Chelly National Monument**. Here you can view the Indian cliff-dwelling ruins that date back to the twelfth century, at the base of sheer red cliffs and in canyon walls on scenic rim drives, four-wheel-drive vehicles, horseback or on foot. Phone 520-674 8443 for details. Rich with history, the Anasazi Indians lived here until 1300 and the Navajo arrived in 1700, using it as a base to raid nearby Indian and Spanish settlements.

Then take Highways 59 and 163 past **Monument Valley**, probably one of the best-used locations for Westerns including John Wayne's *Stagecoach*. To the left of this area is the **Navajo Nation**, the largest of all the Indian reservations – extending across 25,000 square miles, it is bigger than the state of West Virginia – which is home to just 175,000 Indians who welcome visitors for sightseeing and shopping (buy silver and turquoise jewellery, exquisitely woven rugs, intricate kachinas and other crafts). The land encompasses mile upon mile of desert and forest land, interrupted only by spectacular mesas, buttes and rock formations. The Indians provide hiking, horseback or four-wheel-drive tours through some of the most popular sites such as Canyon de Chelly and Monument Valley.

From this area, take Route 98 up to the shores of **Lake Powell**, a 25-million-acre lake with more shoreline – 1,960 miles – than California, which was formed by the completion of the Glen Canyon Dam in 1963.

Watch the birdies!

You've seen them in cartoons, now you can see the birds of the deserts and mountains of Arizona in real life. The south-eastern corner of the state is the most popular bird-watching area of North America and more than 400 species can be found here from migratory water fowl to native birds, nesting birds, grassland birds and mountain birds. You can watch greater roadrunners chase lizards across the desert floors, black-chinned hummingbirds buzz around like bees, acorn woodpeckers drill holes in roadside telegraph poles and painted redstarts flit in the dappled light of oakwoods with Ornitholidays (01243 821230). The company organises a three-week-long-trip at the end of April/beginning of May when the desert is comfortably cool and many birds are nesting while others are starting to migrate to their breeding grounds in the north. All this *and* spectacular views of the Grand Canyon. Another favoured time of the year is in August when the city of Sierra Vista has a birding festival complete with bat stalks and owl prowls.

11

Howdy pardner!

Arizona is real cowboy country and if there is one way to see the stunning scenery, wide-open expanses and narrow gorges, it is on the back of a horse – as a cowboy. Nowadays it is very easy to be a real 'city slicker' as a whole host of ranching options are available, depending on your riding abilities and needs for luxury items, such as a bed. The type of ranches are:

Guest ranch: This is where you live as a 'guest' of the ranch owners in an environment that is designed to entertain you while providing plenty of horse-riding opportunities and Western activities. It's the soft option that will give you a feel for the way of life but no hands-on experience.

Dude ranch: Vacation-based rather than the seriously business-like working ranches, you'll do a lot of riding while Western activities from Wild West shows to rodeo visits, square dances, barbecues and sports provide plenty of fun.

Resort ranch: These offer the Western experience but also have golf, tennis and ballooning, and the whole environment is much more luxurious than dude or working ranches.

Working ranch: These are still in business to raise livestock and breed crops and are home to the real cowboys. Depending on the time of year and the work that is necessary on the ranch, you'll be able to learn to drive cattle, brand and rope steers, eat around a camp fire and sleep under the stars.

Round-ups take place in spring and autumn when the ranchers prepare their cattle to be moved to summer and winter ranges. It's a high-activity time at the ranches so the hours are long and the work is physically demanding. **Cattle drives** follow in which you'll travel six to 12 miles a day but ride at least three times as far as you bring in strays from the flanks. Evenings spent around the camp fire hark back to bygone days in what is a truly wonderful, friendship-forming experience. **Horse drives** are a much faster version as the horses like to travel at speed. Only for very seasoned riders with lots of cross-country experience, but the long-distance gallops are a real thrill.

Offering the full range of ranches are **American Round-Up** (01404 881777) and **Ranch America** (0181 868 2910), while **Equitour**, part of **Peregrine Holidays Ltd** (01865 511642), are excellent for working ranches all over America's West and even provide riding clinics to bring you up to speed!

For horse-riding vacations with a difference try **Outlaw Trails** (01293 529345), who run specially tailored, fully researched trips to the old trails used by outlaws determined to avoid the long arm of the law. Closest to Arizona is the Robbers Roost trail in Utah in which you'll see the way stations and trail used by the Wild Bunch of Butch Cassidy and the Sundance Kid, the Hole in the Wall Gang and Robbers Roost Gang. Robbers Roost land is sprawled across 320 square miles of high desert and you'll ride through pinion, sage and cedar flats, a maze of rock gorges and canyons, plus long mesas, arches, pinnacles and high-shouldered buttes. If you attempt any of the 'climbs' used by the outlaws, you'll get a pretty good idea of what brilliant horsemen they were! The seasons and numbers are limited because of the weather and nature of the trips, but the trails are perfect for lovers of the historical West who want a great big chunk of adventure.

Today it's a home for houseboats and pleasure craft that explore the 96 canyons discovered and mapped by intrepid, one-armed explorer John Wesley Powell in the nineteenth century. **Rainbow Bridge Natural Monument**, a natural stone arch carved by the relentless forces of wind and water, only became easily accessible after the lake came into being. It is an amazing 290 feet high and 275 feet wide. Now boat rentals, tours and accommodations are all available at the Wahweap Lodge and Marina on the lake's southern-most shore. Glen Canyon Dam offers self-guided tours and day-long and half-day float trips on the Colorado River from the base of the dam, from March to October. For details phone 520-645 2471. The town of **Page**, founded as a construction camp for crews building the dam, has plenty of restaurants and accommodation.

INSIDE TRACK

★★★★ ★★★
★ ★
★ ★
★ Did you know that more people ★
★ have died of drowning in the ★
★ desert than of thirst? It's all due ★
★ to flash floods, and the reason ★
★ why they've got such a high ★
★ mortality rate is that they are so ★
★ violent and so quick you literally ★
★ have no time at all to react. ★
★★★★★★★★★★★★★★★★★★

Adventures: So you can see how the area from Monument Valley and the Grand Canyon to Lake Powell, and beyond to the Colorado Rocky Mountains, Zion and Bryce Canyons offer a fabulous array of opportunities for those in search of real adventure. Going white water rafting, mountain biking, walking, hiking, riding amid red rocks, waterskiing on Lake Powell and taking jeep tours around Indian country before camping cowboy-style all provide wonderful thrills. Good tour operators for all these activities

include **Hemmingways** (01737 842735), **North American Representatives** (01344 890525) and **Trek America** (01295 256777).

Now you need to be on your way again! From Page, take Highways 89 and 9 east, past Zion National Park to Interstate 15, heading south-west to Las Vegas. This journey will take around 4½ hours. From Las Vegas to Death Valley is about 1½ hours.

Death Valley: At the bottom of the 300-mile-long Sierra Nevada mountain range that stretches to Lake Tahoe in the north, this is the hottest place on earth. In summer the average temperature is 45°C/131°F and the rocks almost reach water-boiling point. In the heart of the valley is the lowest point – 282 feet below sea level – in all of America. Wimps can visit in March and April when it is just 18°C/61°F and admire the desert spring blooms that shoot out of the sculpted rocks. But let's face it, the whole point of going to Death Valley is to drive through it at the hottest time of year! I would, however, advise giving yourself – and your car – an even chance of making it through in one piece by setting off early in the morning and making sure both your car radiator – and you – have plenty of water. The National Parks of California warn you not to stop your car in the heat of the day (it'll probably not restart until night-time) and don't drive too quickly, again to prevent overheating. Just bear in mind that if you do break down you'll be on your own for some time as there is no public transport in the Valley and not many Americans are daft enough (mad dogs and Englishmen and all that) to go through in the summer. However, if you're sensible you will survive and will be amazed by the

11

Some people opt to stay at Furnace Creek, but frankly I can't see the point of being boiled alive for quite so long! Allow about one hour from Death Valley Junction on the 190 to Lone Pine, and about two to Big Pine on the west and north-west of the valley, where you can make a pit stop for lunch before heading on up to the majestic world of Mammoth Lakes, 1–1½ hours north on 190 and 136.

breathtaking beauty of the miles and miles of sand and rocks that have been hardened into a sea-like landscape by the melting sun. For more information contact **Death Valley National Park** on 760-786 2392. **Mammoth Lakes**, at the gateway to Yosemite, is one of the best places in the Sierra Nevada for outdoor acitvities and is second only to Tahoe as a ski resort in winter. The magical setting and 50-mile trail make it popular with mountain bikers, while expert guides offer climbing, kayaking and hang-gliding. The whole area is also good for golf, canoeing, swimming and searching out wildlife, gold mines and ghost towns. Recent investment in Mammoth Mountain mean there is now a new 18-hole championship golf course and a pedestrian resort, **Gondola Village**, with shops, restaurants, a skating pond and gondola connecting the centre of town to the heart of the mountain for unmissable views. Possible lodgings include: **Mammoth Mountain Inn** (1 Minaret Road, 619-934 2581); **Minaret Lodge** (6156 Minaret Road, 619-934 2416) and **Sierra Nevada Inn** (164 Old Mammoth Road, 619-934 2515). Or you can write to the **Mammoth Lakes Visitor and Information Service** at 437

Old Mammoth Road, Ste Y 93546 (fax 760-934 7066) for a free vacation planner. Other useful contacts include **Devil's Postpile National Monument** (760-934 2289); **Consolidated Gold Mine** (760-924 5500); **Mammoth Museum** (5489 Sherwin Creek Road, 760-934 6918); **Mammoth Mountain Bike Park and Adventure Challenge Course** (1 Minaret Road, 760-934 0706); **Mammoth Mountain Ski Resort** (760-934 2571) and **Tamarack Cross-Country Ski Area** at Mammoth Lakes (760-934 2442).

Depending on how much time you have, the Lakes are likely to be somewhere you stay at overnight, view in the morning and take the must-have photo of before whizzing off to Yosemite.

Yosemite: After the Grand Canyon, this has to be one of the most stunning natural wonders of the world. Mile-high cliffs gouged out by glaciers thousands of years ago are topped with pinnacles and domes from which waterfalls cascade. Coyote and black bears roam the valley floor, which is never more than a mile wide. In winter, roads in the park get blocked by snow and in summer by the thousands of tourists who flock to the area. Guided tours, including trips around the valley and into the mountains, are bookable through most of the hotels in the area. Full details of mountain biking, fishing, boating at Bass Lake, steam train, the historic park and Native American museums are available from

★ ★ ★ **INSIDE TRACK** ★ ★ ★
★   ★
★   ★
★   Fill up with petrol on your way   ★
★   into Yosemite as there are no   ★
★   petrol stations at all in the park. ★
★ ★ ★ ★ ★ ★ ★ ★ ★ ★ ★ ★ ★ ★ ★ ★ ★ ★

Yosemite Sierra Visitors' Bureau.
Write to them at 41729 Highway 41,
Oakhurst 93644 (209-683 4636) for
a visitors' guide.
Another useful office is the **Yosemite
Area Traveller Information Center**
(369 West 18th Street, Merced
95340, 209-723 3153), which can
give you all the latest information on
park and surrounding road conditions
(essential at all times except summer),
transport, recreation, lodging,
camping and dining options.
Yosemite View Lodge, adjacent to the
wild and scenic Merced River, will be
opening **Camp Grizzly** early in 1999.
Based on a theme of a 1950s
summer camp, it will provide
educational nature trails, barbecue-
style dining, country line dancing and
other special events. To book and get
more information on motels in the
area, write to **Yosemite Motels**, PO
Box 1989, Mariposa, CA, 95338, or
phone 209-742 7106.

★★★ **INSIDE TRACK** ★★★
★   ★
★   ★
★   Some roads close from late ★
★ autumn to early summer – check ★
★ in advance and have tyre chains ★
★   at the ready if driving in winter. ★
★★★★★★★★★★★★★★★★★★★★

Other useful numbers include
**Yosemite Mountain Sugar Pine
Railroad** (209-683 7273) which runs
steam trains through the Sierra
National Forest near Yosemite Park;
Yosemite Sightseeing Tours (209-877
8687); **All-Outdoors Whitewater Trips**
(800 24 RAFTS) for half-, one-, two-
and three-day rafting trips from April
to November; and **Whitewater
Voyages** (800 488 RAFT) for
wonderful runs down the Merced with
guides, food and equipment.

> **About 2–2½ hours north on
> Highways 395 and 89 is Lake
> Tahoe.**

Lake Tahoe: You're in danger of
getting landscaped-out here as you
arrive at yet another stunning natural
wonder. The lake, 22 miles long, 12
miles wide and 1,645 feet deep, is
6,000 feet above sea level and is
ringed by the peaks of the High
Sierras that rise majestically to
10,000 feet. This was the setting for
Al Pacino's lakeside home in *The
Godfather II* and the Ponderosa
Ranch (*Bonanza*, remember!).
Highlights include **Emerald Bay**,
22 miles south of Tahoe City on
Highway 89 (916-525 7277),
one of the most photographed
natural attractions of Lake Tahoe
and home to Vikingsholm, a replica
of a Scandinavian medieval castle.
From there, it's a one-mile hike down
to the castle (summer tours available)
and a 100-site campsite. **Sugar Pine
Point** (916-525 7982), a 2,000-acre
park, 12 miles north of Emerald Bay,
is the largest park in Tahoe area and
the only one in the lake basin to keep
its campground open year-round.
Washow Meadows (916-525 7232),
next to Lake Valley State Recreation
Area, 2½ miles east of South Lake
Tahoe, is a 620-acre park of
undeveloped meadows and forest
lands. It was named after the Native
Americans who lived in the area for
thousands of years and who used to
migrate from the Nevada desert in
the summer months to fish in its many
streams and rivers. The all-season
resort of **Tahoe** on the north shore is
packed with sailors, anglers, hikers
and bikers in the summer and skiers
in the winter – five miles north is the
former Winter Olympic ski resort of
Squaw Valley, which is now home to
California's largest ski resort. Peak
seasons are mid-November to April
and July to September. This area
tends to attract younger people and is
much more vibrant than **South Lake
Tahoe**, which draws an altogether
different crowd. Here the town
straddles California and Nevada, so
its casinos attract coachloads of
weekend gamblers from the state

11

capital of Sacramento. The upside, though, is that the place has hundreds of budget rooms with brilliant midweek discount rates.

Contact **Lake Tahoe Visitors' Authority** (1156 Ski Run Boulevard, 96150, 1-800 AT TAHOE) for details of cabins and casino resorts. Other useful contacts include **Hornblower Cruises** (900 Ski Run Boulevard, 530-541 3364) for dinner, lunch and cocktails cruises of the lake that give breathtaking views of Emerald Bay and the mountains; **Heavenly Tram** (50 Ski Run Boulevard, 530-541 1330) for dramatic views from Monument Peak; and **Emerald Bay/Eagle Falls Visitors' Authority** (1156 Ski Run Boulevard, 530-544 5050).

If you're on a brief visit, why not stay overnight in South Lake Tahoe and drive north around the lake past Emerald Bay, Sugar Pine Point and Tahoe City before joining Interstate 80, the fastest and most direct route to San Francisco, about four hours' drive away? Alternatively, you can take the 50 to Sacramento through gold-mining country and join the 80 from there. If you plan to end your holiday in San Francisco, try to leave yourself at least one night or so at the end for a bit of rest and relaxation before the long flight home.

12 SAFETY FIRST

Safety, insurance, hints and tips on making the best of your holiday

No one wants to think about anything going wrong with their dream holiday, but it is worth thinking about a few common-sense aspects of safety and security so that you can avoid any preventable problems.

General hints and tips

Don't allow your dream trip to Las Vegas and beyond to be spoilt by not taking the right kind of precautions – be they for personal safety or of a medical nature.

In the sun

Let's face it, most Brits tend to travel to America at the hottest time of the year – the summer – and most are unprepared for the sheer intensity of the sun. Before you even think about going out for the day, apply a high-factor sunblock as it is very easy to get sunburnt when you are walking around, sightseeing or shopping. Also, re-apply regularly throughout the day. It is also a good idea to wear a hat or scarf to protect your head from the sun, especially at the hottest time of the day from 11am to 3pm, so you do not get sunstroke. If it is windy, you may be lulled into thinking that it is not as hot, but this is a dangerous illusion – especially in the desert valley of Las Vegas! If you are spending the day by the pool, it is advisable to use a sunshade at the hottest time of the day, and apply waterproof sunblock regularly, even when you are in the pool, as the UV rays travel through water. Always make sure you have plenty of fluids with you when travelling. Water is best and try to avoid alcohol during the day as this will have an additional dehydrating effect.

At your hotel

In America, your hotel room number is your main source of security. It is often your passport to eating and collecting messages, so keep the number safe and secure. When checking in, make sure none of the hotel staff mentions your room number out loud. If they do, give them back the key and ask them to give you a new room and to write down the new room number instead of announcing it (most hotels follow this practice in any case). When you need to give someone your room number – for instance when charging a dinner or any other bill to your room – write it down or show them your room card rather than calling it out.

When in your hotel room, always use the deadlocks and security chains and use the door peephole before opening the door to strangers. If someone knocks on the door and cannot give any identification, phone down to the hotel reception desk.

When you go out, make sure you lock the windows and door properly and even if you leave your room just for a few seconds, lock the door.

★ ★ ★ ★ **INSIDE TRACK** ★ ★ ★

Use a business address rather than your home address on all your luggage.

★ ★ ★ ★ ★ ★ ★ ★ ★ ★ ★ ★ ★ ★ ★ ★ ★

Cash and documents

Most hotels in tourist areas have safety deposit boxes, so use these to store important documents such as airline tickets and passports. When you go out, do not take all your cash and credit cards with you – always have at least one credit card in the safe as an emergency back-up and only take enough cash with you for the day. Using a money belt is also a good idea. Keep a separate record of your travellers' cheque numbers. If your room does not have its own safe, leave your valuables in the main hotel safe.

★★★ **INSIDE TRACK** ★★★
Be warned – American banknotes are all exactly the same green colour and size regardless of denomination, so familiarise yourself with the different bills in the safety of your hotel room before you go out, and keep larger denominations separate from smaller bills.
★★★★★★★★★★★★★★★★★★

Emergencies

For the police, fire department or ambulance, dial 911 (9-911 from your hotel room).

If you need medical help in Las Vegas you can go to the **Resort Medical Centers** at 3535 Las Vegas Boulevard South, 8th Floor, Suite 1 or 3743 Las Vegas Boulevard South, Suite 106 (702-735 3600 or 702-736 6311). Both are on the Strip, are open 24 hours a day and offer medical care for tourists. There is a *free* shuttle service, no appointment is necessary, medications, laboratory and X-ray facilities are available on site and the doctors will even do hotel calls.

Cars

Most of the advice is obvious, but when we go on holiday we sometimes relax to the point of not following our basic common sense. Never leave your car unlocked and never leave any valuable items on the car seats or anywhere else where they can be seen.

★★★ **INSIDE TRACK** ★★★
Put away maps and brochures in the glove compartment as these will be obvious signs that yours is a tourist's car.
★★★★★★★★★★★★★★★★★★

Travel insurance

The one thing you should not forget is travel insurance when travelling anywhere around America – medical cover is very expensive and if you are involved in any kind of an accident you could be sued, which is very costly indeed in America.

If you do want to make savings in this area, don't avoid getting insurance cover, but do avoid buying it from tour operators as they are notoriously expensive. For instance, I took a random selection of premiums offered by tour operators specialising in North America and found that two weeks' worth of cover for one person varied in cost from £39 to a staggering £82.25. If you're travelling for anything up to four weeks, the premiums go up to nearly £100 per person.

The alternative, particularly if you plan to make more than one trip in any given year is to go for an annual worldwide policy directly from insurers. These can start at around £55 and go up to £112 – a good benchmark to aim for is around £70 – and will normally cover all trips taken throughout the year up to a maximum of 31 days per trip. The worldwide annual policies make even more sense if you're travelling as a family. For instance if you need to insure four people and buy cover from your tour operator it could easily cost you £160 for a two-week trip in comparison with an annual world-wide family policy premium of between £90 and £140.

In all cases, you need to ensure that the policy gives you the following cover:

1 Actual coverage of the United States – not all plans include America.
2 Medical cover of at least £2 million in America.
3 Personal liability cover of at least £2 million in America.
4 Cancellation and curtailment cover of around £3,000 in case you are forced to call off your holiday.
5 Cover for lost baggage and belongings at around £1,500. Most premiums only offer cover for individual items up to around £250, so you will need additional cover for expensive cameras or camcorders.
6 Cover for cash (usually around £200) and documents including your air tickets, passport and currency.
7 24-hour helpline to make it easy for you to get advice and instructions on what to do.

Check and check again

Watch out for **sharp practices:** In some cases your tour operator may imply that you need to buy their travel insurance policy even when this is not the case, or may send you an invoice for your tickets that includes travel insurance unless you tick a certain box. **Read the policy:** Always ask for a copy of the policy document before you go and If you are not happy with the cover offered, cancel and demand your premium back – in some cases you will only have seven days in which to do this so look sharp! **Don't double up on cover:** If you have an 'all risks' policy on your home contents, this will cover your property outside the home and may even cover lost money and credit cards. Check if this covers you abroad – and covers your property when in transit – before buying personal possessions cover.
Look at **gold card cover:** Some bank gold cards provide you with

insurance cover if you buy your air ticket with the gold card, though only the NatWest Gold MasterCard provides sufficient cover for travel in America – and only if you pay for your entire holiday (ie flights and accommodation) with your Gold Card.
Check **dangerous sports cover:** In almost all cases mountaineering, racing and hazardous pursuits such as bungee jumping, skydiving, horse riding, windsurfing, trekking and even cycling are not included in normal policies. There are so many opportunities to do all these activities – and they are so popular as holiday extras – that you really should ensure you are covered before you go. Backpackers and dangerous sports enthusiasts can try **The Travel Insurance Club** on 0800 163518. They specialise in insurance for backpackers aged 18–35 and the cover includes walking holidays, sports and activities, skiing and scuba diving, bungee jumping and abseiling.
Make sure you qualify: For instance, if you have been treated in hospital in the six months prior to travelling or are waiting for hospital treatment, you may need medical evidence that you are fit to travel. Ask your doctor for a report giving you the all-clear (this may cost £25) and if the insurance company still says your condition is not covered, shop around.

Annual policies

Companies offering annual worldwide insurance policies include **AA** (0191 235 6513), **Atlas Direct** (0171 609 5000), **Barclays** (0345 573114), **Bradford & Bingley** (0800 435642), **Colossus** (0990 775 885), **Columbus** (0171 375 0011), **Direct Travel** (01903 812345), **General Accident Direct** (0800 121007), **Our Way** (0181 313 3900), **Preferential** (01702 423393), **Premier Direct** (0990 133218), **Primary Direct** (0870 444 3434), **Travel Insurance Direct** (0990 168113) and **Travelplan**

12

Direct (0800 0188747). Also, **Thomas Cook** (0845 600 5454) offer commission-free foreign exchange with annual travel cover.

Many of these companies also offer straightforward holiday cover for a given period, such as two weeks or three weeks, which will be again be cheaper than insurance offered by tour operators.

By far the most competitive rates are actually available through **NYTAB**, the New York Travel Advisory Bureau (0331 405060). Its annual, multi-trip travel insurance, for worldwide cover including the United States, costs £49.95 plus insurance premium tax. You will then be given a NYTAB card with which you can also make very cheap phone calls to England from America (25 cents per minute). Who knows, you may be stopping off in New York en route to Las Vegas and the West and will then also be able to use the card for discounted entrances to top attractions such as the World Trade Center, harbour cruises, museums and much more.

ACKNOWLEDGEMENTS

The author wishes to acknowledge the help of the following in the production of this book:

Las Vegas News Bureau, Las Vegas Convention and Visitors Authority, Cellet Travel Services, Nevada Commission on Tourism, Visit USA Association, Funway Holidays, Just America, Airtours, Air Vacations, American Connections, The American Holiday, APT Tourism, Bon Voyage, Getaway Vacations, Jetlife, Jetsave, Jetset, Key To America, Kuoni, Northwest Airlines, Page & Moy, Premier, Trailfinders, Travelsphere, Unijet, United Vacations, Virgin, Bally's, Bellagio, Caesars Palace, Circus Circus, Cirque du Soleil, The Desert Inn, Excalibur, Fashion Show Mall, Harrah's, Imperial Palace, Lance Burton, Las Vegas Airlines, Las Vegas Hilton, Luxor, Mandalay Bay, MGM Grand, Mirage Resorts, Monte Carlo, New York-New York, Rio Suite, Stratosphere, Sundance Helicopters, Wet 'n' Wild, World of Coca-Cola™, Joann 'JJ' José and Rob Powers (Las Vegas Convention and Visitors Authority), Myram Borders and Mike Donahue (News Bureau), Stephen Hughes and Kristian Perry (Funway), Mike Easton (Just America), Colin Brain (Table Rock Lake Chamber of Commerce), Diane Court (Cellet), Arizona Tourist Board, San Francisco Convention and Visitors Bureau, Los Angeles Convention and Visitors Bureau, California Tourist Board, Hotel Nikko, Long Beach Area Convention and Visitors Bureau, Disneyland Resort® in California, Universal Studios, Warner Bros, San Diego Convention and Visitors Bureau, Sea World of California, Palm Springs Desert Resorts® Convention and Visitors Bureau, Palm Springs Tourism Board, Margaret Melia (Disneyland), Stacey Litz and Carol Martinez (LACVB), Makoto Earnie Yasuhara (Hotel Nikko). Plus special thanks to the divine Kirsty Hislop, gullible traveller Bob Maddam, Barbara Wilson and Simon Veness.

Picture Acknowledgements

The author and publisher gratefully acknowledge the provision of the following photographs: Front cover: Alan Benoit, Las Vegas News Bureau, Universal Studios Inc. Back cover: Las Vegas News Bureau. Page 33: Eric Figge (Caesars Palace); Las Vegas News Bureau (Excalibur exterior at dusk, Luxor exterior). Page 34: Las Vegas News Bureau (Fireworks at the Stratosphere, New York-New York). Page 68: Las Vegas News Bureau (Cirque du Soleil). Page 103: Las Vegas News Bureau (Desert Inn Country Club, Horseback trail ride through Red Rock Canyon, Sailing on Lake Mead). Page 104: Las Vegas News Bureau (Desert Princess Cruises paddleboat on Lake Mead, Dolphins at the Mirage, The Hoover Dam). Page 137: Las Vegas News Bureau (Fashion Show Mall Entrance). Page 138: CDT (Bixby Bridge, The Golden Gate Bridge, San Francisco's night-time skyline); Robert Holmes (Monterey Peninsula, Neptune Pool at Hearst Castle™, Vines in the Napa Valley). Page 171: J Paul Getty Trust/John Stephens (Getty Center); J Paul Getty Trust/S Frances Esto (Getty Center); LACVB/Michele and Tom Grimm (Melrose Avenue); Santa Monica CVB/Nik Wheeler (3rd Street Promenade). Page 172: © Disney 1998 Disneyland® ('it's a small world', Tomorrowland); Elmar Baxter/Long Beach ACVB (Queen Mary at Long Beach); LACVB/Michele and Tom Grimm (Universal City Walk); Robert Holmes/CDT (Gondola ride at Naples); Universal Studios Inc (Jurassic Park). Page 173: CDT (La Jolla beach, Old Town State Park, San Diego's night-time skyline); LACVB/Michele and Tom Grimm (Watersports at San Diego). Page 174: Alan Benoit (The Grand Canyon, Jeep tour in the desert); Kathleen Jo Ryan (Colarado river, Hiking down the Grand Canyon). Page 207: Alan Benoit (Canyon de Chelly, Monument Valley, Navajo guide through Monument Valley). Page 208: Alan Benoit (Lake Powell, Rainbow Bridge at Lake Powell); Robert Holmes (Yosemite National Park)

12

INDEX